BOBBY: THE CROOKED HAND OF THE LAW

HILDA STR

Copyright © 2017 by Hilda Stroganovsky.

All rights reserved. No part of this publication may be reproduced, distributed or transmitted in any form or by any means, including photocopying, recording, or other electronic or mechanical methods, without the prior written permission of the publisher, except in the case of brief quotations embodied in critical reviews and certain other noncommercial uses permitted by copyright law.

Publisher's Note: This is a work of fiction. Names, characters, places, and incidents are a product of the author's imagination. Locales and public names are sometimes used for atmospheric purposes. Any resemblance to actual people, living or dead, or to businesses, companies, events, institutions, or locales is completely coincidental.

Bobby: The Policeman That Lied/ Hilda Stroganovsky. -- 1st ed.

ISBN 978-1975675097

PROLOGUE

1966

Robbie Crowe approached the lamppost that marked the start of his quieter, more exclusive part of town, where the school bullies were not such a problem. It wasn't his fault he was a vicar's son. He often got the feeling that he was an eight-year-old boy living in someone else's skin. He didn't fit in at home and he certainly didn't fit in at school.

The boys packing the pavement behind him, some of whom he knew, were in high spirits, what with it being a Friday afternoon in July. Even the teachers had been happier than usual, maybe because there was only one week left until the long summer holidays began. He enjoyed this time of year. He even enjoyed walking home, with his mind bursting with thoughts of long summer nights, but when he reached the lamppost, things changed. True, he felt out of harm's way, which came as a relief more than anything else, but the illusion he'd been building up from one o'clock onwards suddenly shattered. He wasn't going to have a great night, followed by a weekend's family time with his folks. No, he was going to get home, open the door and immediately wish he was back at school. That's when he remembered about the brown envelope in his satchel. Feeling tears rush to his eyes, he paused to sit on a neighbour's wall, dropped his bag onto the pavement and sunk his face into his hands.

Eyes screwed to stop the tears overflowing, he sat with the sun blazing down on his neck, trying to pluck up the courage to continue on his way home, until his thighs felt tender and sore under the weight of his elbows.

"Hello there, Sonny."

Robbie looked up, and slowly began to roast under the shame of his tear stained face. It was a neighbour, the man whose wall he was sitting on. "Oh, hello."

"Have you been crying?"

"No."

The man smiled and laughed amicably. "Didn't think so. Not a big boy like you, master Robbie."

Robbie liked this man. He didn't know his name, but he'd seen him at a few church functions. Once he had some kids with him, whom Robbie had bonded with. He bought them all an ice cream and took them to the park. That was the previous summer, and he hadn't seen those kids, the man's nephews and nieces, again since that day. Shame.

The man patted Robbie's shoulder. "Go on, on your way now. The Reverend will be worrying about you."

Robbie could feel his face betray his thoughts.

"Oh, well, err—. "

"No, you're right. I should be on my way." Robbie got to his feet, dusted down the back of his legs and ran his hand along the brick wall's imprint. The man was right. He should be on his way. His eyes and legs were sore, and he felt hungry. Things might turn out OK after all.

The door creaked open and he put a foot across the threshold. The man had shown him some affection, and it had somehow made him feel much more positive about things. "Hi, Veronica," he said to his father's second wife, who was busy preparing the evening meal. He approached confidently, waiting for her to stop what she was doing and acknowledge his presence. When he got close enough to smell her scent, he tried again. "Veronica, hi. I'm home."

Robbie knew from the way her upper body inched round that this was going to be bad. Her eyes were ablaze with anger. "Do you have any idea what time it is?"

Robbie glanced round at the crockery on the shelves, half expecting the sheer volume of her piercing anger to smash them into a thousand pieces.

"Answer me when I'm talking to you, young man. Everyone has been out looking for you, they still are. Oh, I get it, that's what you wanted, wasn't it? You can't stand not being the centre of attention, can you?"

"No, Veronica, I just—. "

"Robert!"

"Daddy!" Robbie felt genuinely pleased and relieved to see his father; he just hoped he hadn't shown it.

If looks could kill, the look Veronica gave her husband would have sent the six feet three-inch reverend crashing to the floor. "Samuel, everyone has been out looking for him. Things can't go on like this. When are you going to do something about it?"

"What can I do?"

"Boarding school."

"Well, maybe that might be one solution. But I looked into that before, and his grades were just not good enough."

"Oh yes, I remember. He promised you he'd try harder. Well, go on, ask to see his report. Not that he'll have improved at anything. How could he possibly with a mother like—. "

"Robert, do you have your end of term report?"

"Y—yes." Veronica was right—things hadn't improved. Moreover, this wasn't the first time she'd made insinuations about his mother, and he didn't like it one bit.

"Come with me." Reverend Samuel led his son through the living room and up two flights of uncarpeted stairs, to the study. Robbie hated this room. He only ever had cause to go in there when he was in trouble.

The Reverend pulled the oak chair from under his writing bureau, turned it round to face Robbie and sat down. Without uttering a word, he outstretched his arm, turned his palm upwards and parted his fingers. Robbie nervously fumbled about in his bag until his hand collided with the brown envelope.

"Come on, I haven't got all day."

"Here. Here it is, Daddy." Robbie placed his report in his father's hand and felt his mouth drain of saliva. The sound of tearing paper filled the room, before the Reverend delved inside and extracted the single sheet of paper. The teacher had written in blue ink, which Robbie could see from the other side.

The Reverend put on his spectacles and read mostly in silence, nodding here and tutting there, while he became increasingly angry. Once he'd finished reading for the second time, the Reverend folded up the report, slammed it onto his desk and glared at his son.

"Daddy, I'm sorry . . . "

The Reverend raised a hand. "Mathematics and English language are both much better. Your teacher is very pleased with your progress." Robbie struggled to contain his relief.

"But, before you get too ahead of yourself, young man, I should remind you that we had a deal. We agreed that you'd improve to meet the entry requirements of boarding school."

"But, Daddy, I did my best."

"Well, it's not good enough. I defended you to Veronica over and over again, when she said you'd come to nothing." He got to his feet and took a step towards the far corner, where the book case met the window.

"Daddy, no, please. Please."

The Reverend reached into the corner, grasped the cane and bent it round into a loop.

"Daddy, please, I'll do better, I—. "

"Oh, stop your whining and take your punishment like a man." He took hold of Robbie's hand and turned his palm upwards. "I'll teach you to make a monkey out of me."

Robbie gritted his teeth and waited as the cane swooshed through the air.

The room was just beginning to spin when his father stood back and asked if he'd had enough. Robbie knew from experience that, providing he held back his tears, his father wouldn't go on. "Yes, Daddy."

"Have you learnt your lesson?"

"Yes, Daddy."

"Are you going to get the grades you need for boarding school? So I can be shut of you once and for all?"

"I'll do my best, Daddy."

"What? What did you say?" The Reverend seized his son by the hair, dragged him down the stairs, through the kitchen and pushed him into the closed door. As his face pressed into the glass panel, he became aware for the first time that the rain was pounding through the dark.

"Go on, get out."

"What? Why? Daddy, it's raining."

"You made a monkey out of me boy, now I'm going to make an animal out of you. Outside, with the dogs."

"What, but I thought God made man in his own image so he can live apart from the animals."

"That's true, but you're not worthy to be branded a man. Go on, get out with the animals."

"But Daddy, it's raining, I—." Seeing the Reverend raise his hand, Robbie opened the door and made his escape.

The rain was so hard that he couldn't tell if he was crying or not. He spent a second examining his surroundings before he heard a noise in the far corner of the yard. He looked through the rain, past the puddles until his gaze rested on Chester and Lester. They were apparently scared of the rain and cowering to take cover, but knew instantly that Robbie needed solace. Chester, the black Labrador, headed across first, Lester, who was golden, in his trail.

Robbie sat on the doorstep and waited, noticing for the first time that the yard was covered in faeces. Leaning forward, he outstretched his throbbing hand and patted Lester's soaked head. Lester lowered his head and licked Robbie's hand, his tongue getting to work between the fingers that wouldn't straighten out.

When the rain took a breather, the dogs laid on the filthy yard by Robbie's feet. Robbie got to thinking about his future. When he grew up, he wasn't going to be a vicar like his dad. Nor did he want to be bossed around in a shop or office or to drive a bus. He wanted a job where people would respect him, and he'd get to tell others what to do. He looked down into Lester's big dark eyes, and the dog moved towards him.

Robbie stood up, took a step forward and swung a boot at the dog. "Here, take that. I'm a man, not an animal. You'll do as I say."

Lester yelped and hobbled backwards, Chester following him to the corner on the far side where they'd been hours before.

Robbie slumped back onto the doorstep, rubbed his tired eyes and, noticing how hungry he was, began to cry. He became so engrossed in his thoughts that he didn't notice the dogs cross the yard. Only when he felt the cold nose on the back of his hand did he look up, startled. The dog immediately dropped on Robbie's feet.

Breathless with rage, Robbie stood up and kicked the dog onto its side. "Why you, I'm a man. How dare you sit with me!"

The dog stayed on its side as Robbie swung back his boot for a third time. "Take that you . . ." Robbie kicked the dog hard on its underbelly. The dog let out a loud, piercing yelp and hobbled back across the yard, where it lay down and whimpered in agony for the rest of the night.

With daylight approaching, Robbie noticed Lester had gone quiet and crossed the yard to investigate.

"Lester, you OK?" Robbie bent down and prodded the dog, curious to see if it would move. When Lester's cold, lifeless body inched backwards, Robbie stood up straight, puffed out his chest and grinned, his eyes glinting like cats' eyes in the road.

CHAPTER ONE

The minister put down the phone in her private office, glanced through the window at the dull grey sky and sighed. This was big news. She'd only been in the position a matter of months, and the situation seemed to be getting worse by the day. She didn't want to go down in history as the woman that lost the UK millions of pounds' worth of investment from some of the world's biggest and most powerful companies. Owing to her academic background, she'd been given the relatively junior post of Minister of Science and Research, but this was going to have a knock-on effect, the ramifications of which would involve just about every senior minister, including the PM himself.

This wasn't the first time she'd taken a call from Leo Schelling, but it was by far the most worrying conversation she'd had with him. The calls started soon after her appointment and so far, she'd done a good job of appeasing him. But this time he wasn't standing for any nonsense. It was with the words, 'Put a stop to it, Miss Hunter', still ringing in her ears that she dried her palm on her skirt and lifted the receiver for the second time that morning. Alex, the Minister for Trade and Investments, had been around the block a good few times, and had so far helped her over each and every hurdle that had presented itself. He was also directly involved in the situation, as it was his department that dealt with investments of this magnitude.

If it was reassurances she was after, she was left disappointed. On this occasion, her friend and mentor did not tell her to continue fobbing them off until the police finally got their act together. He too had received a phone call from Schelling and confirmed to the Minister for Science and Research that the situation was, indeed, grave. He stressed that the country could not afford to lose the investment under any circumstances. To do so would be nothing short of catastrophic. So, five minutes after her second telephone conversation of the morning, she found herself being whisked across London in a black cab to a secret location that ministers always used when they didn't want anyone to get wind of the story.

This was the first time she'd been invited to attend such an emergency meeting. Indeed, some of her colleagues on the back benches had even doubted the secret hideaway existed. In a way it made her feel exhilarated, like she was acting out a plot from an Ian Fleming book. Her father and older brothers had been James Bond nuts when she was a girl.

On the other hand, she knew full well what was at stake. The next hour could well decide her own future political fate as well as the government's fiscal policy. If what Alex had told her was true, it might even force an interim Autumn budget, and that would let the whole world and his wife know that the country was in serious financial peril. Alex was a smooth operator though, and if anyone could buy more time, then he could. He'd done well to get Schelling to agree to meet them like this at such short notice. Had he not intervened, the information would have gone straight to the PM and the story would have been broken by the BBC.

The taxi left the City of Westminster and headed towards one of Europe's busiest shopping districts. She leant forward, rapped on the window and gave the driver the code name once again, just to ensure they were on the right track.

The driver turned round, smiled and said, "Not long now, it's just along here." Then, completely out of the blue, he pulled up outside the entrance of a shopping precinct. "Get in the lift and give the attendant the code name. He'll show you where to go."

She found the lift on the left-hand side of the building as she walked through the glass sliding doors. She'd been in this precinct several times and never before noticed the lift by the entrance. This was especially strange as she knew the precinct to be on one level only. There was a man in a suit stood by the lift, who smiled and nodded in her direction. This was getting more and more like a James Bond book by the second. She wasn't surprised to find the lift could only go in one direction.

The lift descended two floors and came to a halt. The man in the suit opened the door and murmured some directions in her ear. She stepped out into a dark corridor full of what looked like secret offices. Right at the end of the corridor there was a light, and if she held her breath, she imagined she could hear voices. Waiting for the lift to move on, she set off in the direction of the light. The corridor wasn't too dissimilar to the underground dungeons on Silence of the Lambs. Only the rooms and, she hoped, their occupants, were different.

"Kate, do come in." Much to her relief, Alex was there already. She didn't fancy sitting there alone, wondering if Hannibal Lecter was about to come breezing in at any minute.

She smiled politely and pulled out one of the three chairs that were tucked under a circular wooden table. She hadn't seen a table or chairs like these since she was at school. Alex glanced along the corridor before returning to the centre of the room, leaving the door wide open, and took the seat opposite her. Neither of them got chance to kick off an awkward and tense conversation before they heard footsteps resounding along the corridor.

"Schelling." Alex said with a grin, and immediately rose to his feet. The sound of the metal chair legs scraping on the floor made her want to cover her ears.

Schelling was nothing like she expected. About six feet tall, blond hair, shifty blue eyes. Looked like he could be a body builder or something on the side. She felt her hand creak under the strain as they were introduced.

Alex was the first to speak. "Leo, thanks for agreeing to see us at such short notice. So, I understand that your client is threatening to withdraw their investment in the UK economy?"

"Not threatening. They're done with threats. It's happening." His German accent sounded different in the flesh. Maybe he was Swiss.

"And is there nothing we can do to change your mind?"

Schelling sighed. "Alex. Miss Hunter. I believe you are both acutely aware of the damage these—protestors are doing to the image of the companies my client represents."

Kate cleared her throat. "People have a right to air their views, Mr Schelling. It's part of our Constitution."

"But there are ways and means of silencing them, are there not?"

"There are," said the UK Minister for Trade and Investments, "but the trouble is—the trouble is that people are on their side."

"Then maybe they need to hear the truth."

"That wouldn't wash, I'm afraid. In fact, if the people found out that the companies involved contribute so much to the economy, there'd be outrage. Might even bring the government down."

"Then maybe they need to hear a different version of the truth."

Alex glanced at Kate before replying. "Mr Schelling. What are you suggesting?"

"You British, you're all the same. You're obsessed with fair play and all that. Aren't the lives of a handful of protestors worth sacrificing for the good of the country as a whole?"

Kate opened her mouth to remonstrate, but was beaten to it by Alex. "Protestors? Don't you mean terrorists?"

Schelling smiled. "I'm glad we understand each other, Minister."

Kate was indignant. "No. You can't just ruin the lives of innocent people."

"I can see I'm clearly wasting my time." Schelling shook his head and rose to his feet. "I'll advise my clients to go ahead with the withdrawal," he added, hand on the door handle.

Alex scraped back his chair and rushed across the room. "Wait. I'll sort it. Just give us a few weeks, that's all I ask."

"Very well, Minister, I will advise my clients to delay the withdrawal of funds until the New Year. If progress hasn't been made, then 2005 may well turn out to be Mr Blair's annus horribilis."

"Thank you. I owe you a debt of gratitude."

"Indeed you do. I know I can trust you to ensure your fellow members of the cabinet see it in the same way."

CHAPTER TWO

The second the door opened, the chatter ceased and all eyes focused on the figure making an entrance. "Oh, good morning, Prime Minister," someone, the person nearest to the door said. The others soon followed suit, nodding and smiling in turn.
"Good morning everyone," the PM replied, taking his seat at the head of the rectangular table and shuffling his papers into order before placing them on the polished table top in front of him. "Alex, you're the one that called for this meeting, would you like to tell everyone what it's all about?"
"Yes, Prime Minister, certainly Prime Minister." Alex Hurd cleared his throat before breaking the news. "This morning I was rushed to an emergency meeting with err, Leo Schelling, who, as I'm sure you all know, is the lawyer representing ABC." The minister waited for the murmuring to subside before continuing. It's about the money the organisation contributes to our economy in exchange for the promotion of products which their member companies provide."
"I had no idea," someone said from the opposite end of the table, "I choose to go private." At that, everyone fell about laughing.
 Alex just sat there, feeling a little awkward, waiting for the commotion to die down. "Well, compensation, back-hander, bribe, however

you want to dress it up, the fact is that we've come to rely on this money."

"Absolutely," the PM interjected, "we can't afford to lose it. Not at any cost."

"Yes. Thank you, Prime Minister," Alex said, glad that he'd finally got everyone's undivided attention.

"Well, go on, get on with it for heaven's sake. Don't tell me they want the poor unsuspecting bastards to consume even more of their— products."

"If only that were true, Prime Minister. No, they are threatening to withdraw the payment altogether."

"What? They can't do that. I'm relying on that money to fund the campaign in Iraq. Don't tell me they're pulling the plug, now. My God, if it wasn't for this money, I'd never have gone in to begin with."

"Well, I managed to delay them until the New Year. But, I'm afraid it looks like they mean business this time."

"This Time? How long has this been going on?"

"I'm afraid for quite a while, Prime Minister. Kate Hunter's been dealing with it. It's all to do with these bloody annoying protest people that have been splashed all over the news lately."

"I see. And where is Miss Hunter?"

"She asked me to pass on her apologies and give you a message. I'll err, come to that later, if I may."

"Yes, yes, go on. Do tell me what all this is about, Alex."

The Minister for Trade and Investments gave everyone the specifics.

"So what has Miss Hunter been doing about it?"

"She's been keeping them at bay, explaining about their legitimate right to protest providing they remain within the law."

"And have they? Been remaining within the law?"

"Yes. That's the problem. They just turn up once a week and protest peacefully, using nothing more threatening than placards."

"Mmmm. Shit. So what've the local authorities been doing about it?"

"There's a police presence there every week, watching them, waiting to pounce the minute anyone steps out of line."

"What about the press?"

"Completely onside. It's a conservative rag called The Burton Mail. They'll print whatever we tell them to print."

"Well, that's something at least. What have they tried to date?"

"All the usual. Calling them terrorists, intimidation tactics, bomb threats."

"And nothing's worked?"

"No. Problem is that the people are on their side. Whatever we print is, in their eyes, at least partly justified."

"I see. Well, we can't go getting heavy handed with them. That will only create more publicity for their campaign. Play right into their hands." The Prime Minister paused for a second to read the notes in front of him. "Alex, what do we know about these people? Do any of them have criminal records?"

"Not as far as I know, Prime Minister. Although I do believe most of them are known to the Staffordshire Constabulary."

The Prime Minister turned to his Home Secretary. "David. Your department, I believe."

The Home Secretary got to his feet. "Would you excuse me for ten minutes, Prime Minister? I just need to go and make a few phone calls. See what I can find out."

"Yes, of course. Tell you what, let's all adjourn for, say, thirty minutes, shall we?"

After a swift drink, they all began filing back inside the Downing Street meeting room. The Prime Minister brought up the rear, alongside the Home Secretary who was looking decidedly smug.

Once the chatter and shuffling of papers had died down, the PM raised a hand and recommenced the meeting. "David. So, have you had chance to carry out some investigative work during the break?"

"I have indeed, Prime Minister, I have indeed. So I did some ringing round and discovered that the ringleader, a Miss Jane Thomas was arrested—"everyone looked visibly lifted—" without charge"—their faces dropped again—"last year. What's more, she filed a claim for compensation and was awarded three thousand pounds."

"Quite a strain on the tax payer then," a minister across the table chipped in.

"My sentiments exactly."

"So, there's nothing on any of them then, is that what you're saying, David?"

"There is one thing, Prime Minister. This Jane Thomas, the ringleader."

"What about her?"

"She's got breast cancer."

"Shit."

"No, no, you don't follow me, Prime Minister. She's receiving Chemotherapy."

"Still not with you, David. The British people love a good sob story. They're famous for it. Don't get me wrong, it would be perfect if we were trying to make people like her, but—. "

"Chemotherapy is—."

"Aah. Of course. How stupid of me."

"Not at all, Prime Minister."

"So we could make her out to be a hypocrite for being alive, is that what you're saying?"

"Well, some faiths do prefer death over treatments they don't believe in. Such cases have been well documented. It's what people are used to. OK, I know it's a bit south of the border, Prime Minister, but desperate times call for desperate measures and all that."

"Mmm. I'm just not sure it would work, David. We need something to really make people's skin crawl. But we could keep it on the back burner, just in case we need it later. Was that all you could find on these people?"

"I'm afraid so, Prime Minister. However. The Staffordshire Chief Constable is a close friend of mine, and he reliably informs me that one of the inspectors in Burton Upon Trent, a Robbie Crowe, might be willing to err, play ball."

"Play ball? Little boys you mean?" Said a minister along the table that had been until that point listening quietly.

"Afraid not. Wouldn't wash with a woman, would it? No, the old paedophile game's out of the question, regrettably."

"So what then?" Asked the Prime Minister.

"Well, this, Robbie or Bobby Crowe has a bit of a reputation. His father was a vicar, so has close links to the church. The perfect, upstanding member of society. Just the very person we need to err, instigate a slur and make sure it stands fast.

"And do you think that this Bobby Crowe can come up with something so repugnant that they'll never be able to show their faces in decent society again?" Asked the Prime Minister.

"By all accounts, he is the perfect person. Rumour has it that he killed his dogs for the sheer fun of it when he was eight."

"Good grief. So he's hardly likely to shirk at the thought of —."

"Exactly, Prime Minister. There's err, just one thing though."

"And what might that be?"

"We need your written consent to take whatever measures we feel necessary."

"Oh yes, of course. No problem."

"Thank you, Prime Minister."

"So, if that concludes the matter, you were going to give me a message from Kate Hunter?"

"Oh yes. She's asked me to give you her resignation."

CHAPTER THREE

Holding on to speak to the editor, Crowe sensed he was about to run out of patience. "It's about time that we put a stop to this. Can't you just print the story as I tell it to you, for crying out loud? These people are terrorists. They're trying to get their way using intimidation and blackmail."

"We're doing our best, Inspector. Lots of people—including some of our readers— are on their side."

"On their side? On their side? Are you telling me that everyone in Burton is as stupid and misguided as you clearly are? God made men in his own image for a reason, you know. He intended for us to—."

"That's your view—."

"That's God's view. Although many people around here would say that amounted to the same thing." Inspector Crowe tittered. A knock. "Oh, I've gotta go. Just get it right, for God's sake. Print the damned story exactly like I said it for once, and before you know it they'll be history."

"Very good, Inspector Crowe."

"Inspector Crowe?" A woman's voice called from the other side of the door.

"Yes, what is it, Oplitova?"

"You've err, got a visitor, Sir."

"A visitor? It's nearly lunch time. Can't they come back later?"

"Afraid not, Sir. It's quite an important visitor, Sir."

"Well, unless he's carrying a juicy burger, I'm not interested."

"Bobby?"

"Oh! Chief Constable Sexton? How nice to see you, Sir. Do come in." Crowe strode across his office to open the door for his superior officer. "Come in, come in. Hope you were amused by my little joke earlier, Sir."

"Very good Bobby, very good." The Chief Constable sat down at the desk, facing the window with his back to the door and stretched his legs.

"Take a seat. What can I get you? Glass of water, cup of tea—cognac?"

"A cup of tea will do fine, thanks."

The inspector poked his head around the door and glanced along the corridor. "Oplitova, two cups of tea, pronto." Crowe closed the door and walked around the room to sit facing the Chief Constable. "Good journey sir? She won't be a minute with your cuppa."

"No problem."

"So, what can I do for you, sir? I take it this wasn't just a social call, however pleasant that might be."

The Chief Constable smiled. "I'll err, wait until the tea arrives before I begin. I don't want to be interrupted."

"Oh, wise decision, Sir. Very wise of you, if you don't mind me saying so."

After five minutes of awkward small talk, something that neither man was keen on, there was a knock. "Ah, tea's here at last," said the Inspector as he rose to his feet.

Waiting for the chief constable to swallow his first mouthful of tea, Inspector Crowe repeated his question from earlier. "So, what brings you down to these parts? You have better things to do, surely, then to come checking up on us?"

"Oh, that's not necessary. You run a tight ship here, Crowe, a very tight ship."

"Why, thank you, Sir. Glad you noticed."

"No, it's about those lunatics that have been making the news. The ones on your patch."

Keeping his head still, the inspector looked up at the ceiling. "Lunatics, lunatics, no, not quite with you."

"The protesters, damn it."

"Oh, those lunatics. We've got things well under control there, Sir."

The Chief Constable shook his head. "No. Bobby, they need stopping. I've had instructions from the Home Secretary."

"The Home Secretary?"

"On a matter of national importance. They need stopping. I told them you would be perfect for the job."

"Me? Oh, surely not, Sir."

"And I want to make one thing absolutely clear."

"What's that, Sir?"

"You have licence do whatever it takes. Anything bar having them bumped off. This has come from the PM himself."

"I understand completely, Sir."

"So can I leave it in your capable hands, Bobby?"

"Oh, absolutely, Sir."

"Splendid. Well, I'd best be making tracks."

"Do you have to leave so soon, Sir?"

"I'm afraid so, things to do. You know how it is, Bobby. Oh, but just one more thing."

"What's that, Sir?"

"This needs actioning immediately. You'd better get your thinking hat on. And your skates."

"Well, you can rely on me, Sir."

"Oh, I know that, Bobby. I knew you'd be perfect for the job the minute Blunkett told me about it." Sexton rose to his feet. "So, I'll leave you to do your worst then."

"Oh, absolutely. I'll keep you informed."

"Oh, no need for that. In fact, the fewer people know about it, the better."

Once the Chief Constable had closed the door and he was alone in his office, Crowe sat at his desk, with his back to the window and listened to the receding footsteps clapping along the corridor. Waiting for the car engine to roar into life and fade into the distance, Robbie sprang to life.

Knocking on the various doors as he marched along the corridor, he called out, "Team meeting, my office, ten minutes." Noticing one of his sergeants was reading a book, he took a step inside the room and leaned over his shoulder. "What's that you're reading?"

"Oh, just a detective novel, Sir. I'm still on my lunch hour."

"Well, sorry to disturb you. What's it about?"

"It's about . . . "

Crowe sniggered. "My God, that's ridiculous."

Five minutes later, Robbie Crowe opened the staff meeting. "OK everyone, as you know, I just had a visit from none other than his royal highness, the Chief Constable himself. He's tasked me, us, with sorting out a matter of national importance. . . "

Once he'd relayed to his staff his conversation with the Chief Constable, he looked at each of them in turn and said, "So does anyone have any ideas?"

Seeing they'd drawn a blank, he shook his head and said, "Oh come on, one of you must have something. My God, at this rate, we'll be taking a leaf out of your book, Sergeant. " He laughed at his own joke, waited until he had everyone's undivided attention and declared, "That's perfect. Sergeant, would you care to share with everyone the plot of your book? "

"Certainly, Sir . . . "

Oplitova was the first to speak up. "But, Sir, surely you're not seriously suggesting we act out a fictitious crime just so we can blame it on the protesters?"

"Not us, Constable. I have a contact."

Oplitova shook her head. "I don't like it. Let me talk to them, please."

"Afraid it's too late for talking, Constable. Now, if that's everything, I have a phone call to make to an old friend of mine."

Everyone began filing out of the room. "Sergeant?" Inspector Crowe called out, standing in the doorway.

D.S. Mellor looked over his shoulder. "Yes, Sir?"

"Keep an eye on Oplitova. I mean it, I want you to watch her like a hawk."
"Very good, Sir."
"Oh and Sergeant?"
"Yes, Sir?"
"Keep tomorrow morning free. I may well have an errand for you."
"Very good, Sir."

CHAPTER FOUR

Reverend Percival Jeffries put the top on his fountain pen and placed it, centred lengthways, over his draft of the report he'd been working on. Being the Director of Education for the Diocese of Lichfield, he always had one form of paper work or another to occupy his time with.

 He'd been up since the crack of dawn and made good progress too, but suddenly, the draught coming in from the window, which he'd opened at six am, and had been so invigorating at first, was now starting to give him a sore throat. It was October after all, and he wasn't as young as he once was. He just knew that once he got up and walked across the room to the window, he wouldn't be able to help himself from admiring the view and then that would be that. He'd be distracted from his work for hours. Still, he knew that if he suffered in silence, putting his work before his well-being, his wife would not be best pleased with him.

He knew himself very well. Letting the windowsill take his weight, he leant forward and gazed through the sparse branches of the huge oak tree that stood at the foot of his back garden, across the playing fields that were dotted with swings and climbing frames, at the glorious English countryside that lay beyond. A bird, perched on a branch in the vicarage tree, sang up, catching Percival's attention. For a second they each looked into the other's eyes and Percival was whisked away into another world, a world where the events of ten and a half years earlier didn't haunt every living second of his life, until, eventually, the cold breeze sunk its teeth in and the spell was broken.

Percival sank to his knees, joined his hands and, looking through the window, said his prayers. He prayed every day for forgiveness and on this occasion, told God he'd endure any penance that was bestowed on him.

When the aroma of fresh coffee began to mingle with the smell of the countryside, Percival reached up and closed the window, being careful not to let it slam. He'd only just got back to his desk and removed the cap from his fountain pen when there was a knock, and his door opened.

"Brought you some coffee," his wife said, carrying a white China cup and saucer on a wooden tray.

"Thanks, Loretta, Love. What would I do without you?"

His wife, Loretta was the appointed Vicar of St Peter's church in Yoxall. He loved this life, and he loved the countryside. He'd always lived in the country and was more than grateful when, following the events in Northumberland, the opportunity arose to start afresh in the Staffordshire village of Yoxall. This part of the country was really beautiful, but somehow less wild than his previous patch, the place he'd grown up in. Deep down, his heart was still there, but he knew he could never return. The most he could ask for was God's forgiveness for what he'd done. And, given the gravity of his crime, he knew that he still had work to do before he could look his maker in the eye.

This was the burden that he had to live with and he was starting to toil under the weight.

"How's it going?" Loretta said, one hand on the door handle.

"Oh, very well. I needed this though." And it was true. The bitter black liquid had, temporarily at least, stopped the chill from manifesting itself on his chest.

"That's strange." Loretta made a beeline for the window and stood looking out, brow furrowed.

"What, what is it?"

"There's a police car. Heading this way." She stood at the window looking out, while the engine got gradually louder. When the wheels began crunching the gravelly driveway, Percival joined his wife at the window.

Once the car stopped, Percival returned to his desk and Loretta went to hover by the front door. Reading over his report, an idea came to Percival's mind. He was just about to start writing when his study door door opened. "In here," he could hear Loretta telling the visitor from the hallway.

Percival looked over his shoulder to see a large man stood in the doorway. "Can I help you?" Percival said, with a polite smile.

"Oh, yes." The man extracted a badge from his inside pocket. "D.C. Mellor, I just need a quick word with you. Shouldn't take too long."

"Of course." Percival glanced at a chair by the wall. "Take a seat."

D.C. Mellor carried the chair across the room and made himself comfortable on the opposite side of Percival's desk. "Nice place you got here. You landed on your feet, wouldn't you say?"

"Well, thank you, yes, it is nice—" he paused— "what do you mean?"

"I have it on good authority that you relocated from your Northumberland parish following some rather sensitive allegations."

Percival's head dropped. "Yes."

"Must be difficult for you, you being a man of the cloth and all that."

Percival nodded.

"You ever thought of clearing your name?"

"Only God can forgive me, Sergeant."

"True, but it would help, wouldn't it, if the truth came out. Or should I say, the right version of the truth?"

"Lie, you mean? Oh, I could never do that."

"Well, you wouldn't be lying. You'd just be putting an alternative version of events to people, leaving you to make things up with God."

"Oh—what do you have in mind?"

D.S. Mellor grinned. "Nothing much, really. Just a small favour."

"I don't like the sound of this. What type of favour?"

"Well, there are some protestors. Have you heard about them?"

"Yes, of course I have. It's a bit hard to miss them, isn't it? What about them?"

"Well, they're making rather a nuisance of themselves, and we've had orders direct from the PM himself to put a stop to it. Trouble is, they're not breaking any laws."

"So, what does this have to do with me?"

"We need your help convincing people that they're bad news."

"You want me to lie, you mean?"

"Not lie, just do something under cover."

Reverend Jeffries got to his feet. "Mr Mellor, I may not have a perfect track record, but I'm a man of honour. I'm afraid I have rather a lot on at the moment." He held the door open. "Thank you for stopping by, but I'd like to graciously decline your offer."

D.S. Mellor stayed put. "Jason, that was his name, wasn't it?"

Reverend Jeffries felt himself drain of colour.

"We can help the guilt go away. It must be terrible, carrying that around. You being a religious man and all."

Jeffries glanced at the crucifix on the wall and remembered his prayer earlier in the day. Maybe this was God's will.

Gently closing the door behind him, he walked back to his desk. "What do you want me to do?"

D.S. Mellor cleared his throat and explained, while Reverend Jeffries listened in silence. Five minutes later, D.S Mellor asked him how he felt about what he'd just said.

"Oh, I don't know. My wife does all the—. "

"Do you want your name clearing or not?"

"Yes, yes. It's just that . . ."

"What?"

"Nothing. So if I do this, you'll see to it I get my name cleared once and for all and I can return home to Northumberland, head held high?"

"Yes. We'll have to arrest you first, of course, so it can go to trial."

"Oh."

"But, it won't be anything to worry about. Honestly, we do this kind of thing all the time."

"I can believe that Sergeant Mellor, I really can."

"So, you'll help us out then?"

"Yes. But I'll need my wife's consent."

"That shouldn't be a problem though, should it?"

"No, not at all."

Sergeant Mellor pushed back his chair and stood up to leave. "Well, it's been a pleasure doing business with you, Reverend Jeffries." He offered his hand.

The Reverend shook his hand with an awkward smile and showed him to the door. It wasn't until the police car had turned out of the vicarage driveway and he'd closed the front door, that he realised he was alone in the house. The perfect opportunity to immerse himself in his work and forget all about what he'd just agreed to do.

Almost an hour had passed by the time he put the top on his fountain pen and placed it beside the writing pad. He read his work back and decided it was one of his better efforts. For a minute, he felt content with his lot, then he remembered. He remembered all about Jason, what he'd agreed to do and what the consequences would be for the protestors. These people could easily be members of his wife's flock, and then what would he do? Would he ruin their lives just to clear his name, if not his conscience? Possibly not. Loretta would know what to do, she always did. But this was something he couldn't involve her in, one battle he'd have to fight alone. He'd asked God for guidance, and he'd been given a sign. This was his penance and, If he ever hoped to clear his conscience, he had to pay his dues. God obviously had other plans for the protestors. He would take care of them, and if not, they deserved whatever they got.

A car turning onto the road leading to the vicarage caught his eye; it was Loretta, on her way back from the Mother's Union meeting. He couldn't help but smile as he watched her car gradually grow until it was near enough to catch a glimpse of the driver. He got to his feet, walked to the window and waved away his blanket of depression.

"Percival! Is everything alright, Dearest? You looked white as a sheet from the window."

Reverend Jeffries found himself deep in thought, staring unflinchingly at the crucifix and so jumped out of his skin when his wife entered the room. "Err, yes. Sit down a minute, I want to talk to you."

Waiting for his wife to make herself comfortable, he began. "That policeman earlier, he wanted me to do him a favour."

"A favour—for the police? I hope you said no."

"Well, not exactly. He said he can do something for me in return. And besides, it's only a small thing. They want to . . ."

Ten minutes later, Loretta took a deep breath and exhaled slowly through puffed cheeks. "And what will they do in return?"

"He said he can help. Clear my name, I mean."

"Oh, Percival. Are you sure it's worth it?"

"Yes. It's the will of God."

"Well, that's good enough for me. So, you'll be wanting to know the location of the —?"

"Yes."

"Oh, I know exactly where she is. Pass me a pen and paper, and I'll draw you a map."

***

Sat in the living room, watching the clock on the wall approach ten pm, the one above his wife who was reading silently, Reverend Jeffries heard a car approach. "That's him, he said, rubbing his eyes."

"Oh, are you sure you're up to this?"

"Yes."

"Have you got the map I drew?"

"Yes, it's in my pocket."

The car pulled up outside, and the passenger door opened. Reverend Jeffries fastened up his jacket and walked along the hallway to the front door. "D.S. Mellor," he said after opening the door and seeing the police officer standing there, shielding his eyes from the glare of the headlights, "nice to see you again."

"Come on, follow me." Mellor held open the back door of the car, and the Reverend stepped in, sitting beside a burly looking constable who just nodded in his direction and continued to stare through the window blankly. In the front, Sergeant Mellor sat beside the driver and behind were two more policemen. All of them wore jeans or scruffy looking trousers, like they were expecting to get dirty.

***

Little over half an hour later, Jeffries said goodbye to Mellor and immersed himself in the warm, comforting glow of the vicarage.

It might have been the fresh air or just sheer coincidence, but Reverend Jeffries slept better that night than he had for years.

CHAPTER FIVE

11TH OCTOBER 2004

"Have a nice morning, Dear." Percival Jeffries kissed his wife on the cheek and watched her walk along the garden path, past their car and turn onto the tree-lined road that adjoined the vicarage with the rest of the village. After closing the door, he turned to make the short journey to the study. The delicious smell of bacon intermingled with his wife's perfume and the bitter taste of coffee to create the illusion that his wife was still present. Although the silence, only broken by the birds singing while perched on the rustling tree branches, told him otherwise.

Despite the fact that he had the perfect opportunity to get his head down and make a start on the mountain of paperwork that had accumulated, Jeffries hated being without his wife. She'd gone to tend a sick parishioner, so, in all likelihood, wouldn't be back until lunch time. Jeffries opened the window of his study before making a start. He loved the lingering breakfast smell, but without some fresh air there was a chance it might outstay its welcome. Once at his desk, Jeffries opened the first, most urgent document and began to read. He'd only made it to the third paragraph when a car turned onto the road that led to the vicarage. Jeffries looked up through the window and waited, hoping beyond hope that his plans weren't about to be ruined. When a police car came into view, he placed the document he'd been reading back on the pile and prepared himself for the inevitable. Jeffries led D.S. Mellor into his study and offered him a seat, making sure the window was firmly closed before joining him at his desk.

Mellor had with him a black leather brief case, which he stood on the table beside him before explaining to Jeffries the reason for his visit. "Good to see you again, Reverend," Mellor said with a smile. "I just wanted to give you a progress report and, if you don't mind, ask for another tiny favour."

Jeffries' eyes widened. "Oh? What's that?"

"All in good time. Now, don't know if you heard, but we made an arrest last week."

"I read about it in the paper. A woman with cancer or something."

"Yes, well. We had to let her go."

"Sorry to hear that."

"Lack of evidence. The problem is, your wife identified a 5' 10 " male, with not dark hair. We need her to change her statement. We need her to identify this woman . . ." He pulled out a photo and a newspaper article. "Here. Her name's Jane Thomas and she's a 5' 4" female. As you can see, she has no hair."

Jeffries nodded. "Chemotherapy. I see the problem."

"So do you think you can swing it, Reverend?"

"To be honest, I don't know. She was reluctant to do it to start with. I feel bad for asking her to—."

"We had a deal."

"The deal didn't involve making a blatant lie that anyone with half a brain will see through."

"It does now."

"No one's going to believe it, though."

"I would."

"Say no more."

Laughing off the insinuation, Mellor said, "Reverend, if your wife doesn't change her statement, the deal's off. Furthermore, we can make things very difficult for you round here."

"What are you talking about?"

Grinning, Mellor reached into his brief case and extracted a picture of Jeffries with the word 'Paedophile' emblazoned across the top. "You've got a nice set up here. What would your parishioners say if they found out the truth?"

"You wouldn't."

"Wouldn't I? Want to try me?"

"If I—my wife does this, do you give me your word that this will be the end of it until the time comes for you to return the favour?"

"Of course."

"Well, OK, very well then. Give me the photos and I'll see what I can do."

"That's what I like to hear. Oh, just one more thing before I go."

"What? Now?"

"Inspector Crowe released a story to the press, encouraging them to err—go with the hypocrite angle. It's been all over the nationals."

"I know."

"Well tonight, Thomas is appearing on the BBC. It might be a good chance for your wife to err, get a good look."

"I'll look forward to it. Now, if there's nothing else, I have things to do before my wife returns from her rounds."

"Of course. Don't want to outstay my welcome."

***

Loretta Jeffries, on hearing from her husband about the deal he'd struck with the police had reluctantly realised she'd identified the wrong person. Sat together watching the evening news, Percival Jeffries stood up and exclaimed to his wife, "That's her!"

"Who?" came the reply.

Percival disappeared into his study, re-emerging two minutes later holding a photograph which D.S. Mellor had presented to him earlier that morning. "This is the woman they're trying to frame."

Loretta held out her hand. "Let me see." Looking from the photo to the T.V., and from the T.V. back to the photo, Loretta watched the interview while trying to figure out if they were one and the same person. Five minutes later, she handed the picture back to her husband and agreed with him.

"So, I made a mistake with my identification, did I?" she said apologetically. In an act of faith, she'd got up early the previous Wednesday morning to offer up an authentic identification to the police. To her mind, she'd done her very best under the circumstances.

"Afraid so."

"So what should we do? I don't want all this to be for nothing."

"No, nor do I." Percival lifted the phone, which was on the table beside him, and handed it to his wife. "Better tell him you want to change your statement."

Far from being put out, D.S. Mellor was only too pleased to make the short journey, despite the late hour. They took him into the living room, made him a drink by way of an apology and waited for him to make himself comfortable before Loretta made a start with her new statement:

On the evening of 11th October 2004, I was at home, watching the early evening news when I became aware of the reporter interviewing the female who was a spokesperson for the group. I was immediately struck by the build of this woman and also her features and instantly thought that the male I had earlier described standing by the gate was in fact this female.

Twenty minutes later, D.S. Mellor handed the statement across to Loretta to sign. When he had the paper back in his grasp, he waved the ink dry and gave a smile of deep satisfaction.

"Will that be sufficient, D.S. Mellor?" Percival asked.

"Will it be enough to get us a conviction, you mean? It should be." He stood up to leave. Well, thanks, to both of you for doing the right thing. Inspector Crowe will be most pleased and believe me, he is a man that remembers those who do him favours."

Percival Jeffries leant across and extended his arm. "Pleasure doing business with you, Sergeant."

"Likewise," D.S. Mellor replied, shaking Percival Jeffries' hand. "I might have to pop round again tomorrow, just to get some more signatures."

A day later and the Jeffries' smiles had faded somewhat. Whereas at first, the guilt had been all Percival's, now Loretta felt just as burdened. In the dark of the night, she'd laid awake thinking, wondering how she could look her parishioners in the eye after having been so dishonest.

Sitting in silence, staring at the fireplace in front, completely shutting her husband out, Loretta waited for D.S. Mellor's car door to close. When the thud finally came, she walked across the room in silence to the window, just in time to watch her integrity and indeed her soul, drive away into the distance.

"Let's hope that's the last of him for a while," Percival said with a hint of desperation.

Loretta shrugged and re-joined her husband on the couch, where she sat staring straight ahead in silence.

Percival reached across and grasped his wife's hand. "Thank you. And sorry."

"No. I'm sorry, Dear, it's just a lot to come to terms with. It isn't me that should be getting an apology really, is it?"

"The woman has been terrorising the village for years. God wanted me to do this as my penance."

"Your penance? But you are completely innocent. At least that's what you've always told me anyway. Why would God hand you a penance for a sin you didn't commit?"

Percival had to think fast. "Just because I didn't commit that particular sin, it doesn't mean I'm without sin completely."

"I suppose not. But that doesn't make it any easier to bear. Now I'm the one that needs forgiveness."

"No. God knows, Dear. He knows that you did it for me and to rid your parishioners of an evil influence."

"Do you think so? Do you think God understands?"

"Absolutely, I do. I think you've risen in his estimation as a result of what you've done."

Beaming, Loretta pressed her face into her husband's shoulder and squeezed his arm. "Oh, Honey, you always know just what to say."

Percival gently kissed his wife's crown and sat back, wearing a smug grin.

CHAPTER SIX

It was approaching mid-November when Jane, sat in her flat reading a book, was startled by a loud knock. "Who can this be?" she said to Suzie, who had been settled beside her on the couch and was not best pleased with the disturbance. A sudden thought hit Jane; she hadn't been approached by any reporters for a while or worse still the police, who had promised her they'd be back in touch. With the foreboding increasing with each step, she walked across to the window and breathed a huge sigh of relief when she saw a lorry with the words 'Parcel Force' emblazoned along the side.

On opening the door, the postman presented to her a large box. She glanced down, puzzled, trying to catch a glimpse of the sender's name and address.

"Want me to take this upstairs for you?"

Jane nodded and led him upstairs, grateful that she hadn't had to ask for any help with the box. She was starting to get short of breath climbing the stairs as it was, so lifting the box had been a concern.

She waited for the postman to descend the stairs and leave the building before taking a knife from the kitchen drawer and cutting through the tape. With both top flaps stood up vertical, she peered inside the box and, on seeing the contents, still felt none the wiser.

Two minutes later and the box was empty in the corner of the room. In the middle of the room she counted nine full ring binders. They were from a solicitor called Timothy Lawson-Cruttenden, and they detailed a High Court application to have the protest stopped.

After reading and re-reading each one, she got on the phone to her fellow campaigners. In all, seventeen of these boxes had been delivered.

As far as the campaigners were aware, they were still legally within their rights to continue protesting. So that is what they did, every Sunday throughout the month of November. Although, something was different. As the daylight hours got shorter and they spent more and more time in the dark, freezing hands in pockets, watching their breath spiral upwards as they chatted amongst themselves, they noticed that fewer passers-by were tooting their horns in support.

The locals too were less friendly than before, although not entirely hostile at that stage.

On the final Sunday of the month, the atmosphere changed once again, perhaps because local shops had started early with the Christmas lights and so engineered an early festive spirit. At the back of their minds was the impending court case, which blocked their pathway to Christmas like a great boulder on a country lane. This was due the following Thursday, meaning this could be the last time they'd be protesting.

CHAPTER SEVEN

TUESDAY 30TH NOVEMBER 2004

Inspector Crowe waltzed into the weekly staff meeting, ten minutes, late carrying a pile of papers under his arm. Slamming the door behind him, he took his place at the head of the table, put the papers in front of him and silently acknowledged everyone present, paying particular attention to D.S. Mellor.

Waiting until he had everyone's undivided attention, the Inspector said good morning and formally opened the meeting. It had been a relatively quiet week. Nothing of meaning to report, just the usual drunk and disorderlies, late night punch ups and drug related crime. When it transpired that no one else had anything more to contribute, he looked at his agenda and announced Any Other Business. The time had come for him to tell everyone about the task the Chief Constable had given him, which was starting to become critical.

"OK, everyone, just before I leave you to go about your business, there is something I need to tell you about. You may recall a few weeks ago when Sexton came to pay us a visit."

Everyone nodded in silence.

"Well, he gave me a special task that had come direct from Downing Street."

A collective gasp of disbelief swept around the table. Only D.S. Mellor looked unphased.

"Apparently, the campaigners at—."

A collective groan swept round the table.

"Yeah, them again. Apparently, some major players didn't appreciate them exercising their right to protest, so threatened to pull the plug on a bung they'd given to the treasury. They issued the government with an ultimatum. Stop the protest by the New Year or else they wouldn't get their millions. So Blunkett and Blair between them got on to the Chief Constable and asked him to find the right man for the job, to ensure they get what's coming to them. I have great pleasure in telling you that not only was I deemed to be that man, but we have licence to do whatever we please, bar knocking them off."

A female D.C. at the opposite end of the table leant forward and chipped in. "But, they may have solved the problem for us. No one's going to support them now, Sir"

Crowe looked at Mellor and smirked before the two of them broke out into a fit of laughter. "Honestly, don't be so bloody na ve," Crowe said, once he'd composed himself.

The female D.C.'s jaw dropped. "You mean— "

"Yes, I mean precisely that, Constable."

An ambitious male constable smiled and shook his head. "You wiley old fox, you, Sir."

"Well, sadly, I can't take all the credit for this. D.S. Mellor made a contribution too," he turned to face the Sergeant, "isn't that right, Sergeant?"

D.S. Mellor shrugged. "Well, not really, Sir. Only a tiny one."

"Nonsense. How's the book progressing?"

"Very well, Sir. Almost finished."

Noticing all the quizzical looks, Crowe instructed the Sergeant to fill them in.

Everyone fell about laughing. "Stuff of legends, Sir, stuff of legends." Said the ambitious constable as he initiated a round of applause.

Basking in his moment of glory, Inspector Crowe raised a hand in the halt position. Having once again acquired everyone's undivided attention, he got down to the real business of the day. "Now, as I said, we have to find a way to stop them by the New Year. It just so happens that I've had a tip off about an application for a High Court injunction to make it illegal. Problem is, these judges, they're sticklers for the law—aren't they?"

Everyone nodded their agreement.

"So what we need is something to persuade him, just to make sure he interprets the law in the right way. So what I was thinking was, wouldn't it be perfect if the ringleader was nicked the day before the hearing?"

"Oh, absolutely, Sir. Good thinking."

"Which is why I've been saving this until now."

"Saving what, Sir?"

"Thirteenth of October, after some good work by D.S. Mellor, Loretta Jeffries changed her description. She identified Jane Thomas." He passed round a handful of photos, which each of them examined carefully.

"So rather than have her arrested on 13th October and allow time for the case to shift from the centre stage, I thought I'd bide my time. First thing in the morning, I want you, you and you to go round and bring her in for questioning. I'll get in early, make a statement to the media before you go at eight o'clock sharp."

"Good idea, Sir. Give her the jitters."

"Precisely, Constable, precisely." The Inspector shuffled his papers back into the neat pile they were in before and tucked them under his arm. "Well, thanks for all your contributions. I'll let you go about your business now. Oh and um, good luck for tomorrow morning!"

***

True to his word, Inspector Crowe arrived at the station bright and early the following morning. In fact, it was so early the streetlights were still illuminating the road outside. "Morning," he said to the constable on reception duty, "you can go home now if you like."

"Oh, thank you, Sir."

"Anything I should be aware of?"

"Nothing, Sir. A completely incident free night."

"Oh, splendid."

He waited for the constable to leave the building before having a stroll round, just to check that he was, indeed, all alone in the building. Once satisfied, he sat at his desk, lifted his phone, and called one by one all the journalists and reporters that he knew would be sympathetic to the cause.

He'd been sat in his office, imagining all the accolades he was about to receive, for almost an hour when people began to arrive. Mellor was the first to come knocking on the Inspector's door.

"Morning, Sir."

"Morning, Sergeant. You ready for the big raid?"

"Yes, Sir. I heard about it on the radio coming in. A very well worded statement, Sir. I'm sure she's there now, quaking in her boots."

"Just one thing, Sergeant."

"What's that, Sir?"

"There's a hell of a lot riding on this for everyone involved. So do your best not to balls this up."

Mellor tittered. "I'll do my best, Sir."

"Oh, I know you will. You do remember what I told you about D.C Oplitova, don't you?"

"You asked me to keep an eye on her, Sir."

"I did, so just make sure she doesn't let the side down in any way."

"You can count on me, Sir."

"I know. Come in, why don't you take a seat until the others arrive?"

Feeling honoured, Mellor strode confidently across the room and sat on the same side as the inspector, leaving a good meter and a half between them. After about ten minutes of awkward small talk, which neither of them did well, the first of the D.C.s showed up.

"Morning," the inspector boomed, "all ready for the big day? You could get a commendation for this if you play your cards right."

"Do you really think so, Sir?"

"Oh, I do. Come on, take the weight off your feet while you wait."

After two minutes of awkward silence, the inspector noticed the constable was slightly more subdued than usual. "You alright, Oplitova? You seem a bit, I dunno, quiet."
"Oh yes, I'm fine sir, it's just that . . . "
"Come on spit it out. We're all friends together in here. Isn't that right, Mellor?"
"Oh, absolutely, Sir. I can tell you anything."
"See? So, come on then, spit it out."
"Well, it's nothing really, it's just that—I'm not entirely comfortable with this, Sir."
"Not entirely comfortable with what?"
"This. Arresting an innocent person."
"Oh. We all go through that phase, don't we Mellor?"
"Oh yes. Wait till they're handcuffed in the car and you'll soon forget about your conscience." Mellor and the inspector laughed.
"Well, I hope so, but I'm not quite sure—."
A knock.
"Come in," the Inspector called out.
The door opened and the second female D.C. entered the room.

Once all three of them were in his office, Inspector Crowe wished them luck, reminded them once again how much was at stake and sent them on their way. Through a gap in the blind, he watched them get in a car and turn onto the road, before thinking once again about the accolades he was about to receive.

CHAPTER EIGHT

Jane had been up and down all night, tossing and turning, trying to make herself comfortable. At around six am, she'd given up all hope of getting some sleep and switched on the TV. That's when she first discovered she was about to be arrested. It hadn't come as a great shock. From the moment Jeffries changed her statement, it had been a matter of when, not if, the knock would come. Inevitability hadn't made her any less anxious, though. It felt a bit like going to the dentist. Knowing what was coming didn't make it any easier. Being a woman of principles and in her condition, she knew it was important not to let them see a sign of weakness.

She'd been sat waiting for over two hours, when she heard the distant rumble of a car engine. Her interest piqued and she followed the sound along the main road until it came to the corner. When the engine suddenly grew louder, she walked to the window, her mouth completely dry. She recognised Mellor as he got out of the car, and one of the two female D.C.s he was with. She quickly retreated to the couch before they noticed her watching. It would have given them great delight to know she was waiting. Why else would they have alerted the media before dispatching the executioners?

So at eight twenty am on 1st December 2004, Jane descended four flights of stairs to answer the door to the police. They weren't there long. In fact, they didn't even come inside, they just stood at the door, arrested her and told her to get in the car. As she was being escorted to the car, some more officers arrived on the scene with a warrant to search her flat. Then, once they emerged having found nothing, they gave the all clear to DS. Mellor and Jane was driven to Burton Police Station for questioning.

It was only a short journey, no more than five minutes, but it seemed to take for ever as Jane imagined the ordeal that lay ahead.

Jane knew something wasn't right the moment she was shoved inside the station. She'd been arrested before and this time sensed a different atmosphere. Usually, you can feel everyone's curiosity as they ask themselves what you've done, trying to foresee the experience that might be waiting. But on this occasion there was none of this. It was more like she was a visitor that everyone was expecting and had spent days preparing for.

Past all the smirking faces doing their best to avoid eye contact, Jane was led to a cell. D.S. Mellor pushed her to the back, told her to sit on the hard wooden bench, clanged the door shut, turned the key, looked at her with a smug grin and informed her she was being incarcerated until her solicitor arrived. "Fine by me," Jane said defiantly. Waiting for silence to prevail, Jane took a minute to inspect her surroundings, her feet clapping against the concrete floor as she took in the damp, musky smell. If she listened carefully, she could just about hear voices coming from a different part of the building. The bench was hard and looked about a hundred years old, as if every criminal that had ever walked the streets of Burton on Trent had sat on it. Her hands sank into the wood as she lowered herself onto the bench.

Sat looking through the bars directly in front at the empty cell opposite, Jane wondered if people viewed her as a common criminal or as a crusader for a just cause.

Roughly half an hour passed, during which time she contemplated her current life situation while constantly toiling to make herself comfortable, before she heard footsteps descending the stairs. As the sound boots on cold hard concrete reverberated around the corridor, Jane sat up straight and tried to make it look like she was feeling ultra-confident, even though, deep down, she was anything but.

Mellor was the first to come into view, but it soon became evident that there was another pair of footsteps close behind. Trying not to make eye contact with Mellor, Jane struggled to catch a glimpse of who else might be approaching and was relieved to see her solicitor.

"OK, Thomas," Mellor said, clattering the key into the lock, "Interview Room One." He turned the key and the door clanged open.

Mellor locked the door of the now empty cell and led the way. Jane walked several paces behind, shoulder to shoulder with her solicitor.

Interview Room One was only slightly more accommodating than the cell had been. A wooden table took centre stage, around which were four matching wooden chairs. There was another chair in each of the four corners of the room. On the far side of the room, behind the table was a grey vertical blind, blocking out a window overlooking the car park at the rear of the building.

Jane sat with her back to the door, facing the window. Smith, her solicitor, took the seat next to her. Mellor announced a D.C. would be conducting the interview and promptly disappeared, leaving them alone for a few minutes to listen to the cars coming and going outside. It wasn't until a D.C. Wilson appeared that, for the first time, Jane noticed how hot and stuffy it was.

It was Smith that began the interview. "What evidence have you got that Jane . . . ?"

D.C. Wilson stroked his stubbly chin, shook his head and said, "I am not prepared to tell you at this time."

"Then Jane will not be answering any questions."

Wilson flashed each of them a contemptuous look and said, "Well, a witness saw a 5'10" male with not dark hair standing at a gate in mid-September."

"Jane's 5'4". She's a woman and has no hair at all."

"The witness has since identified her as a female they saw on TV."

That was it. Both sides dug in, and the D.C. kept on with the same questions over and over again. When Wilson went on his lunch break, Smith opened the blind and let in some fresh air. Jane took a second to look right into the cool fresh breeze and let it wash over her, replenishing her energy levels. Soon, a car approached and Jane was just about to get up and close the blind when Smith grabbed her arm. "Shh."

Jane held her breath, and discovered that the driver of the car was listening to the lunchtime news. As the car got closer, they could both clearly hear what the newsreader was saying:

"Jane Thomas, a sixty-two year old pensioner from Burton on Trent, UK has been arrested on suspicion of. . . "

When the news report had finished, they discovered it was the BBC, meaning the story had made the national headlines.

They were still discussing the implications of this revelation when Wilson returned. The first thing he did was to march across the room, slam the window shut and closed the blind. Clearly, the hot, stuffy atmosphere was a tactical move.

An hour or so later and the cool breeze was a distant memory. Wilson kept on asking the same questions as before, but was showing no signs of frustration. Not until the slivers of light between the vertical slats covering the window turned dark, anyway.

Completely out of the blue, Wilson got to his feet, walked around the table and said over Jane's shoulder, "Do you recall saying to Inspector Crowe, . . . ?"

"What?"

"Did you or did you not say to Inspector Crowe . . . ?"

"I did not. I don't ever recall using those words."

"Well, that's funny, Thomas, because Inspector Crowe has provided evidence that on the day after the incident , you said to him, . . . "

"But I didn't set eyes on the man until the tenth. I did say to him . . . but that wasn't until the 31st October."

"Are you sure about that?"

"Yes."

Jane guessed it to be about six when Smith said, "My client is appearing in court tomorrow and needs to get some rest. Are you going to charge her or not?"

Wilson just shrugged and carried on with his line of questioning.

Around two more hours passed before, finally, Wilson stormed out of the interview room and left them in peace, listening to his footsteps echo along the corridor until they faded into silence. When Wilson returned, ten minutes later, he growled at Jane, "OK, you can go." She'd been released on bail, on the condition that she returned on 21st January.

The P.C. at reception offered to call her a taxi, but she declined the offer, choosing instead to stretch her legs and drink up some more of the cool fresh breeze that she'd experienced earlier. Sat at home, watching TV, she was amazed to discover she was the lead story on the ten o'clock news. Watching in disbelief, she smiled and thought how good the police must be at manipulating the media for their own gain.

Despite everything, Jane managed to sleep soundly that night. Just after nine am, sat in her car, she took out her phone and called her fellow campaigners. She'd been too tired to call them the night before, so they had a lot of catching up to do before the trial. The others were just as amazed as Jane at the extent of the media coverage and could not work out why it was so important. They arranged to meet up at a service station for a proper catch up before they arrived in London.

With the last minute arrangements in place, Jane turned the ignition key and reversed out of her drive. After pulling over at a lay-by to notify Smith of their plans to meet at a service station, she continued on her journey through town towards the motorway.

CHAPTER NINE

Like many people, Jane hated the monotony of driving on the motorway. It came as a great relief when out of nowhere, there appeared a sign alerting drivers to an upcoming service station, their designated meeting place. They'd all be looking to her for a plan of action, so she had to be on the ball. She'd slept well, but the monotony of the drive and the warmth of her car had combined to make her feel decidedly sleepy. The break couldn't come soon enough.

Turning down the slip road, she caught sight of a blue car in front that she thought she recognised, making her feel reassured. At least she wasn't going to be sat on her own, getting herself all worked up. She caught a glimpse of the car indicating and turning left into the main car park, so decided to follow suit.

Once in the car park, she got out of the car, closed the door with a thud and took a second to examine her surroundings. In front of her was a vast ocean of empty parking bays, with a few cars parked together in a row. The car she'd seen earlier was amongst them, and there were one or two others that she thought she recognised too. So it was with an air of confidence that she walked along the path and into the main entrance. A man and a woman were chatting excitedly about something in the red top the man was holding. When they saw her, they both fell momentarily silent until the woman whispered, "That's her." The man looked at Jane carefully and concurred. Strolling past the newsagents on the way to the caf , she strained to catch a glimpse of what they'd been talking about. That's when she saw it. Taking a step inside the shop, she picked up a copy of the newspaper and started to read. Unable to believe the lies that they'd printed, she read the article carefully, getting more and more engrossed until she became aware that she was being watched.

The woman behind the counter curled up her nose and looked at Jane like she was the most vile, disgusting thing in the world. Jane thought about confronting her, but in the end decided to put the newspaper back on the pile and continue towards the cafeteria, where hopefully, there'd be some friendly faces waiting. Seeing a few of the others sat around a table at the far side, backs to the window through which she could see a vast swathe of the green English countryside, she smiled and made her way across. Navigating past the tables of chattering people, who were drinking coffee and reading the news headlines, she could feel their stares and whispers burning her back and face.

"Good morning," she said, taking a seat facing the window.

"Morning, Jane," each of the others said in turn.

"Is it me or is everyone talking about me this morning? You should have seen the look the woman in the newsagents gave me. Looked at me like I was dirt."

The protestor opposite her nodded. "I can believe it. People believe whatever they read, don't they?"

"But why? Is this it? Am I going to spend my life from now on as public enemy number one—like Myra Hindley?"

"No, not at all. Rumour has it that she had sympathisers."

"Mmmm. Think I'll get a cup of tea." Jane walked back through the restaurant that hissed at her like a snake until she reached the counter. There was no queue, so she asked for a cup of tea and smiled at the woman behind the counter that was serving her.

"Here," the woman said, clattering the cup on top of a saucer, creating an orange pond in the process. "Do me a favour, will you? Just drink up and go. All of you."

"I beg your pardon?" Jane said, passing across a five-pound note.

"For what you did, you should be locked up for the rest of your life."

"But I was released without charge."

"So you wormed your way out of it. You had a clever lawyer, no doubt. Just—take your tea and go. Go on, get out of my sight."

Jane walked back to the table, her incredulity this time making her oblivious to the gossips.

"Jane. What is it? You've gone white as a sheet."

"Oh, nothing. The woman behind the counter gave me some grief, that's all." She took a sip of tea. "Suppose I'd better get used to it."

"Nonsense, it'll soon blow over once we win the hearing this afternoon."

Everyone nodded in agreement and the mood lifted. When conversation shifted to the day ahead, in particular what each of them was going to contribute, they soon forgot about the events of earlier. Then the man opposite Jane suddenly looked above her shoulder, puzzled.

"What is it?" Jane asked him.

The man furrowed his brow and rested his gaze above Jane's shoulder. Aware of a shadow, a sweet scent and the heat of a human being, Jane started to turn round to see for herself what was unfolding. She was stopped by a woman, with long hair, who leant right over Jane's shoulder, pursed her lips and deposited a clump of green phlegm in her tea.

"What the . . . " Jane began, but the woman wasn't listening. She was striding confidently back to her seat, taking the accolades en route.

"Come on, let's go. Just leave it." The man opposite Jane said, getting to his feet.

As they made their way back to the cars, Jane began to worry that someone would spot her in the traffic and try to accost her—or worse. Thankfully though, once she'd pulled out of the service station and turned back onto the motorway, the time flew by. Right up until the moment she began the slow crawl through London.

It had been a few years since she'd visited the capital, but one thing she hadn't forgotten was how anonymous you feel. So whereas in small towns and villages someone that had been falsely accused and arrested was big news, in London they were small fry. Hardly worth talking about.

Jane was the first to arrive in the car park of the High Court, so, not wishing to enter alone, she sat in the car and waited for a few of the others to arrive. Smith, her solicitor, was one of the first to show their faces.

After Smith, the others soon followed and so with half an hour to spare, all seventeen campaigners plus a handful of solicitors, walked through the main entrance. Once inside, they were directed to a waiting area, where they all sat in silence and waited to be called.

Just ten minutes had passed when an upper-class sounding man announced their case. Jane hadn't been nervous at all, but as soon as she stood up, felt overcome with the jitters. Stepping forward, she thought of the journey home when it would all be over and told herself that the sooner it started, the sooner she could get it over with. On the front row, on the left, was Timothy, Lawson-Cruttendon, barrister for the CPS. On the right, occupying the front two rows sat their own legal representatives, two of whom turned round and glanced at the benches behind them, just in case anyone didn't know where to sit.

Lawson-Cruttendon was the first to speak. It was all very predictable to start with, going on about how they'd been terrorising the village and preventing them from going about their daily lives. He called Jane a 'stalker' as she'd attended ninety-one protests, before surprising everyone by calling on a villager called Peter Clamp. Clamp informed the judge that he was representative for all the villagers and described how the protestors had been terrorising everyone. He told the judge that they had previously been too afraid of reprisals to come forward.

To Jane, this didn't make sense. Leaning forward, she tapped Smith on the shoulder and whispered to him that when the villagers had appeared on TV, they hadn't appeared terrorised. Far from it, they spoke openly and were never shy of appearing on camera.

Jane was the third defendant to be called. After the cross-examination, Smith asked Lawson-Cruttendon why she'd been called as a witness, when she had no previous convictions. Lawson-Cruttendon reminded him that she had just been arrested.

Smith countered that although she had been arrested, she had been released without charge. A point which the prosecution begrudgingly accepted.

The judge then announced a recess to allow him time to reach a decision and everyone filed back into the waiting area.

There was an air of confidence among them, but no-one was taking the verdict for granted. Everyone had presented their case well, and a few holes in the prosecution's case had been uncovered. Everyone knew, though, that as far as the law was concerned, it came down on the side of the establishment more times than not. They knew that to walk out free to continue their protests, they each would have needed to have played an absolute blinder and there would have to be no doubt at all in the judge's mind. They'd done well, but the question was, had they done well enough?

Half an hour later, a clerk poked her head around the door and invited everyone back into court. Jane's mouth suddenly ran dry. She'd been through so much over the previous twenty-four hours, all of it leading up to this. In a few minutes' time, she might have to quit the protest for ever.

Once everyone had settled, the judge made his way to the front. A hush descended as he began his summing up, before concluding that Peter Clamp could not be representative of the villagers of Yoxall and that the campaigners could continue with their protests.

A stifled cheer went up before the judge packed away his things and left the court. The protestors filed out, back into the corridor and headed straight for the main entrance, feeling, understandably, in high spirits. They were brought plummeting back down to Earth, however, the minute they stepped outside and saw all the people with placards calling them terrorists.

The people outside the court were especially hostile towards Jane as she fought her way through them towards her car. Once she'd reversed out of the car park, she drove to the corner of the road and looked at them all in her mirror. In a couple of hours, she'd be home, relaxing with Suzie and this whole terrible business would be behind her.

CHAPTER TEN

"You what? You're kidding me?" Crowe listened to what the Chief Constable was telling him with an air of disbelief. "So what do we do now?" His ear turned hotter and hotter by the second. When, eventually, he was able to get a word in edgeways, all he could muster was, "I understand that Guv, but the decision was completely out of my hands. They gave us the wrong judge, didn't they?"

Much to the Inspector's surprise, Sexton's tone softened considerably. "OK, tell you what. Sit tight, and I'll be down tomorrow afternoon. See what we can come up with when we bang our heads together. Not literally of course."

Crowe laughed and reverted back to type. "Very funny, Sir. It will be a pleasure seeing you again."

With the phone back in its cradle, Crowe extended his legs, slid down in his leather chair and took a deep breath, exhaling slowly through puffed cheeks. For the first time in his Police career, he felt under a mountain of pressure. He'd been asked to do something of national importance and come up short. He was just grateful that he had been able to make the Chief Constable see it from his perspective. He'd done everything he could to discredit the Thomas woman. It wasn't his fault that the judge saw fit to let her proceed with the protest. He considered if there was something fundamentally wrong with the system. It just didn't seem right that after all their hard work and ingenuity, a judge could go and scupper everything on nothing more than a whim, leaving him to take the blame.

To be brutally honest, this was the least of his worries. Ever since he'd attended a race meeting in his early twenties, he'd had a fondness for betting. It started with the horses. The thrill he felt from seeing them thundering along the grass, barging each other out of the way without a thought for danger was just indescribable. Then, for a birthday treat, he'd gone to see the world's greatest steeple chase, the Grand National. A horse fell and broke its neck, sending him dizzy with excitement. That was the moment it started.

Every weekend for the next two years he went to the races, but he never again experienced the thrill of seeing a horse pay for his entertainment with its life. So in the end, he increased the stakes in an attempt to recreate the thrill. He did have some success, which gave him the encouragement he needed to go on spending, until in the end he was completely penniless and living alone in a studio flat; his wife, Susan, had long since left him and taken their son with him. So far, he'd managed to keep his gambling debts a secret from his colleagues at the station, but he knew that it was just a matter of time before the rumours started and well, as any police officer would say, there's no smoke without fire.

One thing to his advantage was his experience and knowledge of how the police worked. It was all about finding someone to apportion the blame to. He knew that to appease their superiors, someone would have to carry the can. At the moment, being the senior officer at the station responsible, it was his head on the block. Sexton was probably going to give him the axe. What he really couldn't cope with in his rather precarious situation was losing his job or even being suspended, with or without pay. If that happened, he'd be in no position to repay his debts, and his personal life would go from bad to worse. Like many people, Inspector Crowe preferred being rushed off his feet to being sat twiddling his thumbs and that afternoon was the quietest he could remember. One of the reasons he felt so at home in the police force was that, more often than not, he didn't get time to think about his personal life. When it was quiet, he had time to sit and ponder over his problems, and that made him worried. Come five o'clock he glanced down at his chewed up pencil and decided to knock off early. He was the boss after all, and he didn't often take advantage.

He found his nightly commute home particularly depressing, and on this day, when everything was fresh in his mind, it depressed him more than usual. He felt this way because, every night, he had to pass the house that he once lived in. The four-bedroomed detached in a privately owned road. Each night, he tried to resist turning his head to take a good look, but he always succumbed. He just needed to check that it was still standing. On one occasion, he'd noticed that the current occupiers had painted the exterior, which, for some reason, sent a thunderbolt of betrayal right through him.

With his car slotted in between his neighbours', he squeezed out, shut the car door and plodded towards the block's main entrance. Once inside, it was up four flights of stairs. As usual, once on his floor, he could hear music from the far end of the corridor, and the family in the flat opposite were screaming and shouting. To them, it was just a regular night, not unlike any other.

It being December, his flat was pitch black and freezing when he opened the door and stepped in. Fumbling for the light switch on the wall, his breath smoked upwards in the cold air. When he flipped the switch, the lights buzzed before flickering and eventually, reluctantly illuminating his room.

On his way to his coat stand, which stood adjacent to his wardrobe, he paused to look at the photo of Susan, which had pride of place on the mantelpiece, above the two-bar electric fire that his landlord had provided him with. He put the photo back on the mantle, bent down and switched on the fire. The bars buzzed and omitted a smell of burning oil mixed with fish, a smell his senses had become accustomed to since his demise. Sometimes it became almost intoxicating, meaning he had to either suffer a headache or sit and shiver. He'd tried telling his landlord, but he didn't care. When you're a down and out, desperate to keep up appearances, no one cares, they just look to take advantage of your situation by any means they can. Once he got back on his feet, he was going to have his revenge, but to be fair, his landlord had helped him out when no-one else would.

He wouldn't have to put up with the smell for long though, not tonight. It was just a quick change, a bite to eat and then he was off out. After putting the kettle on, he took three steps towards his bedroom area and proceeded to change out of his daytime persona. Sat in a pair of black trousers and a sandy coloured sweatshirt, he looked in the mirror on the wardrobe doors opposite and saw staring back at him the real Robbie Crowe; the person everyone in the force didn't know existed. Chin in hands, he wondered what people would think if they saw him in this exposed state.

After glancing at his watch, he strode across to the kitchen area, re-boiled the kettle, took a Pot Noodle from the cupboard and made his evening dinner. Cooking had never been his forte. At least he was getting something warm inside him on a cold night. Besides, if he had anything more substantial, it might lie heavy during the night ahead, which could prove to be a distraction. This was something Susan couldn't quite grasp.

Ten minutes later, he was descending the stairs in the light of the street lamps, which he could see in the distance through the window as he watched his breath spiral upwards in front of him.

When his car door thudded shut, he focused on the steering wheel and for the first time in a few hours, thought about what was at stake tonight.

After what he estimated to be a further ten minutes had passed, hands freezing as they clutched the wheel, he turned into the more seedy part of town, the part that most people hadn't heard of. Indeed, if it wasn't for his day job, he'd never have found this place to begin with. He'd been accompanying a Sergeant on an investigation and overheard a conversation between two shady looking men about a card game later that night in a caf.

He'd been content, until that moment, with playing poker in online casinos; he'd never given the idea of attending a real card game much thought. Suddenly, he was full of curiosity, his heart beating faster with excitement. After finding a reason to dismiss the sergeant, he approached the two individuals concerned.

They were reluctant to give him the particulars at first, as they'd suspected he might be involved with the police, even though both he and the sergeant were in plain clothes. Once he showed them the colour of his money though, one of them, the one with a Hispanic look and a handle bar moustache, wrote down the time and place on the back of a receipt which someone had left on the table.

It turned out to be a steep learning curve. That first night, he learnt more than he had in the previous year he'd spent playing cards online. Needless to say, he made a loss, much to the delight of the others. As he left with his tail between his legs, he was reminded of that day his father had humiliated him by sending him outside with the dogs. And look at how that had turned out. He'd certainly shown the dogs who was boss, so why couldn't he do the same now? So, on his way out, he turned to face their jeers and smiles of derision and said, "Same time next week, chaps?" Which wiped the smiles off their faces in a flash.

He then set about learning everything he could about cards, practising online until the small hours, getting no sleep at all. The following week, the others were laughing on the other side of their faces when he got his money back, with a small profit.

The next week he returned with more money and upped the stakes. The thrill was quite unlike anything he'd felt since that day at the races all those years before. Once he'd become accepted as one of them, he began attending games twice a week, then three times, until eventually, it was every night. When Susan issued him with an ultimatum, he made, in her eyes at least, the wrong choice.

With his wife and son out of the way, he was free to crank up the stakes even further and within weeks lost his house, then his money, then most of his possessions. Until, eventually, he ended up lonely, penniless and desperate, in a studio flat in the most rundown and notorious part of town.

That was all in the past, though. He'd had some wins, big ones too, but mostly losses. He'd long since run out of money and possessions to feed his addiction, so he'd been forced to be creative with what he offered people. The trouble was that now he'd accumulated a mountain of IOUs and people were demanding he pay up. Tonight was his last chance to win big and get them off his back once and for all.

He pulled up in the car park, glanced through the window, nodded at a man that frequented the card games and paused for thought. It hadn't been the best of days so far, but a big win tonight would change everything. This was something that he loved about poker. You never know how your luck might turn. This time tomorrow he could have his old life—and house—back and he could be focusing on persuading Susan to move back in with him. On the other hand, he could be waking up in the morning in intensive care. One thing was for certain, though. In light of recent events, he couldn't risk providing the favours he'd promised people. His job was already in jeopardy, and If he lost that, then he would be spending his nights on a park bench.

He got out of the car, closed the door and strode towards the club, his heart beating faster with each step until suddenly he was some supremely confident card sharp on his way to making a killing.

After purchasing a whiskey, he took his place at the circular table and mumbled his hellos to people, that, secretly, he despised. Around the table were some of the areas most wanted criminals, many of whom he was now indebted to. He consoled himself with the thought that at some point in the future, when he'd won his way back to respectability, he'd return undercover and deliver the biggest heist the constabulary had ever known. He grinned to himself as he watched the dealer carefully, making sure to shoot a quick glance at the other players just to make sure there was no cheating going on. This was something he'd learnt to do right from day one. You get to know who plays honestly, who are the tricksters and who are the bad losers. He also knew which of them couldn't take the pressure of playing for big stakes, something he was hoping to make use of as the night wore on.

Things began well for Crowe. After the first few rounds, he was ahead. He hadn't made any significant gains, nothing that might prompt him to call it a night and quit while he was ahead, but he was holding his own. He had the means to continue, and at this stage of the night, this was all that mattered.

By the time he rapped down his empty glass and placed it beside the other two that hadn't been collected, he was on the run. He'd been dealt a bad hand and he'd spent more than he'd intended. When it had dwindled down to just the two of them, he was hoping his opponent would bottle it. Glancing at his cards, he knew this was his only hope. Eventually, Crowe saw sense and folded while he still had means to continue, much to the delight of his opponent, who extended an arm and scooped up the mountain of cash.

Crowe was still in the game, but only just. All he needed was one win, however small, and he'd be OK to continue. It might still turn out to be a lucky night. He picked up his new hand and tried not to grimace as he readjusted his sights.

An hour, and two more whiskeys later, and his unlucky streak showed no signs of relenting. He'd lost all his money and was back on the IOUs, taking advantage of his day job to offer favours to the people he despised most.

The door opened and a cold breeze blew in. All eyes turned to face the breeze and acknowledge the new comer. Everyone nodded out of respect; everyone except Crowe that is, who just turned away, trying not to make eye contact.

"Good evening gentlemen," the newcomer said as the two men opposite Crowe parted to make space for him. He glanced round and acknowledged each of them in turn, until he came to Crowe, who he quite noticeably blanked, sparking off a round of murmured curiosity.

"Inspector, I want a word with you." The newcomer said.

"Who, me? What have I done?"

"Oh, don't play the innocent with me. You were supposed to do me a favour."

"Oh. Was I? I—had no idea Pedro, honestly I hadn't." He felt his arrogance giving him away as he spoke.

Pedro got to his feet, bent over and crashed his fist into the table. "Yes. I had a visit today from one of your boys in blue. They have it in their head that some of my cars are stolen. You were supposed to fix it so they'd turn a blind eye."

"Was I? Well, the thing is . . ."

"I've had enough of your excuses, Crowe. We all have. I think it's time I gave you some encouragement."

"No, that won't be necessary—. " But it was too late. The newcomer ran around the table, gripped Crowe around the neck with one hand and bent him over until his face was planted in between his knees.

Still holding the defenceless inspector, the newcomer pulled out a knife.

"Now hang on . . . "One of the others protested. But Pedro wasn't listening. He just lowered his hand and pressed the blade into Robbie's heel." "Here's something to remind you tomorrow," he whispered and ran the knife up Crowe's calf towards the back of his knee.

Pedro released Crowe, shoved him off his chair and watched as he writhed around in a pool of blood, clutching his gashed leg through the slit in his trousers.

The others soon forgot about Crowe and recommenced their game. When Crowe had finally composed himself, he managed to stagger to his feet, falling over after two steps and landing at the bar. "Just one more whiskey for the road, Love." He said through gritted teeth. The barmaid smiled. "Shouldn't you go to hospital with that? You might need stitches."

"No, definitely not. Just give me a whiskey, and I'll be on my way."

"Oh well, go on then, I'll serve you."

Ten minutes later, Robbie rapped his fifth empty glass of the night onto the bar and turned towards the exit. It didn't occur to him until he was sat in his car, seatbelt around him, that he was in no fit state to drive. Maybe the barmaid was right and he should go to hospital, have the gash looked at. The trouble was that everyone knew him and people were bound to start asking questions.

A further five minutes later, he finally mustered up the strength to start the car. He knew immediately that his luck would have to turn if he was going to make it home in one piece, but what choice did he have?

He made it out of the car park and all the way along the road outside before he came to a set of lights. A girl, probably a teenager, looking a bit worse for wear, was crossing over. Robbie knew he had to break, but he just couldn't apply enough pressure. He swerved to avoid her, but it was no use. She collided with the front of his car and crashed down in a heap.

Noticing a man below a street lamp, looking down at his mobile phone, Crowe stepped on the accelerator and turned the corner before anyone had chance to recognise him.

Using the winding bannister as a crutch, Robbie somehow made it up four flights of stairs and into the safety of his own home. It wasn't much, but right there and then he'd never been more pleased be there. As soon as the light was on and the door closed, he sat on the floor for a breather; the comfort of his bed might as well have been ten miles away. Roughly half an hour had passed before he crawled across the floor and somehow managed to haul himself up onto his bed. That's when he examined the damage for the first time.

He knew he really should call an ambulance, but that might spell the end of his career. Just by chance, his periphery vision caught a glimpse of the picture of his soon to be ex-wife on the mantelpiece, causing him to smile with relief. Being married to a nurse, just like being a police inspector, had its perks.

He hung up and with one almighty effort hauled himself round so he could lie on his bed. As soon as his head hit the pillow, the room started spinning, beads of sweat rolling into his eyes. She hadn't been happy at first at being woken in the middle of the night, but as soon as she realised he was in trouble, her attitude changed. This made the pain subside significantly and almost went as far as to produce a smile.

Without saying a word, Susan marched across the studio flat, avoiding the red stains, and sat at the foot of his bed. Leaning across, she placed a soft hand on his forehead. Crowe smiled. "I've missed you," he murmured.

"Robbie Crowe, I'm doing this because, despite everything, I still care about you, but don't get any ideas, OK? What if our son was here and whoever did this got hold of him?"

Crowe winced as he felt the antiseptic sink from the cotton wool into his wound. That was the worst part; the cleaning. The stitching wasn't anywhere near as bad. Once she'd finished, she glanced over her shoulder at the blood and asked where the cloth was. "It's all the way up the stairs," she said, getting to work.

Alone in the dark, for the first time that night Robbie remembered about his meeting with the Chief Constable the next day, and wondered what his wife would say if she knew she might just have saved his job.

By morning, he was feeling much better, only a slight hangover reminding him of what had gone before. It was nothing to worry about though, and so he got out of bed and readied himself for work as if nothing had happened.

As usual, he was the first person to arrive at the station. He marched straight into his office, hung up his coat and sat at his desk, relieved to take the weight off his feet after the walk from the car park. He was slightly later than normal, however, and it wasn't more than a few minutes before the others started to arrive. And then, just after nine o'clock, a constable burst in, waving in front of him the details of a hit and run.

"Give me that constable, let me see. I went for a drive last night, it might ring some bells."

The constable handed it to the Inspector with a puzzled expression.

"Ok, that'll be all. Thank you," Crowe said, without looking at the document.

Waiting for his door to close, Crowe read the paper carefully. He took a deep breath, gritted his teeth, got to his feet and hobbled across the room to the shredder.

With barely an inch of the document still visible, the shredder jammed, omitting a loud and painful screech. Cursing, Crowe ripped the strip from the shredder and tore it manually before proceeding to pick out the offending paper that had become stuck. Once satisfied that the shredder was in working order, he began the slow and painful trek back across his office.

For once, he was grateful to have a quiet morning, as it gave him time to think. The events of the previous night could have forced a lesser man to take his eye off the ball, leaving him off guard for his meeting with the chief constable. He had to prepare himself for the worse and imagine what he was going to say, if Sexton said it was all his fault that they'd let the whole country down. Given his current predicament, he just couldn't afford to lose his job over this.

No, what he needed to do was ensure that someone else took the blame for this fiasco. Assuming, of course, that they couldn't put their heads together and come up with a plan B, then he had to think of someone. Someone na ve enough not to suspect they were being framed. He glanced at the clock on the wall; just enough time to nip out for a sandwich before his midday meeting with Sexton.

It was only a short walk to the sandwich shop. It being midday, there was a queue going all the way to the entrance of the shop next door but one. Crowe smiled to himself as he utilised another perk of the job and pushed his way to the front.

Sat eating his favourite roast beef sandwiches (no onions today), Crowe was feeling better than he had all day. He'd only just swallowed the last crumb and deposited the box in his aluminium bin when there was a knock. It was D.C. Oplitova, announcing the arrival of the Chief Constable. "Thank you, Oplitova, send him in."

Looking down at his feet, he murmured, "Oplitova."

"Afternoon, Bobby," Sexton said, closing the door shut and making his way across the room to the Inspector's desk.

"Afternoon, Sir. Cup of tea?"

"Oh, that would be splendid, Bobby."

"Wait a minute, I'll just go and get Oplitova."

"Oh, yes, Oplitova. The female D.C. if I'm not mistaken?"

"That's correct, Sir."

"Well, she makes a fine cup of tea. Was she involved in the arrest at all?"

"Yes, Sir. She was one of the officers that arrested Thomas."

"Ah yes. Dreadful woman."

"Oh, indeed sir. Indeed, she is."

They both started laughing.

"Funny name that, Oplitova," Sexton said with a grin. "Welsh is she?" Crowe shook his head. "Hungaria, somewhere round there. But she once mentioned that her great grandmother was Chinese."

"Ah, that explains it."

Sexton decided to return to the matter at hand. "Well, you did a splendid job, and if you ask me, you each deserve a medal for what you did."

"Oh, thank you, Sir. Surely not."

"The thing is though, you were trusted to come up with a plan that would leave the judge with no choice."

"I know. And if we'd been able to arrest her, she'd have a criminal record and then—. "

"And then everything would have been different, I know. But you couldn't go through with the arrest and well, you've been in the force long enough to know that someone has to carry the can."

"Well, Oplitova—. "

"Unless of course, we can come up with a new plan of action, pronto. What's happened to the tea, for heaven's sake?"

"Shouldn't be long, Sir." The handle lowered and the door creaked open. "Ah, speak of the Devil."

Sexton dropped two white sugar cubes into his tea, clattered the spoon around a couple of times, took a quick sip and raised his hand. "Oplitova?"

One hand on the door handle, the detective looked over her shoulder. "Yes, Sir?"

"One moment, please. Can I have a quick word?"

Waiting for her to stand up close, Sexton asked her, without consulting Crowe, if she'd like to take charge of the Thomas case.

Crowe's mouthful of tea went down the wrong way, sending him into a coughing fit.

"You OK, Inspector? You don't have a problem, do you? I don't want to tread on anyone's toes."

"Oh, no, of course not." Pausing for thought, he realised the advantages. "Of course not, Sir. A brilliant idea, if I may say so."

"Splendid. Well, that's settled then. OK, Oplitova?"

"Yes. Thank You, Sir."

Waiting for Oplitova to close the door and take a few steps along the corridor, Sexton was the first to speak out. "What say we err, forget about the Thomas woman for now?"

"Not sure I'm with you, Sir. Why would we do that?"

"Well, there must be others that we can dig up more dirt on."

"But what about the ultimatum?"

"Well, that's the tricky part. Tell you what, leave it to me. I'll have a word with the home office and see if they can get us more time."

"Good idea."

"And in the meantime . . . " Sexton leant forward across the desk and lowered his voice. "In the meantime, you'd do well to find someone to carry the can. Cover your own back."

"Oh, absolutely, Sir." Crowe grinned a sly grin.

"You look like you have someone in mind, Bobby."

"Well, Oplitova, she did have some objections to the arrest."

"Really?"

"Yes. Aired her views on more than one occasion. Infected the rest of the staff, no doubt, at least on a subconscious level."

The Chief Constable stroked his chin. "Mmm. That's quite possible, Inspector."

"Do you think we should err, remove her from the case?"

"What? Oh no. I say we give her some rope and see what she does." He laughed.

"My thoughts exactly, Sir. Sir?"

"Yes, Bobby?"

"This might be a long shot, but do you think we could appeal, try and get the judge to change his mind?"

"Depends. You know how it works. We'd have to have new evidence."

"Such as a new identification, you mean?"

"Yes, just like that. If we can get someone else to identify her, we can then apply for a hearing at the Court of Appeal, on the grounds that she should have held a conviction at the first hearing."

"We could organise an identity parade."

"Brilliant. How soon can it be arranged?"

Crowe felt compelled to look at his wrist watch before answering. "Well, there's no time like the present. I'll have Oplitova go and get her while we get the video room set up. Think we have her solicitor's details on file, so hopefully there shouldn't be any holdups there."

"Splendid. Well, I'm glad we've worked something out. It's been a worthwhile trip, Bobby, but I'd better be making tracks."

"Feel free to pop in any time you like, Sir."

CHAPTER ELEVEN

Jane had just got settled with Suzie on the couch and reacquainted herself with the plot of her book, when there was a knock. "Go away," she muttered and carried on reading, hoping it was nothing important. When the knock came again, louder and more insistent, she got to her feet and walked across the room to the window. When she saw the police car, she rolled her eyes, took a deep breath and exhaled her plans for a relaxing afternoon.

"Good afternoon," Jane said with a smile, feigning surprise. It was that female D.C., Oplitova.

"Good afternoon, Jane. Sorry to bother you, but we need you to come to the station to help prepare a video identification parade."

"What? Right now?"

"Sorry."

"Do I have a choice in the matter?"

"I'm afraid not. It shouldn't take long. Your solicitor has already been contacted and is waiting in the identification suite."

Jane was happy to see Smith, who was indeed waiting for her, just as Oplitova had said. "Come on, sit down," Smith said, nudging out a chair from under the table, "I'll just spend a few minutes explaining the process before we get started. It shouldn't take long."

"I hope not," Jane replied, sitting down and casting an eye over the computer screen in front of her.

Five minutes later, Oplitova returned with a camera. After preparing some video footage, they then set about scouring the police database to find some suitable participants for the video parade. At first, they found fourteen candidates, but none of these were suitable, so they widened the parameters and this time came up with nineteen. None of these were deemed suitable either.

So, after a lot of keyboard clunking and resetting of parameters, it was determined that in this instance, a video parade would not be feasible. "I'll let Inspector Crowe know," Oplitova said, perhaps a little sheepishly.

Smith sat with Jane in the identification suite for a minute, explaining the procedure and what they might try next. Jane knew that she should be annoyed at having had her afternoon spoiled, but she just got the feeling from Oplitova that however disgruntled she felt about the situation, Crowe was feeling a lot worse.

Jane listened to Smith, with half an ear pointing along the corridor to Crowe's office. She couldn't resist trying to picture his face when he heard the news.

Back home in her flat, Jane called her friends to share with them her ordeal. It was going to be an eventful New Year, but it seemed that for the time being at least she could forget about the allegations. She put down the phone, lifted her book and once again attempted to pick up where she'd left off.

The following day, a Saturday, she decided to cheer herself up by doing a spot of Christmas shopping. She wouldn't describe herself as religious, nor did she have hordes of relatives and grandchildren to buy presents for, but she did like the atmosphere of a busy precinct in the run up to Christmas.

As soon as the sliding doors parted and she stepped inside the precinct that she'd been shopping in all her life, she imagined everyone to be looking at her. Walking through the packed mall, it reminded her of a few days previously in the service station. With everything that had been going on, she'd forgotten about the way she'd been treated and the woman that had spat in her tea. Still, people had better things to do with their time than gossip and single her out.

After spending a while browsing the shelves of the bookshop, she made her way downstairs with two books tucked under her arm. Stepping off the bottom stair and onto the ground floor, a middle-aged man with a bald head stood in her way, staring right at her. She smiled politely and sidestepped him in an attempt to pass, but he moved over to deliberately block her.

"Excuse me," she said politely, still unsure if he was being malicious or if this was one of those awkward situations where the person you're trying to pass keeps moving in the same direction as you.

When he refused to move, she knew for certain. "Fuck off, you make me sick," he hissed in her ear.

Ignoring him, she made her way to the checkout and paid for the books. It was only once she'd left the shop and thought about where to go next that she realised her day had been ruined, and she just wanted to get home to sit with Suzie.

CHAPTER TWELVE

Inspector Crowe slumped into his chair, feeling like a cartoon policeman that has once again been foiled by his old adversary. The Chief Constable wasn't going to be happy that their plan had failed. Phone in hand, his finger hovered over the quick dial button, while he gave the situation a moment's thought. Then, with a wry smile, he put the phone back in its cradle and switched on his computer.

Bringing up the availability for group identification parades, Crowe cursed his luck. The next available date was well into the New Year. He took out a piece of scrap paper and scribbled along the top, Ways to nick Thomas

He'd only managed to write a couple of lines before his mind ran dry and he put down his pen to stare through the window for inspiration. It felt like an age had passed, when, reluctantly, he lifted the phone and called the Chief Constable, preparing to eat a huge slice of humble pie.

"Hello, Sir, Inspector Crowe here. Just ringing to give you an update."

"Bobby. Don't tell me, you've managed to nail the bitch?"

"Well, not exactly, Sir."

"Oh. Well, what then?"

"The Video parade was called off. We couldn't find enough suitable candidates, Sir. I've always said that the database isn't big enough."

"Oh. Well, not to worry, Bobby. You could always call her in for a physical identification."

"Yes. I thought of that, sir. The only problem is—."

"Don't tell me. No slots available this side of Christmas?"

"Precisely, Sir."

"Mmm. Shit. Well, you'd best go ahead with it anyway."

"I'll get notification sent out, Sir."

"Got stuck in traffic on my way home last night. Bloody horrendous it was."

"Terrible, sir. I expect Mrs Sexton was none too pleased."

"Well, no she wasn't. But it did give me time to think about this."

"Oh, good."

"Precisely. Well, and I had an idea. Have you thought about exploring the civil courts?"

"The civil courts, Sir?"

"Well, they are paying the victim unwanted attention, which is, technically, stalking."

"Oh, very clever, Sir."

"Get on the phone and put it to him. Offer to foot the bill. Then, if they carry on protesting after that, we can have them for breaching a court order."

"Good idea, Sir. But it still won't be easy to force it through in time."

"No. Tell you what, I'll get onto the Home Office, let them know the situation and that we're doing all we can. Hopefully, they'll be able to buy us more time."

Crowe fought off the urge to breathe a huge sigh of relief. "Good idea, Sir."

"So, keep me informed. And if I don't speak to you before the holidays, have a good Christmas."

"Oh, you too, Sir."

He found the victim to be a most amicable man that was only too happy to go to the civil courts.

After telling him to keep him in the loop, Crowe hung up, his eye catching the notes on the scrap paper that he'd been working on before.

With the paper in the shredder, he was about to flip the switch when there was a knock. "Come in," he called out, looking over his shoulder. It was Oplitova.

"Oh, sorry to bother you, Sir, but the mother of the hit and run victim is in reception. She wants to know what progress has been made with the investigation."

Crowe felt his high spirits crumble around him as he was suddenly reminded of his reeking personal life Just like when he was a child, he was going to be spending his holidays wishing he was at work. "Hit and run? What hit and run? Honestly, no-one tells me anything about what's going on. I sometimes wonder what we pay you for."

"I did tell you, Sir. I brought the documentation in yesterday morning. You said to leave it with you—."

"Oplitova, I think you've been over-exerting yourself. Maybe you should take an extended break over Christmas."

Oplitova looked horrified. "Are—Are you suspending me, Sir?"

"No, I'm not forcing you to take time off, it's just—oh never mind."

"So what should I tell the mother?"

"Tell her—tell her you forgot about her daughter's death."

"But that's not true, Sir. I gave you the documentation. You said you'd deal with it."

"Oplitova, are you calling me a liar?"

"No, Sir."

"Then, you're obviously confused. Go and tell them that you've been under a lot of stress lately and you weren't feeling yourself. Hopefully, she'll buy it."

"But, Sir—."

"Do it."

Oplitova nodded silently, looking like she was about to cry, and closed the door.

Crowe flipped the switch and the shredder buzzed into life, eating up his piece of scrap paper until it was roughly one inch from the top. Just like the day before, it jammed, omitting a loud screeching noise and the smell of oil. Crowe switched off the shredder and thought about unblocking it, but suddenly realised he'd made a mistake in instructing Oplitova to deal with the situation alone.

He ran across the room and opened the door.

Oplitova stood there, listening, eyes wide in disbelief.

"That was the shredder, wasn't it, Sir?"

****

For Crowe, weekends were a complete non-event. In the past, he'd survived by taking a huge heap of paper work home to occupy himself with. Now Susan had left him, even that wouldn't keep his mind from wandering.

He did have one piece of business to attend to. That Friday night, when everyone else was eagerly travelling home, desperate to avoid wasting a single minute out of the family nest, Crowe was preparing himself for another poker game. Over the last few weeks, the excitement of a winning hand had come to be all he had to live for. One day, when he'd got back on his feet, he was going to find someone to go to the races with. It had been far too long since he'd gone to the races. He felt it to be a more gentlemanly way of gambling than poker. Susan had even gone with him once, when she was expecting Johnnie.

Crowe looked through the windscreen of his parked car, barely noticing the brick wall that lay in front, beyond the wooden fence that marked the boundaries of the police car park. Oplitova was proving to be a problem. There was something in her eyes and tone of voice when he'd opened the door and she'd asked if it was the shredder making the noise. So what if it was? He'd been meaning to get that shredder fixed, ever since it had jammed when he'd been shredding . . . .

His phone vibrated and rang in his pocket. It was the host for that night's card game. He was ringing round everyone to tell them the game was being put back for thirty minutes. Crowe was not pleased with this news. He'd been building himself up to a nine pm start and now he'd have to readjust his preparations. He turned the ignition key, looked in his wing mirror and reversed out of the car park. Quite typically for a Friday night, the traffic was horrendous, so what should have been a ten-minute journey took almost an hour. Having eaten up the extra time, he arrived home feeling relieved that the game had been delayed.

If there was one thing he hated more than being kept hanging on, it was having to rush before a game of cards. That usually led to him forgetting something, which in turn meant he lost out. Playing for the kind of stakes that Crowe was involved with, the slightest distraction can mean the difference between elation and despair. He'd been on a losing streak of late, so decided that it had to end. Starting from that night, he was going to start clawing back the money he'd lost. He'd managed to do some of the favours he'd promised, so there was no immediate threat of further violence. If he was to stand any chance at all of getting Susan and Johnnie back, he'd have to keep them at bay, which meant changing his luck and embarking on a long and fruitful winning streak. Once he'd won back his house, he could call on Susan and say he'd got his life back together. She'd never approve if she knew how he'd managed to do it, but she didn't have to know. Once he'd got her back, he was giving up cards for good.

It was deep into the small hours by the time he returned to his flat, feeling slightly more chipper than he had earlier. He'd felt over the moon with his win when he'd left the club only ten minutes earlier, but once he'd started the car and turned onto the deserted road, he began to put it into perspective. He was up just over two hundred pounds on the evening. Not much in real terms, but it did signify a change of luck. Next week was going to be when everything came right for him and he'd leave the club with a whole new life awaiting. So after two days moping around his flat, occupying himself with paperwork and not bothering to talk to anyone, he found, much to his relief, that Monday morning had arrived. With his upturn in fortunes, he just knew that this was the week in which he'd finally put a stop to the protests. He'd receive a commendation and most likely promotion for his work. He'd get a pay rise, buy his house back and Susan would come home. Everything was going to be perfect.

Everything seemed to be going to plan, when, at just after ten o'clock, the Chief Constable called, to say the companies involved had agreed to give them more time in exchange for less money. Blair wasn't happy about it, but he'd acknowledged the lengths they'd gone to, to try and put a stop to the protests.

Next on his agenda was fixing a date for the court hearing. Fortunately, a lawyer the constabulary had used before for civil cases was available for a meeting that morning.

After being briefed, the lawyer checked his diary and said he could get to work on the case in the New Year. However, he said there might not be a slot available in court, so if he was hoping to stop the protests quickly, this might not be the best way to proceed.

Crowe swallowed this and held his breath while the lawyer made few phone calls, desperate to hear what was being said at the other end. Eventually, the lawyer put the phone down, said there was a slot available on 17th of January and asked if this was soon enough.

Crowe gave a relieved smile and told him it was perfect. Once he was alone in his office, Crowe personally saw to it that a letter was sent out to Thomas immediately.

CHAPTER THIRTEEN

Despite the events of the previous Saturday, Jane found herself in better spirits than she had been in a long while. She'd managed to surmount every obstacle the police had thrown in her way. Despite being the subject of hate for many people, this was going to be a good Christmas after all. She'd arranged to have a get together with a few of her fellow campaigners to celebrate and, if previous years were anything to go by, there'd be more than a couple of bottles of wine on offer.

Holding Suzie's lead in one hand, she unlocked the front door with the other, pausing to check her mailbox before continuing.

No sooner had she turned the key and opened the flap then a pile of mail fell to the floor. Most of it was junk, some were bills, but right at the bottom, she recognised at least one as being from the police. Stooping to gather them from the floor, she took a deep breath and trudged her way upstairs, not all that impatient to read them.

Back in her flat, she sat down, still in her jacket, and tore open the first letter from the police. There were three of them in all. She was being called in for an identity parade; nothing unexpected there. The second was just a reminder that she had to surrender herself on 21st Jan; again, just a routine letter, to cover their own backs no doubt. The third and final letter turned out to be from a solicitor. She was being taken to court for stalking. The hearing was on 17th Jan. Now, this was interesting. She'd have to get on the phone to the others later to see if they'd also had a letter.

Standing up to remove her jacket, she accidentally kicked the junk mail which she'd placed on the floor, waiting to be thrown out. That's when she noticed underneath, a couple of white envelopes. She examined them carefully before inserting her finger and tearing them open. Inside the first was a hand-written letter, in the same handwriting and blue pen as the address on the envelope. Someone had got her address, probably from the newspaper, and was writing to tell her in no uncertain terms that her and her type were not wanted. In fact, he used exactly the same term as the man in the bookshop had. The other envelope contained a similar letter, but this time they'd taken the trouble to type it. She put both letters back in their envelopes, put one on top of the other and tore them to shreds.

Just like the electricity company, the police had chosen to burden her with the news in the run up to Christmas, at a time when most people were celebrating. She gazed through the window and wondered if this was a deliberate ploy, some kind of psychological trick to put her at a disadvantage.

The following Saturday, Jane revisited the precinct, only to be subjected to further abuse. In the end she'd gone home, amused by them more than anything. It got to the point where she couldn't go out without being recognised, but, thankfully, no-one stooped to spitting at her again. In years to come, when she'd sit with her friends and laugh about all of this, only the woman in the service station would remain etched in her memory.

As the day of their Christmas get-together approached, Jane was in good spirits, there being just one thing preying on her mind. For some reason, her forth-coming identity parade worried her. If, as was the general consensus, the police did have it in for her, then surely, they would find someone to pick her out at the parade. If they really wanted to, they could just pay someone to say they recognised her and that would be that; no more protesting. She might even face a short spell in prison. Then she'd have a criminal record and she'd lose every time they took her to court. But then, given the current tide of public opinion, why would they have to pay someone to identify her? Surely the man in the bookshop or anyone that had written her a nasty letter would do it for free and with pleasure.

CHAPTER FOURTEEN

15TH JANUARY 2005

Jane arrived at the police station at a quarter to eleven, allowing her fifteen minutes' consultation with her solicitor before the identity parade began. He assured her it was nothing to worry about and that the police had to be seen to be doing something. At eleven am on the dot, Jane entered the identity suite and joined the line-up.

This is a surprisingly hard thing to do. Having someone walk up and down the line, knowing it is all about you, creates a feeling of guilt even when you're completely innocent. Jane felt sure that someone in the know would be able to pick out the suspect using body language and facial expressions alone. It was with this thought in mind that she watched the witness walk past, feeling certain that she omitted a magnetic pull that would surely attract her attention. Despite her innocence, Jane felt the relief of a guilty person when the witness failed to make a definite identification. As it turned out, the witness told the police she was unsure if she had seen the suspect or not. Smith, Jane's solicitor, was therefore happy to inform her that he didn't feel the identity parade had progressed the police's case against her very much.

Jane flashed a smile at Crowe and said goodbye to him before she left, feeling like she'd won a minor victory.

The following Monday morning, Jane was up while it was still dark to begin another trek to the High Court in London. Just like the last time, they agreed to meet up at a service station en route, to discuss their plan of action, so that they were each certain what everyone was going to say.

Jane hated driving on the motorway at the best of times, but this morning was particularly difficult. It being a Monday morning, the traffic was heavy as you might expect, but it was also an unusually cold morning. It was so cold that her breath smoked upwards and her hands stung against the steering wheel, even though she was wearing gloves. Still, this did have the unexpected benefit of taking her mind off the hearing and stopping her from turning herself into a bag of nerves.

Approaching the turn off leading to the service station, Jane saw the queue and sighed, sending a great white cloud of breath spiralling upwards in the freezing air. Stuck in the queue, she could hear outside, two men having a heated conversation about some kind of driving disagreement. It wasn't quite road rage, more like Monday morning blues, but they were jabbing fingers in each other's faces all the same.

It seemed to take an eternity for Jane to reach the car park and when she did, for some reason felt compelled to park in exactly the same space as before. Once she reached that corner of the car park, she found that the others had had the same idea. She only hoped that attitudes inside the station had changed more than their parking habits.

Fortunately, no-one recognised her this time. Perhaps it was because it was early Monday morning and people were obsessing about their own problems, but whatever the reason, Jane felt relieved. Not that it would have distracted her in any way. She was far too much of an experienced hand to let that happen.

Just like before, the newspapers had her picture all over the front. This time, in the newsagents, it was a young girl, possibly a student, serving and she didn't smirk or sneer as the older woman had done. Jane bought a copy of the paper for the hell of it though, and managed to leave the shop before the girl realised and got excited.

Once inside the cafeteria, a group of them, sat in the same place as before, saw her and waved her across. It was good to see some friendly faces and suddenly the morning chill didn't feel anywhere near as sharp. The others were drinking tea, which for a second prompted Jane to think about buying a cup for herself. But then, recalling how it turned out the last time she drank tea, decided against the idea.

Once seated, she joined in the chatter. There were seventeen of them in all, just like last time. Jane looked over her shoulder at the counter and decided to buy some beans on toast, just to be sociable. By the time breakfast was over, it was light outside, which kind of created the feeling that the traffic would be sparser. As it turned out, they still had over an hour before they reached the capital, but time seemed to pass much quicker in the daylight.

They hit the traffic again once they arrived in London of course, which was when the nerves started to jangle. Jane felt confident that the hearing would go her way, but she knew from experience never to be over-confident, because, ultimately, it all depends on how the judge sees it, which could be influenced by any number of things outside her control.

Typically, they were subjected to the same delays as before. All seventeen of them plus their solicitors were left in the waiting room for close to an hour before a woman with short dark hair called them in. They all found their way to the same places as before, the solicitors at the front with the defendants, including Jane, in the benches behind.

Timothy Lawson-Cruttenden was the plaintiff's solicitor, just like before, which all of them silently thought to be too much of a coincidence. He did his best to put them all in a bad light, pointing out to the judge that Jane was currently on police bail after being arrested and questioned over the theft of Christopher Hall's mother in law, Gladys Hammond.

In the end, the plaintiff claimed a partial victory when several of the protestors agreed to limit the time and frequency of their demonstrations. However, they all disputed a seventy-seven-mile exclusion zone as proposed by villager Peter Clamp.

None of the protestors left the hearing feeling like they had lost. The plaintiff's victory claim felt like they were clutching at straws in a desperate attempt to win a propaganda war. It was pretty evident to all of them that the police were behind the court case.

Jane smiled at a particularly downcast looking Inspector Crowe as she entered Burton Police Station, as per the conditions of her bail. Alena Oplitova, being the officer in charge of her case, took her away to an interview room where she was again questioned.

There was something likeable about Oplitova that Jane didn't see present in the other officers she'd encountered. She was firm but fair, and Jane just got the impression that deep down she sympathised with their cause.

Nonetheless, she was detained for close to three hours, concluding in yet another stalemate. Eventually, Jane was released, but with her bail extended to 1st April.

Jane again glanced at Crowe on her way out, noticing that he was unshaven. The look of despondency in his eyes told her that he'd taken the verdict personally and for the first time couldn't help feeling a tiny bit sorry for the man.

CHAPTER FIFTEEN

Crowe watched Jane disappear through the doors, waiting for her to descend the steps before cursing under his breath. It seemed that whatever he came up with she had an answer to. No doubt Sexton would be on the phone, breathing down his neck. He knew that if he couldn't find a way to stop the protest then someone would have to take the blame and right there and then it was his name in the frame. He had to act quickly to stop the axe before it fell. He was about to turn around and trudge back to his office when the doors opened and the cold breeze bit the back of his neck. A woman walked in, perhaps in her fifties, looking like she was on the warpath.

As the receptionist was busy seeing to a drug addict that was making a nuisance of himself, Crowe did the honours for her. "Good afternoon, can I help you with anything?"

"I want to make a formal complaint."

For the first time, Crowe noticed that she was holding an A4 sized piece of paper, full of printed text. "Well, I'm an Inspector here. What about?"

"About the way my daughter's hit and run case was handled."

"Oh. Well. " He held out his hand. "Here, let me see that."

He held the paper in front of him and read the text carefully, faking surprise wherever and whenever it felt appropriate.

"So, what are you going to do about it?" The woman demanded.

"Leave it with me. As I said, I'm an inspector. I'll make sure heads roll over this."

"Oh, well, thanks." She smiled gratefully and headed towards the door.

Crowe took the paper and walked back to his office, bumping into Oplitova en route. "Oplitova. Can I have a quick word with you please, in my office? Now?"

"Yes, certainly, Sir."

Crowe led her along the corridor to his office. Once inside, he held the door open for her and told her to take a seat at his desk. He could tell from her expression she was worried. This wasn't the first time that he'd got from her a sense that something was wrong.

"I've just had a run in with Mrs Brady, you know, the mother of the hit and run."

"Oh yes. I explained everything to her, just like you said."

"Well, she's making a formal complaint. Now usually, this wouldn't be too much of a problem, but at the moment, with everything else that's going on, it's an inconvenience we could do without."

"Absolutely, Sir. I understand."

"So, to ensure it goes no further. I have to take action."

Oplitova's face exuded a sense of foreboding. "What action?"

"I'm sorry, Oplitova, but I'm going to have to . . . " He suddenly remembered what she said about the shredder. How did she know about the noise it had started making unless she'd heard him—.

"Going to have to what, Sir?"

Crowe paused for thought before replying. "Tell you what, leave this with me. Just forget I mentioned it.

Oplitova looked puzzled. "Are you sure, Sir?"

"Yes. I'll deal with this, leave it to me. Oh and Oplitova?"

"Yes, Sir?"

"Why don't you take the afternoon off? You've been working hard of late. You're looking kind of, well, a bit jaded."

"Really? No, no, it's alright."

"No, really Oplitova, I insist. Go on, go home. I'll make sure you still get paid, if that's what you're worried about."

Crowe waited until he heard her car turn onto the main road and accelerate before he shredded Mrs Brady's letter. Returning to his desk, he picked up the phone and called the officer responsible for human resources. "Can you give me D.C. Oplitova's home address please?"

"Yes, certainly, Inspector."

Crowe listened carefully, noting down the address before making his next phone call.

"Hello Symons, it's Inspector Crowe."

"Inspector Crowe. How lovely to hear from you, again." His sentiments were genuine. Inspector Crowe was one of his biggest paying clients.

"Are you available to do a job for me, Symons?"

"For you, always."

"Ok, here's what I want you to do." He explained carefully and gave him Oplitova's address.

***

There was no sign of Oplitova the following Monday. Apparently, she'd been roughed up by a protestor and was taking some time off to recover from the trauma. It was approaching lunch time by the time someone came to look at the shredder. It had been making that God awful noise constantly since it had first jammed and it was starting to get on everyone's nerves.

It was an uneventful day, an uneventful week as it turned out. No sign of that Thomas woman for once. Come Friday afternoon, he was getting himself psyched up for his card game when he was informed that Mrs Brady was in reception to see him.

"I've come to see what progress has been made with my complaint."

"Mrs Brady, I said I would look into this matter personally, and I have. The officer in question is taking some time off sick. She remembers you giving her the document, but can't recall what she did with it, as has been previously communicated."

"So, what's happening about trying to find the driver?"

"I've been looking into this too, driving round the area, trying to find someone that saw something. Problem is it was late at night and the road was deserted. I know it's not what you want to hear, but the minute we find anything, we'll let you know." He gave her a politician's grin to follow his politician's answer. "Now if you'll excuse me, I have to go. Can I give you a lift anywhere?"

"Err, no, no, it's OK, Inspector. Thank you."

Getting prepared for his card game later that night, Crowe got a sense that this was the night he'd been waiting for. His luck had turned, even things at work were starting to straighten themselves out, and tonight he was going to have the win he'd been craving for what felt like for ever. For some reason, he felt compelled to look smart, so put on a suit with a pair of black shoes. He arrived in plenty of time so he could confidently greet the others as they arrived.

He had a win with the first hand, just a small one, but it made the others conscious of his upturn in fortunes. Things went his way all night, until there was only him and one other left standing. When the moment of truth came, Crowe felt the palpitations pounding, but held his nerve and managed to remain focused, giving nothing away. When his opponent threw down his cards and declared he was out, Crowe leant forward, scooped up the prizes and stood up to leave. At this stage, he wasn't sure how much he'd won. Maths was never his strong point, but he knew from the numbers they'd been playing for, that it was big. He was, however, half expecting someone to stand up and pull out a gun as they do in the movies. Instead, they just congratulated him.

"Well done, Inspector. Your luck truly has changed. How do you feel about testing your luck again, tomorrow night?"

Crowe stopped in his tracks. He'd almost made it. Just one more night like this and he'd be back in his house with his wife and son. He'd been waiting years for a winning streak like this. He had no idea how long it would last or if it would ever come around again. He had to strike now, while the iron was hot. "OK. You're on."

Back in his flat, Crowe emptied the bag of cash onto his bed, spending the rest of the night counting out his winnings. His estimate was right. He was roughly half way to reclaiming his house and family. All he needed was lady luck to be with him for one more night and he'd never gamble again.

The following night, however, things felt different. Right from the start when his car wouldn't start and he'd got oil on his shirt, fixing the engine. He arrived just in time for the first deal, giving his opponents the early psychological advantage.

The first round didn't go as planned, but that could be recovered. Then the second round and the third went badly too. Approaching midnight and he'd already lost half of the previous night's winnings. Part of him, the part that he was ashamed of, told him to quit before he lost everything, but the other part of him knew that if he did that, he'd lose face and no one would ever take him seriously again. He'd lose all credibility. By the time it was down to him and two others, the regular hardcore, he'd lost everything and was back onto IOUs. He trudged back to his car, a penniless and broken man.

CHAPTER SIXTEEN

FEBRUARY 2005

Percival Jeffries put down the phone in his study, pushed back his chair, extended his legs, gazed through the window in front of him at the lush green countryside beyond the trees marking the vicarage boundary, and let out a long sigh. Seconds later, he heard footsteps approaching.

"Goodness. I heard that sigh from the living room. What's the matter? Who was that on the phone?" The Reverend Loretta Jeffries said, placing a hand on her husband's shoulder.

"That was that police officer. D.C. Mellor. Remember him?"

"Yeah. What about him? What does he want?"

"He wants me to go down the police station first thing tomorrow and surrender myself."

"Surrender yourself? Whatever for?"

"So they can charge me with sexually assaulting a minor."

"What? But, Love you're innocent. Why would you do that?"

"So they can take me to court. It's the only way of getting my name cleared once and for all."

"I see. It just—seems so unfair."

"Well, once it gets out there's bound to be hate mail and all. My name's going to be dragged through the mud again."

"Are you sure there's no other way?

"Not without going round gathering evidence for myself, raking things up again. That could take years."

"Oh, Love." She pushed his head into her bosom and held it there for a minute, trying not to cry. "There really is no justice in this world if you have to go through this and that awful Thomas woman walks Scot free."

Percival reached up and squeezed his wife's hand. "You did your best."

"I know. I know it was God's will, but it just didn't feel right, lying like that to the police. I spent all day praying for forgiveness."

"Yes and this is God's way of showing you that he understands. I know what you did was hard for you, but it was a test. A test which you passed with flying colours."

It was safe to say that Percival Jeffries hadn't slept a wink by the time the alarm sounded to tell him the day he'd been dreading for the past three months had finally arrived. Doing his best not to wake his wife, he pulled back the covers, rubbed his eyes and stepped out of bed. He hated those dark winter mornings when you have to put the light on, which on this day he couldn't do for fear of waking his wife, and wished that spring would hurry up and arrive.

In no time at all, he found himself sat in his car, staring through the windscreen, trying to muster up the courage to start the engine. On more than one occasion he looked over his shoulder at his bedroom window, behind which his wife was still fast asleep, and thought about stepping from the car and calling Mellor to tell him the deal was off. He was not a strong man, not in the sense that he could easily walk down the street knowing what people were saying about him, and, had it not been for Loretta's involvement, he would have gone back to bed. He regretted involving Loretta in all of this, regretted, even more, the fact that he'd never been able to admit the truth to her, but it was the knowledge that if he backed out, she would have gone against all her principles for nothing that eventually persuaded him to turn the key.

It wasn't a long journey, no more than twenty minutes, but on that morning it felt more like two hours. He'd been given this appointment at the start of the day so he wouldn't draw attention to himself, but that didn't stop him feeling as if everyone he drove past knew exactly where he was going and what he was being charged with.

Finding the station car park to be surprisingly busy, he parked in the most corner he could find and, after putting on the hand brake and unfastening his seatbelt, sat watching people come and go for a minute in his mirror. When eventually, it was safe to proceed, he opened the door and walked in silence across the gravel towards the police station's main entrance.

The receptionist was very friendly. She directed him towards some comfortable chairs and telephoned Mellor to say he'd arrived. Mellor appeared almost instantly from a room along the corridor and walked briskly towards him, smiling with his arm outstretched.

"Good morning Reverend, sorry to drag you down here on such a miserable morning. Follow me, this won't take long, I assure you."

Jeffries followed Mellor into a room with a table and two chairs, one of which had extra padding on the back and a cushion over the seat.

"Take a seat," Mellor said, gesturing at the comfortable chair.

Jeffries sat down on the makeshift armchair, feeling slightly awkward.

"Cup of tea, Reverend?"

"Oh, that would be nice, thank you, very much."

"One minute."

Jeffries sat on his own in the comfortable chair, trying to peek through the gaps in the blind while keeping one ear on the corridor and the other on the comings and goings in the car park outside.

He appreciated the lengths Mellor was going to, not to make him feel like a common criminal, but it all felt a bit unnecessary. He somehow doubted if the Thomas woman or any other of the protestors had been offered a comfortable chair or a cup of tea.

When he heard Mellor's heavy footsteps clapping against the corridor, he sat up straight and composed himself. Mellor knocked before opening the door and placing a cup and saucer on the table in front of Jeffries. Jeffries leant forward, picked up the cup and took a sip.

"OK for you, Reverend?"

"Oh, yes, absolutely."

"You don't need more sugar or anything?"

"Err, No. It's fine."

"Good. Well, when you're ready, let's get down to business. Finish your tea first if you like."

"What? Oh, err, no, I'd rather just get on with it, if that's OK."

"OK then, fair enough. I just need to take a statement from you. Make sure you understand the consequences of being arrested, just a formality."

"Well, OK."

"In your own words then, tell me about what happened in Northumberland. Why were you transferred to Yoxall?"

Percival took a deep breath and told Mellor everything that happened. In a way, it came as a relief to finally get it off his chest after having kept it bottled up for all those years. He found himself getting quite emotional when he recalled how he'd felt about the young man, despite knowing how wrong it was.

He got so emotional that he didn't notice Mellor being selective about what he wrote. When Mellor raised a hand and told him to stop, he was surprised to find how few lines there were on the page. "That's fine, thank you, Reverend," Mellor said, with a grin and passed him the form to sign.

"OK then, I'm releasing you pending a court hearing at a date to be arranged. All over. Wasn't that bad, was it?"

"What? Oh, err, no, not at all."

"Come on, I'll walk you to the exit."

Mellor took him along the winding corridor back to reception, where he reached in front and held open the doors for him. "Nice seeing you, Reverend. We'll be in touch with a date for the hearing. Have a nice day."

Jeffries got into his car and drove all the way home with a smile affixed to his face. He couldn't believe how easy it had been and, better still, soon it would all be over.

CHAPTER SEVENTEEN

MARCH 2005

"Chief Constable, do come in, Sir. Take a seat. How was the journey? Cup of tea?"

Crowe held his office door open and waited for the Chief Constable to make himself comfortable, before calling out to a nearby constable to bring in two cups of tea, pronto.

"It's good to see you, Sir. I was expecting, hoping, you'd pay us a visit soon, but wasn't sure when."

"Thought I'd spring it on you. A senior officer did that to me once, and I found it helped keep me on my toes."

"Oh, good thinking, Sir."

The door creaked open and a young constable entered, carrying two mugs of tea on a plastic tray. "Thank you, Constable," said Crowe, "you can leave us now." Crowe took a sip of his tea and waited for the door to close before initiating the conversation. "So, what brings you all the way down here, Sir?"

"Just thought I'd see how things were going, you know, with the protestors. I also have an idea to run past you."

"Sounds intriguing."

"Well, tell me what's been happening and then I'll give you my idea."

"Not much more to report really, Sir. Thomas had her bail extended for another month after the identity parade failed. Oh, and Percival Jeffries' case has been reopened, Sir."

"Percival Jeffries. He's the—."

"The vicar's husband. The paedophile that got moved from his home parish in Northumberland. We agreed to clear his name in exchange for his wife identifying Thomas."

"Oh yes. A stroke of genius, if I may say so."

"Not at all, Sir. Not at all. I just wish you'd phoned before coming down. I could have saved you a wasted journey, Sir."

"Well, we ought to be exploring other avenues."

"My sentiments exactly, Sir."

Sexton pulled out a piece of paper from his pocket and slid it across the desk. "I was thinking about appealing on that Crimewatch programme. What do you think?"

"Crimewatch? Not quite sure what that would achieve, Sir. We know exactly who did it."

"Of course. I just think that it would absolve us of all suspicion. The appeal goes out on Wednesday 17th. Then at dawn on the Thursday morning, you send round a crack squad and make some arrests."

"The names on the paper, Sir?"

"The names on the paper."

Crowe had always wondered if he had what it takes to be a TV star. "Of course, and everyone will think that the arrests are linked to the show and won't ask questions until we've proved they're guilty. Brilliant."

"So you're keen on the idea?"

"Yes, most definitely, Sir."

"Good. And what about the court case?"

"Well, there's another hearing on the 18th. The judge is due to give his decision about the exclusion zone."

"Can we get to him in time?"

"I doubt it, Sir. But we do have a good legal team on board."

"I'll get on to the PM. Get him to offer him a knighthood."

"Good idea, Sir."

"Well, sorry to cut it short, but I have a busy day ahead. I think it's been a worthwhile journey though, don't you, Bobby?"

"Absolutely, Sir."

The Chief Constable rose to his feet and offered Crowe his hand. "Keep me informed of how it develops, won't you? I'll be in touch."

"Yes, Sir. Thank you, Sir."

16TH MARCH 2005

Inspector Crowe lifted his phone, punched in his wife's number, tucked the handset between his neck and shoulder, cradled his head in his hands, dug his heels into the floor and pushed back until his legs were fully extended. Grinning like a Cheshire Cat, he waited for his wife to pick up. "Good morning, Dearest. Guess who?"

"Oh, Robbie. Good morning. I was asleep."

"Did you see me on TV last night?"

"Oh, yeah. The Crimewatch appeal."

"What do you think?"

"Well, I— yeah, you should get some leads from this."

"No, silly. I meant about me. Didn't I do well?"

"Yeah, you were the star of the show."

"Really? What about my shirt? Did you like it? I bought it especially."

"Very nice, Robbie."

"Did it compliment my eyes? Did it make me look handsome?"

"I think we'd better hang up Robbie, because all the top agents are probably trying to get hold of you."

"Very funny." He tittered. "Do you think so?"

No sooner had he put the phone back in its cradle and sat up straight, then a constable knocked before entering.

"Good morning, Sir."

"Good morning, Constable. Nice to see you here bright and early."

"Thank you, sir."

"What can I do for you? Or were you just coming in to congratulate me on my TV performance last night?"

"We've just had a report of vandals, Sir—."

"What? Well, send someone out to it. You don't have to give me a live report. This is why we have team meetings."

"Yes, I know the ropes, Sir. It's just that, this particular incident involves the protestors. I just thought you'd want to know."

Crowe's face lit up. "The protestors, you say?"

"Yes, Sir. Mellor's gone to investigate."

"OK. Well done, Constable. When Mellor gets back, assuming he has the suspect with him, can you let me know? I'd like to sit in on the interview."

"Oh, very good, Sir. I'll inform you the minute he returns."

Crowe had only just finished working through his list of contacts, basking in the glory of his TV performance, when he heard a car pull up outside. Cursing the fact that his office was without a direct view of the car park, he listened in silence, holding his breath. The sudden draught told him the front doors had been opened.

It was Mellor, with what sounded like three other males. A cavalcade of footsteps approached along the corridor until there was a knock. Crowe sat up straight. "Come in."

It was the same constable that he'd seen earlier. "Err, Mellor has returned, sir, with three suspects. I'm conducting the interview now. We're in room four, Sir."

"Oh, thank you, Constable." Crowe rose to his feet, pushed his chair back under his desk and strode across his room to catch them up. By the time he was in the corridor, door closed behind him, the constable, bringing up the rear, was disappearing into the interview room.

"A-hem." Crowe closed the interview room door and cleared his throat, ensuring he was the focus of everyone's attention. "Good morning everyone, I'm Inspector Crowe. I don't usually do this, but I'm going to be sitting in on this interview. Just to ensure it all goes smoothly." He thought about adding *and we get the right outcome*, but in the end thought better of it.

It wasn't often that three suspects were questioned at once, so the interview room felt a bit overcrowded. It didn't take Crowe long to realise that there were no free seats, so he promptly disappeared to the adjacent room to fetch a spare.

He told the constable to proceed as usual and sat in a corner, not quite like a spare part, but definitely on the periphery, while he listened with interest to everything that was said. To his disappointment, but not surprise, most of the talking was done by the questioner. The whole process took him back to the days when he was finding his way through the ranks. He used to enjoy this process. When the suspect finally breaks down and admits to a crime, it is one of those moments that makes life worth living. The police equivalent to a footballer tucking the ball into the net.

However, it soon became clear that these suspects were not playing ball. When the constable had asked the same question for the third time without getting an answer, Crowe suddenly noticed how hot and stuffy the room felt. Five minutes later and he started missing his own comfortable chair in his air-conditioned office. "I err, think I'll take a break," he said, getting to his feet and hoping the relief didn't show through in his face.

He'd only just stepped through the doors of his office, when his phone started ringing. He dashed forward in the cool, fresh air, wincing as his bad leg took the weight.

"Chief Constable. How nice to hear from you, Sir."

"Good afternoon, Bobby. Splendid show last night—."

"Oh, thank you, Sir. You didn't call just to congratulate me, did you?"

"Well, no, I—."

"Oh."

"No, I wondered if you'd heard about the two arrests earlier this morning?"

"No, Sir. I've been a bit pre-occupied with—."

"Well, the Stafford station sent a squad to a house in Gloucester this morning. "Twenty-five of them in all."

"Really, Sir?"

"Yes, don't interrupt. They found and arrested a man and a woman aged thirty-two and thirty respectively."

"On what grounds?"

The Chief Constable filled him in.

"Well, thanks for telling me. I've got some news of my own, Sir."

"What's that, Crowe?"

"This morning, one of my lads single-handedly brought in three of the bastards that were causing criminal damage."

"Really? That's great news. How's it going?"

"Not much progress yet, Sir, but there's still time."

"Well, if you can't make criminal damage stick, try changing the charge. You'll get more time to question them at the very least."

"Good idea, Sir. That's just what I was planning on doing."

"Well, I'll keep you updated. If they make the charges stick in Stafford, I'll call to tell you to let your trio go free. Otherwise, assume the worst case scenario. To be honest, the evidence is pretty flaky, so they'll have to box clever to seal the deal in Stafford."

"I understand, Sir. The last thing we need is for two separate arrests for the same crime. Wouldn't look very good in court, would it?"

"Precisely."

Once he'd finished with the Chief Constable, Crowe decided to take himself out to the sandwich shop. On his way back, he paused outside the door of Interview Room Four and held his breath. They were still at it. The three suspects were experts at avoiding the question. He decided to leave it until mid-afternoon before barging in and suggesting they change the charge.

After lunch, things went quiet, so he decided to make a phone call direct to Stafford Police Station, to get an update for himself. No point in constantly bothering the Chief Constable, he thought. Turned out that they were having just as much trouble making it stick, as the Chief Constable had said, as they were having in Burton. They'd sent a squad, including some forensic experts, round to search the premises and a vehicle, but had no luck in finding any new evidence.

With this in mind, at just after three pm he entered the interview room and called the constable doing the questioning out into the corridor for a private word.

After closing the door firmly, Crowe lowered his voice and said, "Are you making much progress with the questioning?"

The constable shook his head and whispered, "No. I'm flogging a dead horse, here, Sir."

"That's what I thought."

The constable looked embarrassed.

"OK, I think it's time we changed tack with this."

"How do you mean, Sir?"

"I think you should have a break for say half an hour, then come back, with a fresh spring in your step. I also think you should try changing the charges. Try . . ."

The constable grinned. "I know what you mean, Sir. It's just there's not much evidence—."

"But what do we have to lose? They're here, they have a motive and they look as jaded as you do."

"Mmm. Maybe you're right."

"I am right, Constable. Go in there and tell them you're taking a break, then re-emerged in thirty minutes looking totally refreshed and change the charge. It will completely throw them off guard, believe me."

Crowe stood listening through the closed door as the constable made the announcement.

Thirty minutes later, Crowe entered Interview Room Four alongside the constable, to be greeted by grateful looking smiles from the suspects, who clearly thought the game was up. Imagine then, their dismay when, instead of receiving their discharge papers, they were instead informed that the charge was being changed.

The constable, refreshed from the break, patiently ignored their protests, waited for them to tire themselves out and sat down, facing them. Crowe did his best to make himself comfortable in the same corner as before.

As it turned out, all three had water-tight alibis, but Crowe was determined not to let them slip through his fingers, so continued the questioning well into the night, long after the constable had gone home. At around nine pm he informed them they were being kept in police custody over night and they would resume where they'd left off first thing in the morning.

Crowe called for someone to escort them to a cell and left the building, completely oblivious to the curses being hurled at his back.

As usual, Crowe was the first person in the building the following morning. He took great delight in ensuring the detainees were up and ready for action as soon as he arrived. And, as he was in such a good mood, decided to take them back to the interview room and recommence the questioning himself. It had been a long time, and he really missed the thrill of not only seeing, but making them squirm. Part of him, the part that also enjoyed watching the horse fall and break its neck, also hoped he'd be the one to make them crack. He drafted a confession for each to sign before he began, just so there'd be no hold ups when the typist arrived.

He started off with the same line of questioning as the day before; getting them each to go over, yet again, what they were doing on the night in question. Much to his dismay, he found them to be stubborn opponents, sensing straight away that it was going to be yet another long day. When the constable arrived on the scene, he left him to it, deciding to retreat to the comfort of his office and resign himself to another failure.

If this particular cloud did have a silver lining, it was that Stafford had also let their suspects go uncharged, meaning at least, that he was not going to be made to look like an incompetent. Crowe hunched forwards and plunged his chin into his hands on his desk. Sexton was doing his best, but the pressure was on. It was only a matter of time before his attitude changed and he would find himself the scapegoat. He had to act quickly to stop that happening. Then, remembering something else Sexton had said over the phone, he sat back and mustered a tiny smile; the court case was tomorrow. If the judge imposed the exclusion zone, most of his troubles would be over.

CHAPTER EIGHTEEN

17TH MARCH 2005

For the third time in recent months, Jane was up early, getting ready for another trip to the High Court in London. In contrast to the other two times, though, it hadn't kept her awake, and she was past getting herself worked up about it. Maybe it was down to the fact that it was light outside and things always seem better in daylight or maybe these trips to court were becoming routine. The group had agreed to their customary meeting en route, but some, including Jane, didn't feel it was strictly necessary. She agreed to it to be sociable and to lend moral support to those that needed it. It was also a Thursday, which perhaps explained why all the commuters seemed less on edge, more tolerant of each other. There's just something ingrained about Sunday nights and Monday mornings that make them universally hated.

There was no problem entering the service station this time and nor did she have any trouble finding a place to park. However, her instincts took her to the same place she'd parked in previously, and she smiled to herself as she saw that all the others had also been drawn to this corner of the vast car park. And despite there being so many empty bays, she slotted her Micra in between two familiar cars, just as she had before.

She did pause to buy a newspaper on her way to the restaurant. The headlines were all about the arrests of the previous couple of days. Her visit to the High Court was more like an afterthought, although tomorrow, barring something extraordinary happening, she was certain to make the headlines. She bought some beans on toast from the caf, not caring whether anyone recognised her or not. Carrying her tray across to the table where the others were sat, she smiled and looked over her shoulder when a man hissed abuse at her back. She was starting to feel a tiny bit sorry for people that believed everything they read in the newspapers.

The others shared her confidence. There was none of the nervous tension of previous visits. They all knew that as long as they were permitted to continue protesting, they'd emerge victorious, despite the contorted angle the media would inevitably throw on it. They also knew that deep down, that's how the police saw it too.

Heads held high, they polished off their breakfast and made their way back to their corner of the car park, wishing each other luck and offering last minute reassurances on the way.

After leaving the service station, the journey towards London had passed quickly previously, but this time, it positively flew by. Just like before though, progress came to a halt once they hit the London traffic.

When Jane opened the doors of the main entrance, the receptionist smiled and said hello, like they knew each other well. Jane didn't need to be directed to the waiting area, she knew exactly where to go. They were kept waiting half an hour before a middle-aged woman wearing glasses called them into the court room.

The judge cleared his throat and spent the next hour bad mouthing the protestors, calling them everything from guerrillas to terrorists, despite the fact that none of them had been charged with any offence relating to the protest.

Finally, when he'd finished his onslaught, giving the members of the press present all the ammunition they needed, he got down to the point. Despite their collective air of confidence, Jane felt nervous as he read out decision.

He demanded that they cease their hate campaign, but did not enforce the seventy-seven-mile exclusion zone that the police were hoping for. Instead, he said he would grant them a final chance to protest peacefully, warning that if the terrorism continued, he would impose the exclusion zone which would effectively bring a halt to their campaign. For now, the restrictions already imposed would continue to apply. This meant that the protests could not consist of more than twenty-five people and they could only protest on a Sunday between the hours of noon and three pm. All in all, the judge gave them the go ahead to continue protesting peacefully as they were. They didn't have to change a thing to comply with his orders.

None of them said as much on the way home, but with this and the recent failed arrests, it kind of felt like they were starting to gain the upper hand in their battle with the police to exercise their right to protest.

This joyous feeling spilt over into the next day, when Jane decided to venture out for a walk to the shops. She wasn't surprised at the newspaper headlines. It had seemed to her that the judge had repeatedly used the words 'terrorists' and 'guerrillas' to give them the opportunity to contort the verdict and to use words that would impact with people in the way the police desired. By using the media, the police could yet turn defeat into victory.

Being branded a terrorist was, therefore, par for the course and nothing less than any of them had expected. What she felt to be below the belt and what went so far as to hurt her was the way in which one of the reporters had again used her cancer to imply she was a hypocrite. Despite everything, it felt like they were determined to single her out and wage war against her individually.

CHAPTER NINETEEN

Crowe sat alone in his studio flat, staring at the blank TV screen, half an eye on the clock. The ticks pounded in his ears as he tried to shake off the feeling of numbness that he'd been experiencing since he heard the news at around four pm. He was worried. Worried that Sexton was about to turn nasty to save his own skin, worried that he'd lose his job, worried that his creditors would call their debts in, worried that he was going to be found out for being the fraud he was.

The second the clock struck ten pm, he reached for the remote control and turned on the TV. This was the third news bulletin he'd watched, each one making his anger increasingly uncontrollable, turning it into a brewing volcano, steam seeping through the surface, warning of an impending eruption. Maybe that was why he felt compelled to watch it one more time, because he knew he had to find a way of letting it out.

The story was headline news. He watched patiently, smiling even, as he listened to the judge brand them terrorists. Then, noticing the Thomas woman smiling on her way out, he picked up the remote and hurled it across the room at the TV, cracking the glass from top to bottom and sending the batteries inside the remote flying across the floor along with the battery cover.

Not for the first time, he felt like a cartoon character with an adversary that kept on getting away from him. Resisting the temptation to say, I'll get you, Thomas, you see if I don't, he went to the cupboard and took out a bottle of whiskey that he'd been saving for emergencies.

He'd only taken a couple of sips when a thought occurred to him. Alcohol often had that effect. Maybe he'd been too focused on Thomas and he should try and broaden the scope of his enquiries. What he needed was a way to lay the foundations for a fresh campaign. Learn from his previous mistakes and concentrate on enemies he had a better chance of beating.

Crowe grinned as he sat formulating his plan before jotting down some notes. Once he'd finished, he poured himself a second glass of whiskey. The second glass was a celebration and so tasted much better.

CHAPTER TWENTY

1ST APRIL 2005

"Hello, can I help you?"

Jane smiled at the officer behind the reception desk and stepped inside, happy that she wasn't notorious enough to be instantly recognised. Standing inches from the desk, she replied, "Yes. My name's Jane Thomas, and I've been asked to report in today as per the conditions of my bail."

The constable smiled politely and told Jane to take a seat in the waiting area. She immediately turned away and headed for the hard, plastic seats without needing to be told that someone would be along to see her as soon as her solicitor was present. She was an experienced hand now and knew the form. She also knew that her solicitor was likely to arrive before anyone was ready to see her and so it turned out. Only two minutes later, Smith made his entrance, smiled at the receptionist and continued towards the waiting area. He sat on the chair beside Jane, bade her good morning and told her what to expect.

They had to wait for what seemed like an age, but was actually no more than thirty minutes, before Mellor appeared. "Jane Thomas? Step this way, please."

At first, there was no difference in his demeanour. He looked at her, both of them, like they were dirt and proceeded to lead them down the corridor, too disgusted to look back.

Then, approximately half way through the short journey, Crowe appeared from nowhere. "D.S. Mellor, can I have a quick word, please before you begin?"

Mellor looked over his shoulder, curled his nose and said, "Won't be a minute." They watched silently as Mellor followed Crowe into his office. Once they were both inside and the door firmly closed, they each took two steps forward and stood in silence, trying to eavesdrop on what was being said.

It turned out to be much longer than a minute, more like ten, that they were stood waiting in the hot, stuffy corridor. It sounded like Crowe was trying to explain something, which Mellor was having trouble digesting. The door opened and Mellor emerged. Both Jane and her solicitor jumped back, desperate to avoid being caught red handed listening in on what was being said.

"This way," Mellor said, ignoring their embarrassed expressions. Although he stopped short of apologising for the delay, there was something different about Mellor. The curled up nose, the look of sheer disgust was no longer present for a start. Once the questioning started, this difference in attitude became all the more apparent.

He started off with the same questions as before, prompting both Jane and her solicitor to set themselves in for another long and gruelling session, resulting in another stalemate.

However, it soon became clear that he wasn't going to keep on repeating himself. He just took Jane's answer, wrote it down then asked her for a statement.

It didn't take long to complete, and he didn't keep on tutting and shaking his head as if calling her a liar as he had before. They were in the interview room little over an hour when Mellor got to his feet, opened the door and told Jane she was free to leave without charge. Once back at home, she sat on her couch and took a moment to reflect on the situation. It felt good to be a free woman again, with no run ins with the law on the horizon, but she'd been dragged through the mire over this. The police had made people despise her for their own gain. No one was going to care that she'd been released without charge. As far as they were concerned, she was beneath contempt. People in Burton had long memories and it was going to be a long time before she could walk around the shops again without fear of being insulted. No, as far as she was concerned, she had more than adequate grounds to make a complaint.

CHAPTER TWENTY-ONE

7TH APRIL 2005

Inspector Crowe marched along the corridor and into his office with an air of renewed optimism. He'd been lying awake half the night, thinking everything through. He'd allowed his grudge against Thomas to get in the way of what really mattered, which was stopping the campaign. She'd proven to be such a slippery opponent, because she had such a squeaky clean record. But others did not. Anyone with previous would be much easier to convict, and so he was going to go through the files and find the right people to hang it on. In the meantime, he had to get the message across loud and clear to the public and the prospective judge that they were dealing with terrorists that had no place in society.

He pulled out the chair, sat down and glanced at the clock on the wall. He had at least two hours to kill before Sally, his part time secretary, arrived. He placed the notes he'd made the night before on his desk and extracted his notepad and a pen from his top drawer. With any luck, he'd be free of disturbances, which would allow him to concentrate on producing the perfect letter.

"Good morning, Sally," Crowe said as his secretary made her entrance.

"Good morning Inspector. How are you today?" Sally replied, removing her jacket.

"Very well, thank you, very well."

She looked at him quizzically. "Mmm. You seem in good spirits this morning. Has something happened that I should know about?"

"Indeed it has. Why don't you make us both a cup of tea and I'll tell you all about it."

Five minutes later, Sally returned carrying two mugs of tea. She placed one in front of Crowe, casting an eye over the drafted letter on his desk.

"Is that letter what you wanted to tell me about, Sir?" She asked, walking across the room to her desk.

Crowe took a sip of tea before replying. "Yes. I need you to type it up for me."

"Very good, Sir." Sally reached down to switch on her computer, sat back and watched the screen as it whirred into life. It was an old computer that really needed replacing, so it seemed to take an age to boot up. When, eventually, Sally had open in front of her an empty Microsoft Word document with a flashing cursor, Crowe's mug stood empty on his desk in front of him.

"You ready?" he asked Sally, getting to his feet and walking across the room.

She looked up over her shoulder. "Yes, Sir."

"Good. OK, take this down . . . "

There was a distinct glint in Crowe's eyes as he dictated a supposed communique from the protestors. As the lies dripped from his tongue, he felt exhilarated, his heart pounding with excitement.

Roughly ten minutes had passed by the time Crowe looked over Sally's shoulder to read the freshly typed document file. "Mmmm. It's lacking something. A code name to give it extra authenticity. Let me think." He glanced through his window for inspiration, his eyes falling on a horse and cart that was holding up the traffic.

"Red rum. End it with code name red rum."

Sally took a minute to read the letter back to herself, murmuring it aloud under her breath. "Who is this going to, Sir?"

"Oh, the local press. Hopefully the nationals will pick it up from there."

"Do you really think they'll print this?"

"Why wouldn't they? They print everything else we tell them." He smirked and made his way back to his desk as Sally sent the document to the printer.

With the freshly printed letter in front of him, Crowe picked up his phone and instructed a junior constable to take it straight to The Burton Mail newsroom. He told the constable to pass on instructions for it to go out in today's edition.

Later that afternoon, he sent the same constable out to buy a copy of The Burton Mail. Holding the paper in front of him, Crowe made himself comfortable, read the headline and grinned.

After reading the article, he called the editor to thank him personally for his good work.

CHAPTER TWENTY-TWO

Inspector Crowe arrived into work, feeling better than he had done for a long time. He'd had a win at cards the previous Friday, but over the weekend he'd made a decision. A decision for the life of him he couldn't work out why he hadn't come to before.

Arriving home on Saturday afternoon, he'd come across a pile of junk mail. For some reason, something compelled him to take them to the couch and read each one in detail, rather than just throw them straight in the bin. One of them, he discovered, was alerting him to the fact that he'd been pre-selected for a loan. Mainly because he had nothing better to do, he went online and checked it out. Of course, he hadn't been approved of anything; he had to go through a lengthy application process to see if he qualified. Then, the thought occurred to him that if he managed to get a bank loan, he could use the money to clear his debts and buy back his house. However, because of the amount involved, he didn't receive an immediate decision. He'd checked first thing before leaving for work, only to find an email apologising for the delay. By the time he got home later, he should know. This time tomorrow he could have the cash in his account. On Friday, if he could do a deal with Tony, the guy he'd signed his house over to, he'd have his old life back and everything would be rosy again.

He opened the blinds and the window to let in some of the fresh Monday morning spring air, returned to his comfortable executive chair and cradled his head in his hands. He had a routine, which he'd have to get on with. Providing there was nothing urgent to deal with, every Monday morning, he started by going through his in tray. This was important, because Mondays they always had a team meeting and he had to give the impression that he knew what he was doing. He laughed aloud at the little joke he had with himself. Close to the top of the pile, about six inches deep, was a photo-copy of one of the protestors' flyers. He put this to one side, thus forming the beginnings of a 'to shred' pile.

He continued working through the paperwork, until, right at the bottom, he found a copy of a statement Jane had made the previous week. He picked it up, held it to the light, read it, re-read it and read it for a third time, his blood boiling more violently with each re-read. In the end, seething, he placed the statement next to the shred pile, which consisted solely of the flyer, and paused for thought. It was about time that woman was silenced once and for all. She'd made a monkey of the force once before and he wasn't going to let her do it again. It's about time she learnt some respect for the police. He opened his drawer, pulled out a black felt tip pen and placed the flyer in front of him.

After crossing out the final four words of the heading, which was written in bold across the top, he added one extra word to make it read, Save Yourself. Crowe grinned and looked through the window, deep in thought. When inspiration came, he returned to the job at hand, now grinning more widely than ever.

> Jane, UR goin to need you're 3000 pounds compensation, by the time we've finished with U, and that lovely Nissan Micra.

> You'll be lying in a hospital bed with your jaw wired up, U won't be doin ur 'free speech', you fat ugly bitch. Go and get some plastic surgery u fucking need it.

He held it up the light and smiled. This felt good. Not as good as he'd felt when that horse broke its neck at the races, but not far behind. After rereading the caption, he felt something was missing, so added, UR a marked woman, right along the top, making sure it would be the first thing she saw.

He placed the note on his out tray. He'd give it to some plain clothes constable to deliver later, when it was dark. She wouldn't be smiling when she found it on the mat the next morning, that's for sure.

From that moment on, the day flew by. By the time they'd finished the staff meeting at four pm, he was already starting to think of going home and checking his emails. He knew that some people checked their personal emails at work, but he'd never done that. He liked to keep his work and personal life separate in all aspects. Besides, if he had checked, there's a good chance he'd have been too distracted to do any work.

The minute he arrived home, he walked straight over to his PC, pushed the button and took his coat off while it whirred into life. Without bothering to sit down, he leant over his desk and went straight to his inbox, cursing the fact that he was one of the few people that still remained on dial up as his emails took an eternity to download.

After clicking on the emboldened subject line that read 'your loan application – decision', he tried to resist skipping straight to the bottom paragraph, instead reading the small print. When, finally, he came to the line that informed him he would have the cash in his bank account within twenty-four hours, he stood up straight, punched the air and screamed out 'Yesss'.

Straight away, he loaded his bank's online statement facility and confirmed that his balance had received a significant boost. He was back in business. Now all he had to do was get through the next four days. He wished he'd thought to ask for Tony's number so they could have done business there and then, and cursed the unwritten code of conduct that prohibited syndicate members from having each other's contact details.

For once, Crowe didn't arrive first for the card game that Friday. He deliberately waited until the others would have been there for at least an hour, before putting on his jacket and making his way down the stairs to his car. If everything went to plan, this would be the final time he'd be making this journey. The last thing he wanted was to succumb to temptation, join in the game and get himself into debt, thus enslaving himself to the syndicate for one more week at least.

The barmaid smiled and eyed him suspiciously when he walked in. She was most likely surprised at his tardiness, as would everyone else be. She began pouring him a whiskey. "No, not tonight," he said, placing a hand over the top of the glass. Looking bemused, the barmaid apologised and went about her business.

The minute Crowe walked into the room, all eyes fell on him. Some of them friendly, greeting him, making him feel welcome. Others looked put-out, and some of them looked like they were wondering what he was up to. Eventually, Crowe got the impression that his late arrival had been taken as some kind of ploy to give himself an advantage and no-one said a word. They continued with the game, letting Crowe stand at the back, watching silently, waiting for his moment to arrive.

When the cards landed on the table, the money scooped up into a bag, the relieved chatter started. That's when Crowe approached Tony and asked for a quick word.

"Err, yeah, certainly mate."

Tony looked and sounded like your typical Cockney gangster. The two shared a respect for one another, but neither would go so far as to call the other a friend. Tony was about 5ft ten inches, had a shaven head and looked like he had at least four cushions stuffed up his jumper.

Once outside in the fresh air, Tony lit up a cigarette. "Want one?" he said, offering Crowe the packet.

Crowe took a cigarette, placed it in his mouth and leant forward while Tony lit it for him. Taking a long, deep puff, Crowe realised just what he'd been missing out on.

With the small talk over with, Crowe took the cigarette from his mouth, flicked some ash atop the concrete forecourt and said. "Tony, I want my house back."

Tony grinned. "Wife been giving you jip, has she?"

"She's left me."

"Oh, sorry. Never realised. Now, why would I give it back?"

"We had a deal. I give you the money, and you hand back the keys."

"And do you have the readies?"

"I do indeed."

Taken aback, Tony took a long puff on his cigarette and looked up at the cloudy, starless sky. "OK. You got it with you?"

"Follow me." Crowe led him back to his car, where he opened the back door, leant in and pulled out a grey bag full of twenty pound-notes. "You got the keys?" Crowe said, holding the bag firmly by his side.

"Follow me."

Tony took Crowe back to his car, where spent a moment rummaging around in the glove compartment. "Here," he said, holding the keys up, making them shine in the light from the nearby street-light.

Crowe extended his right hand, while with his left, he dropped the bag half way between them. When the exchange was completed, they both turned to head their separate ways. Crowe had only taken two steps when Tony called out.

"You not playing tonight then, Crowe? Lost your bottle have you?"

"I've given it up, mate. Besides I have a big day ahead tomorrow."

"What you doing, tomorrow?"

"Moving into my house."

Tony walked across the car-park so they could converse without the need for shouting. "Could you, err , give me a day to get things ready? I've just got a few things to take care of."

"Of course, no problem."

"Thanks, pal. Pleasure doing business with you." Tony extended his hand.

"Likewise." Crowe shook his hand, walked away, and then realised how one sided the exchange had been. At that moment, he felt more determined than ever not to return to his old ways. "Tony?" He called, walking briskly in the direction he'd just come."

"Yes, Pal?"

"Can I have your phone number? Just in case there are any problems with the house."

Tony nodded. "Yes, Pal. Certainly."

Crowe couldn't wait to phone his wife to give her the news. He felt most frustrated when he called Saturday afternoon to be told by her mother she'd gone out with an old school friend. Crowe couldn't help feeling hurt by this. He'd gone to such lengths to find the money, just to win her back, only to discover that not only was she not missing him, but she was out, having a whale of a time. It was only some time later that he realised he'd been doing the same thing every Friday night since they'd split up. He decided to leave breaking the news until the following morning so he could surprise her, but then remembered how she liked to take Johnny to church on a Sunday, so it would have to wait until the afternoon. Damn it. He didn't mind though, not really. He liked the fact that she took her religion seriously. He'd done well to find a church going girl that his daddy would have been proud of. There aren't that many of them around these days.

He decided to leave it until Sunday afternoon before going to his house. Half way down the concrete stairs, leading from his flat to the car park, he paused, hand on the bannister to recollect all that had happened while he'd been living there. He had to admit that not much of it was good. Looking through the window at the town on a sunny Sunday afternoon, he swore to himself there and then that he was never going to let himself sink so low again, no matter what. And if that meant giving up cards and even the horses, then so be it. This was the start of a new phase in his life and he was determined to make the most of it.

Hearing footsteps ascending the stairs from below, he snapped out of his trance and continued on his journey to his car. Once settled in the driver seat, the clunk of the seat belt still ringing in his ears, he again paused briefly before turning the ignition key, reversing out onto the main road and making the short journey to a different world. Turning down the tree-lined road, he wound down his window to take in the smell of freshly cut grass on an English Sunday afternoon in early May. To his surprise, an old friend, out walking his dog, smiled and waved as he drove past. Crowe smiled to himself as a warm glow engulfed him. He was back among his own kind, where he was known and respected. Catching a glimpse of the purple fence that Susan had helped him paint, he smiled again, but as it got nearer and he began to see things in more detail, the smile gradually faded from his lips. By the time he was parked on the road, looking directly at the house that stood out like a sore thumb in this exclusive part of town, his smile had been devoured by a look of horror. The fence that Susan had so pain-stakingly painted with him on that summer's day when they'd just moved in was now rotten and dilapidated. Towards the end nearest the garage, two panels were missing. He walked along the driveway, fidgeting with the key in his pocket, until he came to the gap in the fence where the end panels should have been. That's when he heard the voices.

Releasing his key, he walked slowly towards the door and pressed his ear to the bubbled glass pain. A man and a woman inside were having a row. And, by the sound of it, there were kids in there too. He rapped gently on the door and waited.

An angry looking woman in her late thirties flung open the door and stood glaring at him. Her face was bright red, several strands of blonde hair plastered to her forehead.

"What do you want?" she snapped.

"I'm errr—My name's Robbie—Police Inspector —Crowe," he said. "This is my house and I've come to reclaim it." It wasn't until she slammed the door in his face that got an inkling as to what they might be rowing about.

Crowe reached into his pocket for his phone. Before he could dial Tony's number, the woman shouted, "There's a f***ing man out there that wants to take our f***ing house away. Now f*** off upstairs and get your f***ing things packed, now!"

Tony had obviously been renting out the place. He paused for a moment to think about what he was doing, but, ultimately, couldn't see a problem in taking his own house back. He did go back to his car before calling Tony though, who apologised and said he'd give his tenants a ring to hurry them along. After being told that hopefully, they'd be out by the end of the day, Crowe went back to his studio flat, his moment of glory postponed for at least another twenty-four hours.

Distracted at work the following day, Crowe felt like he was operating on autopilot, like he was just playing out time until he got home and the day could begin for real. By the time five-thirty came around, he looked at his desk to discover at least six fresh coffee rings. And a glass ashtray that was overflowing. Since he'd had that cigarette with Tony the other night, he hadn't been able to stop and feared he might be becoming addicted. Goodness knows what Susan, who had strong anti- smoking views, would make of this.

Hopefully, it wouldn't come to that, and it was just a phase that would soon pass. Antagonising her after everything he'd put her through was the last thing he wanted. If, indeed, she agreed to come back at all. He hadn't had chance to tell her anything yet and felt relieved that he'd waited until the house was ready for them to move in. He just got the feeling, deep down, that he was going to go back to the house to discover Tony's tenants still there, sat cross legged on the driveway, refusing to budge. Fighting the urge to light up yet another cigarette, he decided he might as well pack up and go home early.

Finding another heap of mail in his letter box, Crowe decided to read it before venturing out to claim his house back. With the top five letters back in their envelopes and cast onto the floor, he came to the terms and conditions of his loan. Holding it up to the light, he couldn't find the motivation to read the seven pages of eight pt.

Times New Roman, but held his gaze for at least ten seconds on the headline emblazoned across the top of the page which read: Your assets are at risk if you don't keep up the repayments.

There'd be no problem making the repayments, not on his salary, none at all. But if anything should happen to make him lose his job then . . . .

Oh, he was worrying about nothing. This was all down to that Thomas woman, and the pressure Sexton had heaped on him to come up with a way of stopping the protest. It was starting to look like this was all in the past now, and finally, he could move on. Recalling the note he'd written her, he sat back on his couch, legs drawn in until his heels touched the upholstery and gave it some thought. He wholeheartedly regretted saying the things he had and for a second considered calling the station to cancel its delivery.

Then he remembered the trouble she'd caused him and the fact that despite everything, she was a rational person. Hopefully, she'd take the hint and wouldn't put him in a position where he had to carry out his threats.

Feeling a sudden urge to stretch his legs out, he remembered the task at hand, so, with a smile, got to his feet and descended the stairs to the car park. After making the short drive to his house, he felt happy to see it empty, this time. Ignoring the missing fence panels, he let himself in and browsed each room, noticing the damage without it actually registering.

Finally, after inspecting each room and doing his fair share of reminiscing in each, he stepped through the patio doors into the garden. It was obvious that this had been neglected. The grass was waist high for a start, and the trees made it look like a jungle further down, near the shed, but at least his table, the one he'd bought to watch the cricket on a few years back, was in good shape. Kicking away the empty crisp packets and crushed lager cans from the flags, he pulled out a chair and sat down. It was a glorious summer's night. Maybe he'd enjoy it for an hour or so before calling Susan. There were, however, a couple of items that he needed from the shop, which he knew to be just around the corner, less than five minutes away.

Placing a packet of cigarettes and a couple of cans of beer on the counter, he weighed up the assistant, trying to work out if she was new. She had long dark, scraggy hair, blue eyes under which were a good few wrinkles and her lips were smeared with bright red lip stick. Moving his eyes down, he came to her name badge which read, Beth. "Nice night isn't it?" Beth said with an awkward smile, obviously wondering why he'd been taking so much interest in her.

"Yes. Yes, it is." He then proceeded to tell her that he was moving back into his house. Beth sounded shocked and declared that she knew the previous occupiers well. Crowe thanked her, picked up his supplies and left the shop, her name etched in his mind.

Half way through his second can of beer and with at least four cigarette butts in the glass ashtray, he looked around him and realised it was starting to get dark. Crowe decided there was only so much thinking you can do before you need someone to talk to. He'd already fought off the urge to take out his phone and see if there was any horse racing anywhere. So, with the temptation still lingering, he finally got round to calling his wife.

Susan was as much surprised as she was overjoyed to hear that he'd got the house back and came over right away. Crowe noticed her face droop when she saw the fence, her expression of disappointment turning to one of despair when she carried out her own internal inspection. Being a woman, she noticed things Crowe hadn't and started making a mental list of all the things they'd have to do to make it their own home again.

It had gotten completely dark outside, and indoors, the curtains were drawn and the lights on by the time she looked him in the eye and said, "OK, Robbie. I'll move back in, but if it happens again—."

"It won't," he said, dropping to his knees and taking hold of her hand. "Thank you."

CHAPTER TWENTY-THREE

The next morning sailed by, despite the constant interruptions. Aside from the protestors, things had been quiet of late, and it had been just a matter of time before this changed. When he returned from his stroll out to the sandwich shop, Jane's complaint caught his eye. This was an annoyance he could do without, with his life finally going in the right direction. So with a sigh, he picked up the phone and called the Independent Police Complaints Authority, the independent body set up to deal with complaints against the police. He'd dealt with them before; they knew when to play ball. After quoting them the case reference, he explained the situation, just to ensure that they reached the right decision.

The woman he spoke to sounded old, and too snooty for her own good. "So, let me get this right, Inspector Crowe. You claim you've had instructions direct from the PM himself to do whatever it takes to stop the protest?"

"That is correct."

The woman breathed down the phone for a few seconds. Perhaps she was asthmatic.

Crowe grew impatient. "And might I also add that should action be taken on this case, anyone finding the police guilty of unethical behaviour will at best be fired. At worst made to carry the can and go to prison for a very long time."

"I see, Inspector Crowe. Well, I have to verify all this of course."

"Of course."

"And if what you say is corroborated, then I can assure you this case will go no further."

"Thank you. It will be."

"Good day, Inspector Crowe."

"Good day. It just keeps getting better and better."

The woman laughed and said goodbye before hanging up.

Crowe's good day was made even better when he arrived home to find all his furniture returned from storage. Susan was busy cleaning what was to be Johnny's room, ready for his return the following day. He had to hand it to her, she'd transformed the house. Even given the skirting boards downstairs a lick of paint. Secretly, he found the smell of paint a bit intoxicating though, so decided to pretend he hadn't noticed. But the best was yet to come. It turned out that she'd been down to the butchers and bought them a joint of beef for dinner. Crowe, who hadn't enjoyed a home cooked meal for over a year, felt a tingling sensation on his tongue as he imagined eating roast beef with gravy. They finished off Johnny's room together while the beef slow cooked.

Much to Crowe's surprise, when they sat down to eat, Susan just had vegetables.

"You not having any beef?" Crowe asked, showing a clump of chewed meat as he spoke.

"No. I bought it for you. I know how much you like your meat."

"Don't be silly." He picked up his plate, held it over the corner of hers and proceeded to push a piece of meat with his knife.

"No." She moved her plate away.

"Sorry."

"Look, the reason I'm not eating meat is I've kind of gone vegetarian."

"What?" Crowe's jaw dropped open, a piece of meat got caught in his throat, and a bout of coughing and spluttering ensued.

"Are you OK?"

Crowe, face red as a beetroot, still coughing and spluttering, nodded. Susan rose to her feet and brought him a glass of tap water.

Crowe drank it down in one gulp, stopped coughing and composed himself. "Sorry."

Susan started laughing. "It's OK. I expect it came as a bit of a shock."

"You can say that again."

"It's a much healthier lifestyle. To be honest—" she glanced at his stomach— "I think you could benefit from going vegetarian too."

"No way. Never."

"You haven't even tried it. You'll like it once you get used to it. Let me cook you a vegetarian meal tomorrow night, see what you think."

Crowe glanced through the glass doors at his twilit garden to imagine the ironic headlines his own hypocrisy would generate if he turned vegetarian.

Susan smiled. "What you laughing at? Come on, tell me."

"Oh, nothing. Look, I really can't go vegetarian at the moment. I'll give it a go later in the year though, I promise."

"Well, OK. Although I still don't understand why. Are you gonna finish this beef off then?"

"Yes, since you've cooked it so well."

Susan smiled and went to the worktop to slice the remainder of the beef joint.

Crowe spent the rest of the week on the crest of the wave. Even his secretary noticed the extra spring in his step. He knew, though, that at any moment his world could come tumbling down and everything he'd worked so hard for could once again be in jeopardy. By Friday lunch time, he was starting to think this moment wasn't going to come after all and he was set to have the best weekend ever. He spent the entire day in a great mood, right up until four o'clock when he came back from his meeting to find a note on his desk that would remove a considerable amount of shine from his weekend.

CHAPTER TWENTY-FOUR

Jane picked up the note she'd found folded in half in her letterbox the other morning and read it one more time, paying particular attention to the grammatical errors. She had an idea who sent it, the reference to her compensation money gave it away, but of course couldn't prove a thing. She folded it once each way and put it in her pocket. The others would be most amused when they saw it; as had she been. Indeed, it was only for her amusement that she found herself repeatedly drawn to it.

It was early May now, and at long last, the fine weather had arrived. Jane relished the Sunday afternoon protest in all weathers, but, secretly, as was most likely the case with all the others, she enjoyed the protest much more when it was sunny.

Glad to be wearing her thinner jacket, Jane left her block of flats and crossed the road to the car park, taking several gulps of fresh air as she soaked up the sun, listened to the birds and smelt the freshly cut grass.

Within about five minutes of setting off, she was already in a different, more rural world. Her part of town was unequivocally urban with lots of tightly packed terraced housing and people that spoke in a multitude of languages. After taking a left turn, she drove up a long and winding hill. This really was the most glorious place to spend a sunny Sunday afternoon. Right in the heart of the English National Forest, it had the capacity to inspire any painter or help a writer overcome writer's block. The houses she'd driven past along the way were all detached and came with a garden that could only be described as vast. Probably they housed doctors, magistrates, politicians or police inspectors. There was certainly no graffiti or drunken teenagers up to mischief in this part of town.

Turning into the side road where everyone parked, she decelerated and came to a complete stop. Stepping from the car, she smiled at Helen, the nurse who had come from Liverpool. She was sat in her car with the door open, eating a picnic. She hadn't been for a few weeks because of staff shortages in the paediatric ward she worked in.

Once everyone was in position, they got down to business, waving placards and chanting as one, making sure they were seen to be protesting peacefully. It didn't take long for a police car to show up. Jane could see Crowe sat inside, seemingly watching her constantly. She even imagined him to smile and wink on one occasion. He was present most of the afternoon, keeping a watchful eye on them, ready to pounce given half a chance. Once he'd decided he'd had enough and left the scene, the whole atmosphere lifted. Jane took the opportunity to take out her letter and show it to everyone. They each reacted with derisive laughter, in exactly the same manner she had. Not only at the schoolboy grammar and childish insults, but also at the very thought that this could deter any one of them from exercising their right to protest about something they felt passionate about.

One of the people around her, who showed more interest than most, was called John. John had acquired a certain amount of infamy, when, in 1984, he'd done something regrettable in the name of their cause.. He'd spent twenty years trying to put that mistake, that rush of blood after one too many glasses of wine, behind him. Despite having been to prison and paid his dues for what he is the first to admit is a despicable crime.

Reading the letter carefully, John shook his head and said, "Can't believe they thought they could scare you off that easily, Jane."

Jane shrugged. "To be honest, nothing surprises me about them anymore. I've made a complaint."

"What? About the note?"

"No, well, there's no proof they sent it, is there? Only circumstantial evidence. No, about the lies they concocted."

"Oh, that." John smiled and broke eye contact, perhaps feeling guilty for what he had done all those years before. "Any news?"

"No, it was only a few days ago. They take their time with things, don't they?"

"They sure do. I'm still on bail."

"You're joking?"

"No. Maybe I'll file a complaint too."

"Yeah. You do that. It might not do any good, but at least it will cause them an inconvenience."

"Yeah, think I might, Jane. Thanks for that."

CHAPTER TWENTY-FIVE

Glancing in the mirror, Percival Jeffries straightened his tie for the umpteenth time that morning. His wife, sat beside him in the passenger seat, reached across and squeezed his hand. "Leave your tie alone, will you? You'll cut off all circulation."
Percival smiled and shifted his attention to the steering wheel. Loretta was doing her best to make him feel at ease. She thought she understood everything, how nervous he was feeling and what was going through his mind. He wished she did understand. He truly did. But the fact of the matter was that she didn't. All this time, he'd been lying to her, telling her that he was completely innocent and that the allegations were all lies, made up to get him out of the way by a bishop that saw him as a threat.
Today was a huge risk. Although his court appearance was a pre-arranged sham, to make it convincing, the crown prosecutor might present evidence that he couldn't wriggle out of later. It might all go horribly wrong, and he might lose not only his good name in those parts, but also his wife.
It wasn't an exceptionally long drive to Birmingham, no more than an hour. Once in court, the nerves really set in. After being made to wait for half an hour, Percival Jeffries, along with his wife and solici-

tor were called in. He could sense the animosity raining down on him from the public gallery straight away.

Jeffries hadn't seen the boy since he'd left Northumberland and, for some reason, was surprised, taken aback even, to see he had grown into quite a handsome man. The very sight of him brought all Jeffries' old feelings flooding back.

The crown prosecutor was on top form and so too was Jason. His emotional recount of events left some members of the public gallery in tears. Percival cast a sideways glance at Loretta and was horrified to see that she'd been taken in. He knew her too well; from that moment on, whatever the outcome, he'd lost out. He cursed himself for not having thought of this before. Surely, he could have dreamt up some excuse to keep her away from the court.

When Jeffries himself was called to the stand, he glanced at Loretta and smiled, hoping for some support. She blanked him, causing his entire body to droop. As he walked to the box, he sensed that the earlier animosity had now transformed into hate. It seemed everyone, his wife included, was baying for his blood. Someone called out that he ought to be castrated for what he'd done and the judge had him removed for contempt of court. It took several minutes for order to be restored and once the prosecutor got to his feet to begin the cross examination, Percival was just praying for it to be over.

For the next ten minutes it was like all his worst nightmares had come true. The prosecutor fired clever question after clever question at him. With Loretta still refusing to look him in the eye, his mind just went blank. He could feel himself cracking under pressure, the urge to make a full confession gaining more momentum by the second. Just when he was about to crack, the prosecutor turned to the judge and said he'd no more questions.

His own solicitor did his very best to rectify the damage, but both men and everyone else present for that matter, knew that the writing was on the wall. At this stage, Jeffries had forgotten all about his deal with D.S. Mellor.

When both sides had finished giving evidence, the judge ordered a recess to give the jury time to reach a verdict.

The Jeffries sat beside each other in the waiting room, a wall of nervous tension between them. All Percival wanted was for his wife to tell him it was going to be OK. Then, no matter what the verdict, he knew it would be. Not wanting to risk confirming his greatest fear, he just sat looking straight ahead at the vending machine, wishing he could get himself a drink without the necessity of speaking to his wife.

By the time the clerk looked around the waiting room door, Jeffries had convinced himself that he'd been found out and he was going down. He got to his feet and, for a minute, thought Loretta was going to stay rooted to her chair, but, right at the last, she stood and brought up the rear.

When the judge asked the foreman of the jury if they had come to a decision, Jeffries held his breath, his mouth completely dry.

"No, your honour," came the reply.

Percival inhaled so deep that he felt a pain in his diaphragm. He closed his eyes, rocked back his head and let out a long, slow breath. After a brief pause, the judge announced that he had no choice but to order a retrial in November. Resisting the temptation to hug his solicitor, Jeffries got to his feet and walked along the centre aisle, feeling pleased with himself for not cracking under the most extreme pressure. He was determined this was going to make him stronger and if Loretta didn't believe he was innocent, that was her look out. In the driver's seat of their car, eyes firmly fixed on the road ahead, Percival couldn't help once again reflecting on how close he'd come to caving in. And what about Mellor? It wasn't meant to be a real trial. This was all for show, so he could clear his name. He would definitely be having words with him. He decided the minute they arrived home he was going to call and find out what was going on. And that wasn't all he was going to do, either. Once the dust had settled, he was going to make a full confession to his wife. Hopefully, he could make her come round in time. As he saw it, this was the only way of making things right between them.

They were roughly half way home when Percival suddenly felt a soft, warm hand envelop his as he shifted gear.
"Sorry," Loretta said, resting her head on his shoulder and squeezing his hand hard.
Percival smiled and kissed her forehead. This was the second let off he'd had in the space of a few hours. Maybe this was a sign from God that he'd been forgiven for what he'd done.
Jeffries did call Mellor as planned. As it turned out, the jury had been briefed, but given the evidence presented, half of them had decided to return a verdict of guilty. He assured Percival that in November, he'd ensure the jury was properly vetted before the trial commences.

CHAPTER TWENTY-SIX

By the time July came around, Crowe was feeling like everything had finally come together for him. He had his wife, son, house, his life back and there'd been little trouble from the protestors. He still regretted sending the note, but as far as he could see, it had done the trick.

One particularly warm and sunny Friday afternoon, Crowe was sat cradling his head in his hands, his legs fully extended. A warm breeze blew in through his open window, making the papers on his desk and in tray rustle. He was thinking about the night and weekend ahead. Johnny was at Susan's mother's house, and they were having a garden party. They used to have such events all the time before the problems started and this was to let everyone know that they were back on the scene. He'd have to try and concoct a story, should anyone ask, that explained where they disappeared to for all that time, but he had faith in his creative powers and his ability to think on his feet. The previous weekend, Susan had mentioned going away on holiday, something that up until a couple of months ago, he wouldn't even have dreamed about.

The garden party was going to be good, but it only occupied a fraction of his thoughts. He'd persuaded a guy that lived on his street to go with him to a race meeting some time ago and tomorrow was the big day. They'd been sat in the conservatory for weeks, planning it while they got slowly inebriated on home brew.

It had been a busy morning. He'd been rushed off his feet with meetings and dealing with one petty criminal after the other. He'd decided to spend a few minutes recharging the batteries while it was quiet, so allowed his thoughts to run riot. Having moved on from the races to the South of France, where Susan wanted to go, he was brought tumbling back down to earth by the telephone. He was having such a lovely afternoon, that for a minute, he decided to let it ring off. However, once it rang seven times, he bottled it and reached forward to grab the handset from the cradle.

"Chief Constable. How nice to hear from you!"

"Hello, Bobby. Hope I wasn't disturbing anything."

"Well, I err . . . "

"Oh, well, this won't take long. I have an update for you about the protest."

"Oh." Crowe hoped he didn't sound as deflated as he felt.

"You remember John Beardsmore, the activist that—?"

"How could I forget?" he mumbled.

"Sorry?"

"Oh, yes. Of course, I remember. What about him?"

"He's gone and made a complaint. Says he's been kept on bail under false pretences."

"The sheer audacity of some people amazes me."

"My sentiments exactly, Bobby."

"Couldn't they just explain the situation to the complaints authority? Like I did when Thomas complained."

"Oh they have and I'm sure that nothing will come of it, thank God. It's just that it's been leaked to the press, and well, it doesn't look good."

"Oh, I see. The old, no smoke without fire thing, again."

"Exactly. Especially coming hot on the heels of your Thomas woman."

"So what's the plan of action then, Sir?"

"Well, there isn't one, not really. I'm just ringing to warn you that all this doesn't look good and well, there's bound to be some sort of inquiry."

"Oh. I—I see."

"Is everything OK, Bobby? You don't sound all that chipper."

"No, everything's fine, Sir. It's just that, I've got myself back on my feet and everything's going well at the moment. An inquiry is the last thing I need."

"Well, sorry to be the bearer of bad news, then. Just thought you should know. If you take my advice, you'll have someone to pass the blame onto when it comes to you."

"I know the way it works, Sir. I'm glad to say that I've been giving it some thought and I have someone in mind."

"Glad to hear it. Oh well, back to the grindstone."

"Indeed, Sir. Thanks for keeping me informed."

Crowe placed the phone in its cradle, sat back and took a deep breath. This was bad news, bad enough to put a dampener on his weekend, but somehow it didn't feel like a catastrophe.

Despite the way his life had been going, he knew his world would come tumbling down around him should he lose his job for any reason or be suspended without pay. If he couldn't make his loan repayments, the debt collectors would come knocking and so far, the only backup plan he had was re-joining the cards syndicate. He could make enough in one night to repay the outstanding amount in full and no-one, especially Susan would be any wiser. Crowe opened his top drawer and took out the half empty packet of cigarettes that he'd bought on his way to work that morning. This was one pleasure that no-one could take from him.

By the time he was stubbing out the butt in the overflowing ashtray, he'd managed to forget all about his conversation with Sexton. True, there was likely to be an inquest, but in his experience, this wouldn't be anytime soon. He had at least six months to devise a plan to ensure he evaded scrutiny, so why let it ruin his weekend?

Glancing at the clock on the wall, he began going through his papers, prioritising things for Monday morning. This was something he always did on a Friday afternoon, just before leaving the office and as such, the task came with a feeling of elation that the working week was finally over.

A knock. "Inspector Crowe, are you in, Sir?"

"Yes. Come in."

A uniformed constable entered, holding a document, the top of which fluttered and rustled in the warm breeze that carried in the sound of the nearby traffic.

"Sorry to bother you, Sir. Thought you might have packed up and gone home early."

"No, no, not me. Things to do." he said, with a grin. "What can I do for you, Constable?"

"A lady just brought this in, Sir. Thought you might like to see it." The constable handed him the document, which he placed on his desk without bothering to read.

"Oh, thank you, Constable." He smiled. "I was just about to go home, you were right. Think I might leave this till Monday morning."

"Oh, I think—."

"Goodbye, Constable, have a nice weekend."

"Goodbye, Sir. Same to you."

The second he heard the constable's first footstep clapping against the corridor through the closed doors, Crowe picked up the document and put it straight on his in tray. Whatever it was could wait. Resisting the temptation to scan the paper at least to see what it was about, Crowe packed away his things and got to his feet. This was going to be the best weekend he'd had for a long time.

After pulling up on the driveway of his four-bedroomed detached house, Crowe stepped out of his car and, with a mischievous grin, closed the door firmly but quietly. He continued to creep along his garden path, before letting himself in and holding his breath. He could just about hear his wife upstairs. Maybe she was getting Johnny prepared before she shuttled him to her mother's for the night. Like a cat sneaking up on a dormouse, he ascended the stairs, crept along the landing and burst into Johnny's room. "Surprise!"

His wife gave a short scream and clapped a hand over her heart. "Robbie. What are you doing back so early? You gave me a fright."

"Oh, sorry about that. I wanted to surprise you. Well, I didn't have much on, and it was a nice afternoon, so I thought I'd come home early. Say hello to Johnny before you take him to your mother's."

"Oh, that's sweet of you. Come here."

Crowe walked towards his wife until he was close enough to hear and feel her breathing.

Standing on tip toes, she leant in and kissed him on the lips. "Thank you."

From that moment on, everything about Crowe's weekend was perfect, his expectations met and exceeded.

Just an hour later, Johnny was at Susan's mother's, and they were laughing and joking in the sun filled kitchen as they prepared the food for their dinner party.

The party was a huge success with lots of new friends made, but that was nothing compared to the race meeting. He arrived home just after ten pm, having won 200 and feeling secretly fulfilled after witnessing a horse injure itself.

He spent Sunday relaxing with Susan and Johnny, even finding time to spend an hour or so in his new best friend's conservatory, where they drank home brew, put the world to rights and made plans for their next race meeting. By the time Monday morning came around, he was struggling to remember anything from the previous Friday.

"Good morning," he said with a smile to the receptionist as he breezed in, still on a high from his win at the races.

"Good morning, Sir."

Just as Crowe was turning into the corridor that led to his room, the main door opened and another constable entered. Crowe could hear panicked whispers behind him, but in his current state of euphoria, failed to take notice. Nor did he notice the hurried footsteps moving towards him along the corridor.

Stepping into his office, Crowe removed his jacket and started scanning his room for clues of what had been happening the previous Friday. His gaze had just rested on his in tray when the doors behind him were flung open, and the same constable that brought him the documents the previous Friday came marching in. She was carrying a copy of The Burton Mail, her expression concerned, almost panic stricken.

"Sir," she said, offering him the newspaper. "Sir, have you seen this morning's headlines yet?"

"No. I've only just got in."

"I think you should have a look."

"Ok." Crowe took the newspaper, unfolded it and flipped it over, grinning confidently.

When he held up the paper and read the headline, the constable looked on as Crowe's smug grin transformed into a look of what he could only describe as horror. "I did try to warn you, Sir."

"I'm Sorry?"

"Friday afternoon, Sir, I brought the statement straight to you, but you—."

"Statement? What Statement?"

"The one you put on your desk and decided to leave for today, Sir?"

"Constable, what are you . . ." He glanced at his in tray.

"Yes, the document on top of your in tray, Sir."

"OK, Constable, thank you. I'll deal with this now."

Once the Constable had left him, he took a minute to consider his options. Eventually, he lifted the phone, dialled the first three digits of the newspaper's press office, hesitated, then hung up.

The document in his grasp told him everything he needed to know. Mrs Brady, the mother of the girl that was involved in the hit and run (lying had become such a natural act that he was now deceiving himself) was filing a complaint. After carefully reading the details, he turned to page three where her statement had been recorded in barely legible black ink. The newspaper had quoted the statement virtually word for word.

Mrs Brady was unhappy with the service she had received in relation to her daughter's hit and run. When she came to report the crime, she'd been palmed off, made to feel like a nuisance. Everyone she spoke to showed a complete lack of compassion, failing to acknowledge that her daughter had been killed. Worse of all was Inspector Crowe, whose only concern was shifting the blame onto the constable that was dealing with her.

In his mind, he carefully went through the events of the previous Friday, even making a few notes on a piece of scrap paper. After twenty minutes' head scratching, he was still none the wiser as to who might have gone public without his consent. In the end, he decided the easiest way of finding out was to phone the editor and ask him.

"Hello Mr Jones, Inspector Crowe here from Burton on Trent Police Station."

"Ah, good morning. What can I do for you?"

"You can tell me why you printed the story about the Brady complaint without consulting me first."

"We're not obliged to seek permission from anyone before printing a story which we believe to be in the public's interest, Sir."

"Then, at least can you tell me who the informant was?"

"You mean it wasn't an official source?"

"Well, if it came from here, whoever it was went over my head, so no. It wasn't an official source."

"I see. Give me a minute please while I go and investigate this."

Crowe fidgeted with some papers on his table that were blowing around in the breeze. He should have had a cigarette before calling. He really fancied one. Maybe if he was quick he might just have time to—.

"Inspector Crowe?"

"Oh, yes? Look, is this going to take long?"

"No, not at all. I'm afraid the informant asked to remain anonymous."

"He asked to remain anonymous? What the hell does that mean? I'm a Police Inspector for—. "

"You're still not above the rules, Sir. I'm afraid it means that I'm not at liberty to name the informant. Not at this stage, anyway."

Now desperate for a cigarette, Crowe lost all patience. "Fine," he snapped, and slammed the phone back into its cradle.

Crowe opened his drawer so quickly and with so much force that he almost pulled it from its rails. He delved straight in and there, right at the back, was his emergency packet of cigarettes. He'd have to make it a priority to buy some more at lunch time.

After pushing back his chair and extending his legs fully, he lit up, and, from the instant he took his first puff, felt overcome with a calming relief. To anyone that tried to dissuade him from smoking, he could say that it cleared his head and gave him time to think. And that could only be good for productivity. He smiled to himself as the cogs creaked into life.

Of Course, he murmured to himself, five minutes later, and leant forward to stub out the cigarette. Still wearing a smug grin, he got to his feet, marched across his office and on into the corridor, closing the door behind him. He knocked twice on each door he passed, opened it a couple of inches, looked in, and said to the unsuspecting officer inside, "staff meeting, my office, thirty minutes."

Once he'd completed his journey, he decided he might as well carry on, past reception, through the doors, across the road to the supermarket opposite. It wouldn't do to use up his emergency packet of cigarettes. He was starting to crave again already.

Thirty minutes later, Crowe was sat back in his chair, legs stretched with just his feet under the desk. In front of him was a fresh packet of cigarettes, with two already missing. Just as he exhaled a cloud of smoke, there was a knock. "Come in," Crowe called, removing the cigarette from his mouth.

A constable walked in, squinting in the thick, toxic cloud that hung over the inspector's desk.

The constable smiled as she sat, doing her best not to breathe in the smoke for fear of causing offence should she have to cough.

They both sat in polite silence until someone else joined them. Once everyone was present, Crowe stubbed out his cigarette and held the front page of The Burton Mail up for all to see. "OK. I want to know who is responsible for this. Which one of you went behind my back to the papers?"

There was a collective bout of head shaking as each of them denied their involvement. "OK, if none of you is prepared to own up to it, I'm going to ask you all individually."

He coughed to clear his throat, emitting a thick, cigarette tasting rustle, before looking at each of them in the eye and asking," Was it you?"

After he had heard seven unequivocal No Sirs, he paused for thought. His eyes widened as something suddenly came to mind. "D.C. Oplitova, I'm going to ask you again. Was it you that went behind my back?"

D.C. Oplitova, wearing a puzzled expression that was matched by everyone else, replied once again, "No, Sir."

"You absolutely sure about that?"

"Yes, Sir. It wasn't me that called the press."

"OK, if you say so. That will be all, folks. Thank you for your time."

Waiting for the last of them to leave the room, the door to close and the clapping footsteps to recede, Crowe kicked back his chair and thought about what had just happened. It was Oplitova; it had to be. She obviously thought she had some kind of hold over him, just because she heard the shredder. On further consideration, he concludede that she had much more about her than he'd assumed. She was a dangerous opponent that had to be stopped. If only there was a way he could silence her for good. He decided that, now things with Thomas had gone quiet, he was going to focus all his attention on getting rid of Oplitova. The problem was, if he was going to frame her for the protest fiasco, he had to time his efforts to perfection.

His phone lit up and emitted a loud, piercing electronic version of the ring the old manual phones used to produce. His mind felt blank as he leant forward to raise the handset to his ear, neither knowing nor caring who might be on the other end.

"Chief Constable. How nice to hear from you."

"Hello, Bobby. Listen, I heard about the press leak. I think it's time I took some action, so I was wondering if we could schedule a meeting this afternoon?"

Crowe, as people always do when faced with a question about time, glanced at the clock. "Err, yes. I can do this afternoon."

"Good. Sit tight. I'm on my way."

Crowe didn't like the sound of this. It usually took him about an hour to drive down. He glanced again at the clock. Their meeting might well last beyond five, meaning he would be late arriving home. He decided to kill time by chain smoking, but his plans were thwarted by a stack of paperwork that suddenly arrived on his desk.

He'd barely skimmed the surface of the paperwork, when there was a knock on his door. Crowe looked up to tell whoever it was to come in, but before he could do so, the door opened and Sexton appeared.

"Bobby, thanks for seeing me at short notice."

"Oh, no, don't mention it. Not at all, Sir."

Sexton paused to shut the door, testing it to ensure it wouldn't open of its own accord in the breeze. "This, err, shouldn't take long."

"Take as long as you like, Sir."

Sexton smiled and pulled out the chair directly facing Crowe. After making himself comfortable, Sexton screwed his nose, gave a short sniff, glanced at the ash tray and said, "Have you err, taken up smoking, Bobby?"

"Oh, you know. Just one or two a week."

Sexton smiled and shook his head. "I know it's not my place to say what you should and shouldn't be doing in your own time, but I hope it is just one or two a week."

Crowe looked puzzled. "Why's that, Sir?"

"Well, for one, it stinks to high heaven of cigarettes in here. Reminds me of a pub. And for another, I'd hate to lose one of my best inspectors."

"Why would you do that, Sir?"

"Oh, come on. You must know the health risks. My brother smoked all his life." He choked up. "Died of lung cancer last year."

"I'm so sorry to hear that, Sir. I had no idea. I'll make sure it doesn't happen to me."

"Well." Sexton smiled awkwardly as if embarrassed at the way he'd opened up. "Down to business."

"Oh, of course. What can I do for you? You wanted a word about the Brady complaint."

"Yes. Listen, as you know, this is the third high profile complaint we've had lately and, despite the fact that the other two came to nothing, mud sticks, so they say. We can't afford for people to start getting suspicious, especially with, well, you know, the instructions from above and all that."

Crowe nodded. "Understand completely, Sir."

"Well, that's why I'm compelled to take action. And unfortunately, your name is in the firing line."

"Me?" Crowe rocked back in his chair as he tried to laugh off the suggestion."

"Yes. You."

Crowe's smile evaporated, and he felt the colour rush from him, like his worst nightmare was about to come true. "No, don't sack me, Sir, Please. I've just got my life back together, I—."

Sexton raised a hand. "No one's going to sack you, Bobby. At least, not over this anyway. As I said, you're one of my best inspectors, and I don't want to lose you."

Fighting the urge to lean across and kiss Sexton's forehead, Crowe took a deep breath and said, "Oh. Well, what then?"

"I have to be seen to be doing something, so I'm ordering an inquiry." Knowing his actions would be central to the investigations, Crowe knew, or thought he knew, what was coming.

"So, until it has been completed, and to prove we are an entirely ethical and transparent organisation, I'm going to have to ask you not to come into work."

"You're suspending me, Sir?" Crowe felt his mouth run dry. If he was suspended without pay, he'd be back to square one.

"I don't want to do that. Why don't you, err—take a holiday. You must be due some annual leave."

"Oh, yes, Sir. I am."

"Well, a month should be sufficient, I think. I'll sanction it today, with immediate effect."

"Oh, err, thank you, Sir. The only thing is, my wife and I were planning on going away in a month or two and—."

Sexton waved a hand. "Not a problem. Go on holiday now." He looked at Crowe carefully. "To be honest, Bobby, you look like you could do with a break. Where were you thinking of going?"

"Well, Susan, my wife, wanted to go to the South of France, but, to be honest, I'm running a bit short on funds, so we'll probably end up at Skegness."

Sexton shook his head. "Go to the South of France, old boy. Have it on us. Call it a long overdue bonus."

"Really, Sir?"

"Really."

"Thank you."

"Not a problem. You go home, pick a resort then fax across the details."

"Thank you, Sir. I will."

"I don't suppose you have any annual leave forms hanging round, do you, Bobby?"

"I don't have any in here, Sir. I'll just err, nip and get some."

Crowe left Sexton alone in the office, while he went to the stationary cupboard in the store room. Two minutes later, he returned with the form. Sexton took a pen from his top pocket, clicked it into life and proceeded to fill in the dates before signing a big swirly signature at the bottom. He passed it to Crowe. "You need to sign it next to mine."

"Thank you, Sir," Crowe said, signing the form. His signature looked minuscule compared to Sexton's.

Glancing at the clock, Sexton said, "I'll take this. Personnel don't go home until six. I'll make sure they process it for you."

"Thank you, Sir."

"Not at all. Grasping the form, Sexton rose to his feet. Well, best be going. Why don't you knock off early, give your wife the news?"

"Oh, yes, Sir. Think I will."

Sexton offered Crowe his hand. "Thanks, Bobby, for your cooperation and your—understanding."

Shaking his hand firmly, Crowe replied, "Not at all, Sir. Any time."

Sexton walked to the door, rested his hand on the handle and looked over his shoulder. "As I said, just choose where you want to go and fax it across for my attention. You do have a fax machine, don't you?"

"Well, No, Sir. But I believe they have one at the library, so it will have to wait until they're open tomorrow."

"Not a problem. Well. I must be making tracks. Enjoy your time off Bobby, you've earnt it."

"Thank you, Sir."

Crowe returned to his desk and listened to the receding footsteps, voices in reception and, eventually, the car door thud. Once Sexton's engine had changed gear and been consumed by the surrounding traffic, Crowe put on his jacket, locked his door and walked along the corridor for the last time in a while. He paused at reception to brief the sergeant on duty who, despite the surprise being written all over his face, just took it in his stride and said he'd convey the message to everyone that needed to know.

Once in his car, the door closed and his seat belt firmly in place, Crowe took a second to think about what was happening. Of course, he was pleased that the Chief Constable had been so generous, but there hung over him an air of caution. He just got the feeling that this whole episode might come back to haunt him and this was not the jaunt Sexton was portraying it to be.

Still, Sexton had always treated him fairly, and he had no reason to doubt him. He was after all, taking some annual leave; there was nothing wrong with that. With this thought in mind, he started the engine and left the car-park. He couldn't wait to get home and give Susan the news.

Susan was delighted. She screamed in excitement and ran across the room to the computer, which was on a desk in the corner.

"What are you doing?" Crowe asked his wife.

"Oh, come on, no one goes to a travel agent these days. I'm looking at holidays to the South of France online. Did he give you a budget?"

"Oh, good idea. No, but don't go mad. I don't want to be accused of taking advantage of his—The Force's generosity."

"Of course."

After spending most of the evening excitedly browsing the Internet, weighing up the pros and cons of the various villages, they finally settled on a resort and printed out the booking form. Susan was disappointed that it couldn't be finalised there and then, giving Crowe the impression that she, like him, suspected that this was too good to be true and something would surface to scupper their plans.

Crowe, therefore, took the initiative and printed out their itinerary to give her something tangible to look at until the trip could be confirmed. She appreciated this and went to fix them a bite to eat, leaving Crowe alone at the computer. Old habits die hard, and he couldn't resist having a quick look at the news headlines.

Much to his dismay, the newspaper report had attracted the attention of the TV networks and was given a mention alongside the other stories deemed to be of lesser importance. The report contained a link to the article on the newspaper's website, which Crowe clicked on.

It suddenly struck Crowe that he hadn't actually sat down and read the article in detail. All he'd done was taken in the headline and skim over the story, which, to be fair, was enough to determine that he was in a sticky spot. Now in the comfort of his own home, he focused on the screen, shut out the noisy kids outside and read the article from start to finish.

It turned out that Mrs Brady had worked at Simons' dry cleaners for almost thirty years and, surprise, surprise, was a model employee. Crowe smiled to himself at the journalist's selective use of the information, clearly designed to distort the story to give the subject a favourable perception. They applied exactly the same trick on the protestors of course, so he was hardly in a position to complain.

Crowe navigated away from the page to find the library's opening hours. They were open all day the following day, a Wednesday, but he wanted to get it sorted out early. He then searched for Simons' dry cleaners and discovered that they didn't open until ten, which meant he'd have some time to kill in the morning if his trip into town was to fulfil both of its objectives.

Finally realising that the light was getting bad and he was straining to see, he glanced at the clock on the corner of the screen. Johnny was at an age where he went to bed early and if he didn't see him to say goodnight, he wouldn't get another chance. So, feeling awash with satisfaction, he switched off the computer and trudged up the stairs. His son, who was in bed but not yet asleep, smiled as their eyes met.

***

Much to Crowe's frustration, the fax machine was being used by an elderly gentleman wearing a green cardigan when he arrived at the library the following morning. Never famed for his patience, Crowe paced up and down between the nearby tables, looking and smiling at the old man whenever the opportunity arose. When the old man went to fetch an assistant, because, apparently, it had jammed, Crowe pulled out a book from the shelf and started reading, making sure he always had half an eye on the fax machine. The last thing he needed was for some old dear to jump ahead of him in the queue. When the old man returned with an assistant, they spent a good ten minutes poking and prodding the poor machine, but still couldn't get it to work. In the end, Crowe's frustration was exacerbated when she went to fetch a technician, who came with a screwdriver and a box of tools.

The technician fixed the machine in no time. With the offending piece of paper in the waste paper bin, the old man was fit to go. Fortunately for Crowe, and the machine, the library assistant smiled politely and asked the old man for the number.

"Sorry for the delay," she said, stepping aside to give Crowe access to the machine.

Crowe smiled and said it was fine, but couldn't help slipping in a subtle glance up at the clock, just to let her know that he didn't have all day. Fortunately, Crowe did not experience any of the old man's problems and the fax went straight through without any glitches. With the original printout folded away in his trouser pocket, he left the library and headed straight for Simons' dry cleaners. It was one of those shops that he passed practically every time he went into town, but he'd never had reason to enter. Maybe that was his problem. One of the things he liked about his job was that no matter how long you've been doing it, how experienced or accomplished you think you are, there's always one more trick to learn.

Crowe couldn't help rolling his eyes when he saw the queue, hoping that no one else saw his frustration. He joined the back and, having thought about it, realised this wasn't such a bad thing, providing no one else came in after him. The last thing he needed was to find another front page spread about him. Sexton would not be best pleased if that happened, especially after being told to keep a low profile.

When, finally, he got to the front of the queue, and the assistant asked how she could help, Crowe glanced over his shoulder before replying. Her puzzled expression told Crowe that if this was Mrs Brady, she was more perceptive than most people.

"Are you Mrs Brady?"

"Mrs Brady? No, I'm not. She works in the back."

"Could you go and get her, please? I need a quiet word."

"Oh. Err, who should I say is asking for her?"

Crowe hesitated before replying. He didn't want to give his identity away, but he just got the feeling that this woman was going to refuse to comply if he didn't. "Tell her it's Inspector Crowe."

"The police? Oh."

"Please, I just need a quick word."

"Well, OK, wait there."

Once the woman disappeared, Crowe, for the first time, became aware of a constant low-pitched buzzing noise coming from a back-room, that abruptly stopped after a mumbled conversation. Crowe had about ten seconds to bask in the glorious silence before Mrs Brady arrived.

"Inspector Crowe?" she said with a distinct chill in her voice.

"Mrs Brady. Sorry to disturb you at work. This won't take long, I just want to know if it was you that went to the press with your complaint?"

"Went to the press? What are you talking about?"

"Don't you read The Burton Mail?"

Mrs Brady cast her eyes down at the counter. "No. I don't get time."

"Oh well, sorry to have troubled you then," Crowe said, with an air of resignation.

The other woman reappeared and said quietly to her colleague, "Mr Simons is on his way."

Mrs Brady nodded in acknowledgement and turned back to conclude her dealings with Crowe. "Look, I have to go. Sorry I couldn't be of any help, Inspector."

"Mr Simons? I always thought there was a man called Simon. Well, you live and learn."

Mrs Brady laughed. "A common misconception." She reached to the shelf below the counter. "Here's a business card. Just in case you need to get hold of him for anything."

Crowe held the card between his thumb and index finger. "Symons. Spelt with a Y."

"Yeah. It was young Mr Symons' idea. He liked the play on words." She laughed.

"Young Mr Symons?"

"Yeah, father and son, they run it together. Old Mr Symons is ready to retire, but between you and me, his son isn't the most reliable person to take over the business."

"Why not?"

"Well, he's friendly enough. It's just he goes away for long periods and seems to have some unsavoury friends."

"Interesting. Well, thanks for your help, Mrs Brady. And I'm sorry you were unhappy with the service you received."

She shrugged. "Well, better get back to work."

"Of course."

Leaving the dry cleaners', Crowe got a feeling he was on to something. Needing some extra thinking time before he went home, he decided to call in at the caf next door for a cup of tea. Carrying his cup and saucer, he noticed some of the tables had an ashtray instead of a no smoking sign. He allowed himself a smile after recalling the way he'd put some emergency cigarettes in his brief case. Just in case he needed them.

With his mug half full, he lit up, sat back and relaxed. This, he'd discovered, was his thinking pose. Ideas always flowed through his mind when he relaxed with a cigarette. He couldn't believe he hadn't started smoking earlier.

The name, Symons, it sounded familiar. He took out the card and had another look. Symons with a Y, not an I. "Of course," he murmured to himself and drained his tea in one gulp. Symons had been insisting he was owed money. Now he could go on holiday in peace.

***

A month later, Crowe breezed into his office on a warm Monday morning, feeling like a different man. He'd had a great time in France, whiling away the hours on the beach reading crime mysteries. He'd decided that he was the kind of person that never did things by halves. First with the gambling, then the cigarettes and now the crime novels. Once he found something that he enjoyed there was no stopping him. Reflecting on this and a great many other things, Crowe smiled, opened the window and reached down to switch on his PC. The PC in his office had a particularly loud fan and he'd almost forgotten what this sounded like. Crowe found that noises, like smells, become less noticeable once you get used to them and it was going to take a while to reacclimatise himself, not just to the noise of his PC , but the demands of being a busy Police Inspector. Just as it had taken a couple of days to adjust to being on holiday.

The thing most prominent in his mind was the inquest. He had a feeling that everything had gone OK with no serious glitches, because otherwise, Sexton would have been straight on the phone to him. There might also have been some press coverage. In hindsight, Crowe was surprised at the lack of press coverage. Whoever had been in charge had done a first rate job of keeping everything under wraps.

There was bound to be other things that required his urgent attention too. Crowe shifted the stack of papers from his in tray to his desk. When he stood up, the pile almost reached to his neck. He was going to have his work cut out getting through them, and he was going to have to stay late for a few nights. Susan, it seemed, had become more accommodating to his work needs, even than she was before. Perhaps for the first time, she realised that it was his work that afforded them the lifestyle that she loved so much. She'd been impressed with Sexton's generosity and was even keen to meet him. Crowe had just smiled when she'd said this and returned to his book. He got on well with Sexton, but he just got the feeling that he could have a nasty bite. Make no mistake about it, he would have no hesitation in putting Crowe back in the firing line should the need ever resurface.

Despite the constant interruptions, Crowe made swift progress with his back log of paper work. By lunch time he was nearly half way through. That was when, for the first time that day, he looked up and decided he needed a cigarette.

Sitting back in his chair, legs fully extended, in his now customary smoking pose, Crowe considered that he had at last found a disadvantage of smoking. On this occasion, there was nothing to think about, and the cigarette break had only served to halt his steady progress. Maybe this was the first time his need for a cigarette was psychological rather than practical and was perhaps the beginnings of an addiction. He laughed to himself at the thought of him being labelled an addict of any kind, stubbed out the remainder of his cigarette and continued with the paperwork.

He'd only managed another two or three documents when he was interrupted by the telephone. Cursing, he reached across his desk and picked up the phone. "Inspector Crowe," he said, hoping he didn't sound as reluctant to talk as he felt.

"Bobby, welcome back."

"Chief Constable." Realising the possible implications of this phone call, his mouth went dry. "How nice to hear from you." He flicked his tongue around his mouth, trying to generate some saliva.

"How was the South of France?"

"Oh, fantastic, Sir."

"And do you feel refreshed? Eager to get back to work with an extra spring in your step and all that?"

"Absolutely I do, Sir." Crowe smiled to himself as he considered how unusual it was to say something like this in honesty.

"Good. Because I have some good news."

"What's that, Sir?"

"The inquest is finished and has found nothing untoward happened. Not by you or The Force in general."

"So, I'm in the clear, Sir?"

"You are indeed, my friend."

"Oh, that's fantastic news, Sir. A huge weight off my mind." Crowe covered the mouth piece, turned away and gave a short laugh. In contrast to his earlier statement, this was a complete lie. He'd known all along the inquest would find in the police's favour. They always do. Still, it was never good to make assumptions, and he had to be seen to view the system as completely fair and transparent.

"Well, I'll leave you to get on. I expect you have a mountain of things to do."

"You can say that again, Sir."

"Well, keep up the good work. Just—remember not to get carried away."

"What do you mean, Sir?"

"Well, we've got over one barrel, but there might be another on the way in the form of the protest thing. I've heard rumours that the companies involved are once again getting a bit err, disgruntled at the bad press."

"Yes. I understand." Truth be told, this had slipped Crowe's mind.

"You can either find another way to stop them or find someone else to blame."

"I understand, Sir."

"Well, I'll leave you to it then. I'll call in on Friday to see how things are going."

"I'll look forward to it, Sir."

Crowe hung up and immediately buried himself in the pile of paperwork. He would be working late that night and the Chief Constable's phone call did little to help in that respect. But in another way, he felt a certain reassurance that everything was going to work out well and the protest fiasco was going to end with him unscathed.

Providing he kept his eye on the ball, he could relax for now and just see how things panned out. He still felt bad about writing the note to Thomas, but she hadn't been shooting her mouth off since. Maybe his approach had been too softly-softly and, when faced with the threat of violence, these people listen. This was an interesting thought and one he'd certainly bear in mind for future reference.

Crowe knew though, that he had to do as the Chief Constable said and either find a way of stopping the protesters or prepare himself for the backlash. He just wished it could all be over so he knew which avenue to pursue.

CHAPTER TWENTY-SEVEN

SEPTEMBER 2005

Jane sat back on her chair and reflected on what had been so far, a pretty eventful year. She soon realised that most of the action had been in the first half of the year. Things had been relatively quiet since her complaint in July, which she'd heard nothing from yet. She knew that her old adversary, Crowe, had been in trouble, and in a way felt sorry for him when she read about Mrs Brady's complaint in The Burton Mail. He was just a pawn in the plot to tarnish her good name and was perhaps just as much a victim as she was. The real perpetrators were much higher up the chain. Everyone else was just carrying out instructions. She knew this only too well. On the other hand, though, Crowe had some kind of personal grudge against her. He'd made that pretty obvious with the hilarious note he'd sent. She'd taken a copy and left it on her writing desk, to be read every time she felt in need of a pick me up.

Although things had gone quiet since July and they were peacefully protesting every Sunday afternoon as the judge had ordered, she knew that she could wake up to find herself splashed over the newspapers again at any moment.

The forthcoming Saturday, 3rd September, was a date she'd noted in her diary months before hand. They were holding a march through Burton town centre, to increase awareness. They had the support of the public, which was why the police had no choice but to give them the go ahead. They were expecting a good turnout, around two hundred people, and, by the looks of it, the sun was going to be out. Jane had noticed how town was always busier when it was sunny. The warm weather created positive vibes, meaning people were more likely to stop and listen to what you have to say. People were going to be handing out leaflets and—.

The phone. "Who could this be at this time?" Jane muttered to Suzie as she made her way across the room to her writing desk, where she'd been sat talking, earlier. "Hello?"

"Jane, have you heard the news?"

"What news?"

"You haven't heard?"

"Heard what?"

Jane could hardly believe her ears as her friend told her the news that she, all of them, had been hoping for, but in all honesty had never expected to hear. And it was all down to the work they'd done over the years.

Hardly able to contain herself, Jane punched the air and shouted 'Yipee'. When she finally said goodbye to her friend, the phone rang again, and again.

As elated as she was, part of her though, urged caution. The march had been planned months in advance and was aimed at spreading awareness and recruiting more protestors. She knew from experience that the police and journalists would try and twist it round to portray them in a negative light. A sense of injustice, after all, sells newspapers. She tried to convey this to everyone that phoned. They'd won a partial victory, but the war was far from over. They had to be clever and make sure the publicity the march was bound to generate, was all positive.

The weather was just as great as forecast, and the march generated a lot of support. People were willing to stop and talk. Almost everyone went home with a leaflet, although the police, being the police, did sour the atmosphere by arresting someone's thirteen-year-old daughter, just to show they disapproved.

None of them were particularly surprised, the following morning, when all the newspapers reported the march as a victory parade. Of course, they took the opportunity again to show them in a bad light and had distorted the story to drum up outrage at the miscarriage of justice.

CHAPTER TWENTY-EIGHT

"Bobby. Good morning. Sorry to bother you so early. I wasn't entirely sure if you'd be in yet."
Crowe glanced up at the clock on the wall to see that it was approaching quarter to eight. "Oh, nonsense, Sir. I've been in a good half hour at least."
"Splendid. Now, I have some news . . ."
Crowe listened in silence to what the Chief Constable had to say. "Oh, not that old chestnut again, Sir."
Sexton roared with laughter. "Couldn't have put it better myself. Yesterday, there were some arrests. Don't know if you heard about it?"
"No. Tell me, Sir. Please do."
"Five of them. A thirty-five-year-old man in Manchester, a thirty-six-year-old man in Birmingham, a thirty-eight-year-old in Wolverhampton. Two women too. One in Wolverhampton and one in Burntwood."
"Good idea, Sir. If you cast the net wide enough, you're bound to get a conviction sooner or later."
Sexton laughed. "Knew you'd say that, Bobby."
"Oh, am I really that predictable, Sir?"

"Predictable no, reliable, yes. And that's just what we need in a case like this. Someone that understands the consequences of getting a conviction or, as the case may be, not."

"Thank you very much, Sir. So what can I do for you?"

"Well, we got our heads together down here and decided that we'd have the most chance of getting a conviction out of this if they were questioned together. In the same building that is, not simultaneously."

"Yes, I understood, Sir."

"So, what do you say?"

"What? Here you mean?"

"Well, where better? You have been taking the lead on this case, after all, Bobby. It's only right that you should be the one that takes the glory."

"Thank you, Sir. Yes. Send them here. I'll make the preparations. What time can I expect everyone to arrive?"

"Some time in the afternoon, so it'll probably be an overnight job."

"Oh, not a problem, Sir."

"I knew I could rely on you, Bobby. You know, if you do get a conviction out of this, I'm going to recommend you for promotion."

"Me? Really, Sir?"

"Yes. You deserve it, you really do."

"Oh, thank you, Sir."

"Not at all, Bobby. Not at all. Well, I'll leave you to get things ready and to get on with catching some criminals. I'll call again tomorrow to see how it's going."

"Any time, Sir. I'll look forward to it."

"Cheerio then."

"Cheerio, Sir. Thanks for ringing."

Crowe put the phone down, lit a cigarette and sat back in his chair. He liked the Chief Constable, they'd always got on well, but just recently, he was starting to think that maybe, just maybe, to an outsider, he might sound a little sycophantic? If he was made chief inspector, they would surely be on a more even footing, and the dynamics would have to change.

Much like a lecturer he'd once had that informed Crowe of his inability to do any work until he'd had a coffee on a morning, Crowe could not now operate without a cigarette. Of course, he'd lit up the minute he'd walked in, but now, still under an hour later, the urge for a second had proven to be irresistible. Taking a deep puff, he considered that some time soon, he'd have to face up to the fact that he had an addiction. With the gambling thing too, maybe it was in his blood and he just couldn't help it? After allowing his mind to wander and deciding that if he adopted this philosophy, he'd have to apply the same principle to criminals, he shrugged off the idea, put out his smoke and got to his feet. He had more important things to do than spend all day philosophising.

He had intended to brief everyone individually, but by the time he'd left the confines of his office, he'd already changed his mind. Taking two steps along the corridor, he moved his left ear towards the first door, held his breath and, after establishing it was occupied, rapped on the door. Without waiting for a reply, he opened the door, poked his head round and said, "Team meeting, my office, ten minutes." The officer inside nodded and continued with his work.

After walking through the building and repeating the process seven times, he walked briskly back to his desk. He flirted with the idea of having a quick cigarette before the meeting, but decided against it, telling himself that this show of strength was proof he did not have an addiction.

However, as he sat impatiently waiting for his doors to open, the craving became stronger and stronger until all he could think about was the taste of nicotine. He began impatiently drumming on his desk with his fingers, until, just as he was about to give in to his craving, the doors opened and one of his sergeants walked in.

Once everyone had arrived, Crowe clapped a hand against his desk to get everyone's attention. "Ok everyone, I'm going to keep this as short as possible . . . "

He had to keep the meeting short, because his urge to light up again was all that he could think of. Briefly, he considered the implications of smoking a cigarette there and then, but decided against the idea. He didn't want to demonstrate any signs of weakness to his staff. This was despite the fact that some of them had screwed their nose, faked a cough and waved their hand in front of their faces as they approached his desk. He suspected that they might be calling him an addict behind his back, even though none of them would ever say it to his face.

"I had a phone call earlier from the Chief Constable. There've been five arrests concerning the protestors, spread far and wide across the Midlands and North West." He waited for the chatter to stop and the news to be digested before continuing. "The good news is, folks, that we have been chosen to ensure they are not let off the hook."

"What does that mean, Sir?"

"It means, that they, all five of them, are coming here to be questioned."

A collective groan went up.

"Now, now. This is a great opportunity for everyone to shine."

"What are they being charged with, Sir?"

"Good question. Brilliant. Conspiracy to blackmail."

Everyone looked visibly lifted by this change in angle.

"And, should any further incentive be needed to bag a conviction, then I have it on good authority that, should we succeed, yours truly will be in line for promotion."

"What time will they be coming?"

"Don't know for sure, but the Chief Constable told me the motley crew will be arriving some time this afternoon." He paused to let the news sink in. "Are we excited?"

"Oh, yes, Sir." Everyone nodded and put on a fake smile.

"Then, that will be all. Good luck." All he could think about was lighting a cigarette.

"Sir?"

"What? Now?"

"I don't get the link between the protestors and conspiracy to blackmail, Sir."

Crowe got to his feet, threw back his head, held his arms out wide in a V shape and said to the ceiling, "Lord, why have you surrounded me with idiots?"

While moving his head downwards, he noticed his drawer, the one where he kept his cigarettes, to be open about half an inch. He took a deep breath, hoping to catch a whiff of sweet nicotine. Sounding like a patient headmaster that was just about at the end of his tether, he said, "There is no link, you imbecile. You'll just have to get creative with your questioning, won't you?"

"Oh, yes, Sir."

"Comprendez?"

The constable nodded.

"Then on your way. Honestly, you'll have to buck your ideas up if you ever want to progress in The Force. You could do a lot worse than take a leaf out of my book."

"Oh, yes, Sir."

Crowe left his desk and marched across his office, to usher them all from his room and to ensure the door was firmly closed behind them. Once the last of them had gone, and the footsteps began to recede, he ran to his desk, flung open the drawer and pulled out the cigarette packet, which he found to be empty. "No, it can't be," he said aloud and began rooting through the drawer, looking for a rogue that might have slipped out by accident. With the drawer upturned atop his desk and the contents scattered across the floor, Crowe sat down, leant forward and dropped his face into his hands. Just what was happening to him?

After taking five minutes to compose himself, Crowe got to his feet and walked calmly across the road to the shop.

Much to his annoyance, there was a queue. At the front was a young mother with a pushchair, so pushing in was out of the question. He waited impatiently while the old man in front of him chatted to the assistant until, finally, his turn came around. He pressed a five-pound note into the assistant's hand and left without uttering a word.

He politely strolled through the station, nodding and smiling en route, but the second his door was closed, he dashed across to his desk, pulled out his chair, sat down, took out a cigarette and lit up. Closing his eyes, he sat back, inhaled deep and breathed out. A smile spread right the way across his face as he considered how all the craving had been worth it for that one moment of sheer ecstasy.

Opening his eyes, he was still feeling on a high when he noticed his answer machine was flashing. Whoever it was could wait, he told himself, at least until he'd finished his cigarette.

He'd only just stubbed out the cigarette when there was a knock. A constable had some kind of problem with a drug addict that was making a nuisance of himself. Didn't know what to do with him. Just the kind of annoying routine thing that he didn't really need on a day as important as this.

It was early afternoon when the visitors arrived. Crowe was in his element, overseeing the process and making sure that each of them was interviewed by the right officer. Once all five were being questioned separately, Crowe went back to his office and wished, not for the first time, that he could be more involved with the questioning. He thought about sitting in on an interview, but knew from experience that this was hardly helpful. All it did was serve as a distraction and if his officers were anything like he used to be, they'd resent the intrusion. The questioning process was an intimate affair, a battle of wits almost, between the police officer and the accused. Any outside interference could distort the process. No, despite his need for closer involvement, Crowe decided to stay put and sit on his hands to stop himself passing the time by chain smoking. This had worked for approximately five minutes before he succumbed to his craving.

When his stomach started rumbling, he knew the afternoon must be drawing to a close. After glancing up at the clock, he decided to take a stroll through the building, to see what progress each of his officers had made, to inform them he was going home and to tell them to ring him should they need anything.

He nudged open his front door in high spirits, feeling positive that at some time the following day there'd be at least one arrest. However, the minute he set eyes on Susan, he began to panic. "Susan, what—what is it?"

"It's Johnny."

Slightly later than usual, Crowe arrived at the station the following day, still reeling from the events of the night before. Susan had claimed she'd been trying to get hold of him to tell him that Johnny had been sent home from school, feeling sick and short of breath. Crowe had disputed this, telling her he'd been in his office all afternoon and if she'd rang he'd have answered. Then, out of the blue, he'd remembered seeing his flashing answer machine and told her how he'd been distracted. Needless to say, this hadn't washed at all with his wife and as far as he could tell, when he'd left that morning, he was still in the dog house.

He had learnt a valuable lesson though. He'd learnt that being in a position where he craved a cigarette so much that it consumed everything else, was not the most desirable of situations. That's why he'd decided to put in his briefcase one of the vast multi packs of cigarettes that he'd bought at the duty-free shop on his way back from France. If Johnny was unwell, he might need a cigarette to calm his nerves occasionally. It was his way of coping. Taking the cigarettes from his bag, he held them to his nose and took a deep and glorious whiff. From now on, no matter what, he was always going to have a friend by his side, ready and waiting to help out in his hour of need.

Feeling strangely reluctant to cut through the cellophane wrapping, Crowe instead rummaged through his bag, looking for any spares that might have fallen out. It took him a good five minutes to get right to the bottom of all the loose documents, pens, paper clips and empty sandwich boxes, but eventually, when his fingers met the long, slender prize, he grinned. After spending a few seconds examining the cigarette carefully, holding it up to eye level between finger and thumb like it was some kind of precious stone, he lit up, put the cigarette in his mouth, closed his eyes and relaxed.

He'd only taken two puffs when he remembered. With all the furore surrounding Johnny, he'd arrived into work having forgotten just what an important day it was. Laughing to himself, he decided to finish his cigarette before doing his rounds. He almost felt like he owed it to everyone to do this, just to ensure he was operating at his optimal level.

However, he didn't get chance to see for himself how the visitors were keeping, because, just as he was putting out the stub, there was a knock. Furrowing his brow, he glanced at the clock; he'd forgotten that he'd been delayed and therefore arrived at work later than usual. He was unprepared and so decided there and then not to let it happen again.

"Come in."

"Good morning, Sir. Thought you might want to see this . . ."

The constable extended his arm, offering Crowe a piece of A4 paper, with writing on both sides. "Oh, thank you," Crowe said, casting an eye over the contents, noticing that the handwriting was hardly neat and tidy.

As soon as the door had banged shut, Crowe lifted the paper up to the light and examined it carefully. It appeared to be a summary of each interview's progress. As his eyes moved slowly from left to right and then from top to bottom, he felt his optimism turn to concern and then slowly give way to despair.

The noises and chatter in the corridor told him that everyone had arrived, so he got to his feet and went to see each of the officers involved. Despite his despondency, he did his best to gee each of them up. If he didn't encourage them, he knew the opportunity to lay this thing to rest and to land himself a promotion would inevitably slip through his fingers.

Throughout the morning, he couldn't resist popping in on the hour, despite the obvious annoyance of the officers doing the questioning. He could tell though, just by looking at them. From the way that, by lunch time, the accused were all sat grinning smugly with their arms folded, while the officers all had their sleeves rolled up and their top buttons unfastened.

At midday, he'd only just got back to his office when one of the officers he'd just seen knocked and entered. "Sir, I'm going to have to let this one go."

"No."

"There's no evidence. He has a water tight alibi."

"Keep trying."

"But I've been trying for almost twenty-four hours now. It just feels like I'm going over and over the same stuff. Once they see they have you on the run, they dig in and then you've lost them."

"Well, undig him, damn it. Do anything. Just don't tell me you're releasing him on bail."

"I might have to, Sir."

Crowe thrust his hands over his ears and started humming the signature tune to one of Johnny's favourite TV programmes."

"Sir!"

"Sorry, did you say something?"

The officer turned round in disgust, banged the door shut and marched back to the interview room.

As soon as he was on his own, Crowe leaned forward, folded his arms on his desk and rested his forehead atop of them. He couldn't believe what he'd just done. He'd known earlier that the writing was on the wall and had secretly resigned himself to the facts. Getting to his feet, he plodded along the corridor, pausing when he heard the voice of the sergeant he'd just been talking to.

"Can I have a word please, Sergeant?" Crowe said, looking in around the door.

"Certainly, Sir."

Once they were in the corridor and the door firmly closed, Crowe apologised and told him to release the accused on bail if he thought it the right thing to do.

"Oh, very good, Sir."

An air of abject failure hung over the entire station when, at just before four pm, Crowe picked up the phone and told The Burton Mail he was releasing all five without charge on bail.

Later that afternoon, Crowe trudged along his garden path, feeling the weight of the world on his shoulders, looking forward to his wife's welcoming smile and a hug from his son.

"Hello, I'm home," he called, scanning the hallway for signs of life.

"I'm up here."

Crowe climbed the stairs, feeling uplifted at the sound of his wife's welcoming voice. The minute he opened his son's bedroom door and saw the look on her face, he knew it wasn't good.

"He's been sick all day. First with his breathing, then stomach pains. He's gone right off his food."

"What? You should have called me."

Susan shook her head. "Didn't want to bother you at work. I'm sorry about yesterday. I was just worried."

"Oh, I know. Do you think we should get him to the doctor?"

Susan nodded. "I've made an appointment for twelve o'clock tomorrow."

"I'm coming with you."

"Oh, you don't have to. It's probably nothing. You know what they're like at that age."

***

Despite not having slept a wink, Crowe got into work bright and early the following morning, just as he'd planned. For the first time since joining the force, his mind wasn't on the job. It felt like all the criminals walking the streets, Sexton, Thomas, The Burton Mail, they belonged to another, increasingly distant world and his only connection with this other life was the multi pack of cigarettes that he'd thoughtfully brought with him the day before. He opened the cupboard, reached inside, held the box to his nose and smiled. It was like he'd been reunited with a good old reliable friend that would never let him down.

By the time he heard footsteps in the reception area, the glass ashtray, which he'd instructed the cleaner to empty on a daily basis, was overflowing. He felt so heartened by the sound of life that he did something that he'd never done before. Rather than waiting for whoever it was to come in, bearing news, good or bad, he got to his feet and walked through the building, just to say hello.

The duty sergeant looked at him inquisitively. " Good morning, Sir. Is err, everything OK?"

"Well, no. Not really, Sergeant. My err, little boy's a bit poorly. I was awake all night."

"Oh, sorry to hear that, Sir."

"I was just about to make a cup of tea. Would you like one?"

The sergeant fought off an amazed grin. "No, it's OK. I'll have one in a bit."

Crowe trudged straight back to his office, bypassing the kitchen. Once at his desk, he lit another cigarette and did his best to shift the smog that was clouding his mind. He knew he'd have to focus himself quickly because at any minute—.

The phone rang. Leaning forward, he placed his cigarette in the ash tray, gripped the phone and froze. This was Sexton. He wasn't going to be happy. Feeling overcome with a sudden panic, he let the phone ring eight times while he tried to think up an excuse that might save face.

"Good morning, Bobby."

Crowe was determined not to sound as despondent as he felt. He knew that his tone of voice would define the course of the conversation and that above all he had to inspire confidence in his senior officer. "Good morning, Sir." Crowe hung his head in despair and waited for the backlash.

"Oh, dear." Sexton started laughing. "Sounds like you have the weight of the world on your shoulders there, Bobby. I know things look grim, but you have to put a brave face on for the sake of the troops."

"I know that, Sir. Sorry." Knowing full well that Sexton had a young son of his own, Crowe decided to play the sympathy card. "It's just that, my son wasn't very well yesterday. I was awake all night, Sir."

"Oh. I didn't realise, old boy." A moment's awkward silence followed before Sexton, sounding choked up, said, "I can imagine just how you feel, Bobby. Tell you what, we'll postpone the conversation I was calling for. You just concentrate on getting your thoughts together. Have you taken him to see a doctor?"

"No, Sir. Susan—my wife— is taking him today at twelve. I was—. "

"You're going with her, I hope?"

"Well, I wasn't sure if that would be OK, Sir."

"It's a question of priorities. Take all the time you need."

"Thank you, Sir."

"Don't mention it. Just one thing."

"What's that, Sir?"

"You do remember, what I said, don't you?"

"Not sure. Said about what, Sir?"

"Oh, nothing. You go to the doctors'. I'm sure it will work out fine and he'll be right as rain."

"I certainly hope so, Sir."

"And about the other matter. I'll phone you—this time tomorrow?"

"Perfect, Sir."

It was safe to say that that was the longest morning of Crowe's working life. From the second he put the phone down, all he could think about was Johnny. He felt most relieved when the clock finally approached eleven thirty. By this time, even the thought of another cigarette made him feel nauseous.

It was only a short drive to the surgery, and he had to wait five minutes in the car park for Susan to arrive before leaving his car. Quite typically, they were made to wait forty minutes beyond the appointment time, meaning that by the time they were called, they were more nervous than ever.

Once inside the doctor's room, they both sat, and Crowe left his wife to do most of the talking. The doctor did some tests, listened to Johnny's heartbeat, and addressed them with a puzzled expression. He told them that he couldn't be certain what was causing the respiratory problems and they should keep an eye out for bruising and bleeding. He also said to make an appointment immediately, should they notice any unusual swelling or glandular problems.

Sensing that the consultation was drawing to a close, Crowe was the first to get to his feet. That's when the doctor said he would give Johnny something to take away the pain, make him more comfortable. Susan smiled a mother's smile, but Crowe was horrified. "No." Susan glared at her husband. "What do you mean? Why?"

"He doesn't need them."

"What? Why?" Susan looked perplexed.

"He's being paid to—. "

The doctor decided it was time to reassert his authority. "Mr Crowe, you don't have to give your son treatment to make him more comfortable, but by all accounts, he has been in a lot of pain recently and—."

"Aren't there any alternative treatments?"

Susan's jaw dropped. "Robbie, what's got into you?" She turned to the doctor. "Doctor, I must apologise for my husband's behaviour. He's been under a lot of stress at work lately. What with the protests being all over the news and all."

The doctor nodded. "Oh yes. I read about that. Mr Crowe, you are of course at liberty to give your son alternative medicines, but I cannot recommend nor condone such a course of action. Herbal practitioners are renowned fraudsters and their methods have not been proven."

Susan smiled triumphantly. "Thank you, Doctor."

"So, would you like me to write out a prescription or not?"

Susan nodded. "Yes please, Doctor."

The doctor scribbled down a list of meds, signed a long and swirly signature and handed the green prescription to Susan.

"Thank you, Doctor."

Taking the prescription in one hand and her son in the other Susan marched out of the room and along the corridor, leaving her husband to follow like a puppy.

"Susan, wait!" Crowe called, the minute they were outside in the car park.

"What?" Susan called angrily over her shoulder, one foot inside the chemists.

"How many pain killers did he prescribe?"

Susan held the prescription to eye level and counted. "Five."

"Don't you think that's a little excessive?" He said softly, finally catching her up.

"No. I don't. He isn't well."

"Oh, well do whatever you think's best. I have to get back to work now. I'll see you later."

Susan shrugged. "Whatever."

Once back at the station, Crowe, feeling somewhat relieved that at least it wasn't bad news, soon got down to business. It was a busy afternoon and soon passed. Come six o'clock, Crowe's usual knocking off time, he'd forgotten about his disagreement with Susan, only remembering once he'd parked on the driveway and was about to step out of the car.

It hadn't been a great day, but it suddenly felt a whole lot worse. If there was anything Crowe hated more than the protestors, it was arriving home to a sour atmosphere. It was at times like this that he missed the solitude of his studio flat.

Nonetheless, he opened the door and called out to his wife, sounding hopelessly optimistic that she'd come running down the stairs to meet him, as she often did when she was in a good mood. The silence told him everything he needed to know.

Unsurprisingly, he found her in Johnny's room. She'd placed a dining chair by his bed and was sat reading him a story. On the windowsill were five separate types of pain killers. All open, all missing some of their contents.

"Hi," Crowe said, approaching his wife and sick son. "How is he?"

Susan glanced at him and shrugged.

"I want to explain, about before."

"No need."

For a second Crowe smiled as he imagined himself to be in the clear. "I understand. You were thinking about the cost. That's all you ever think about."

"What? No, you're wrong."

"I'm not wrong, Robbie. Sometimes I think I should have stayed at my mother's."

"You don't mean that."

"No. Maybe not. But I was ashamed of your behaviour. For the first time ever, you made me ashamed. So go on then, tell me, what would make you speak to a doctor in such a manner? Like he was some kind of—trainee dog handler?"

Crowe opened his mouth to explain, but soon closed it again when he asked himself if she would understand or if she would dismiss the idea that doctors can't be trusted.

"What? You were going to say something."

"No. It doesn't matter." Weighing up his options, Crowe glanced through the window for inspiration. He could either spend all night trying to explain or he could just confine himself to the dog house and get some peace and quiet.

"Well?"

"No. You were right. I was just thinking about the money. Five items felt a bit over the top. Have they made any difference?"

"A bit. He's still had stomach pains but his breathing's improved."

"Well, I'm sorry, OK?"

"OK."

Susan smiled and squeezed his hand.

Crowe fetched a chair from downstairs and spent the rest of the night sat with his wife at his son's bedside. Not long after it got dark, Johnny fell asleep, and their conversation was reduced to whispers. Despite having patched things up with his wife, he was still worried about his son, and when the prospect of Sexton's phone call crossed his mind, he lost the desire to sleep. And so, for the second night running, got up in the morning with his eyes stinging.

No sooner had he stepped into his office then the phone started ringing.

"Good morning, Bobby."

"Oh, good morning, Chief Constable."

"How's your son?"

"Better. The doctor couldn't find anything serious the matter, so that's a relief."

"I can imagine. So anyway, down to business."

"Chief Constable, I want to offer my most sincere apologies for having to release all five of them on bail. My officers tried everything, every line of questioning imaginable, but they couldn't find anything on any of them. They all had alibis, Sir."

"I understand, but you must understand this. It will soon be a year since we were handed this task and we have precious little to show for it. Eventually, someone will have to carry the can."

"Of course."

"What about your Thomas woman? What's she up to these days?"

"Nothing incriminating. Unfortunately."

"Well, she's the only thing we have anything on. Why don't you send an officer round to rough her up a bit? Then, once she's vulnerable, have her brought in on a charge of conspiracy to blackmail."

"Oh, I don't know, Sir. Feels like that's come to a bit of a dead end."

"Well, as I said, she's the only person to have been identified."

"Do you think it could work, Sir?"

"I think it's worth a try, Bobby. Because if you don't do something then . . . Look, it's getting to the stage where pretty soon it will either be her head on the block or yours. There I've said it."

"I understand, Sir."

"Good man."

The second he'd hung up, Crowe reached for his cigarettes. For some reason, he didn't detest Thomas quite as much as he had a year or so before and since yesterday, he was actually starting to sympathise with her. More than anything, he felt he had been taught a lesson for what he told the newspapers and if he went against her again and against his own moral judgement, then the consequences could be a lot more severe. Sitting back, Crowe lit up and asked himself if his time in the force was in fact about to come to an end. But what else could he do? Having laughed off the idea that he might be cut out for anything else, he stubbed out the cigarette and delved into the pile of paperwork that was getting angry.

CHAPTER TWENTY-NINE

NOVEMBER 2005

Percival Jeffries looked up from his report and peered through his study window at the breath-taking countryside that surrounded the vicarage. Nothing could ever compare to his Northumberland home that he grew up in, but it had become like a home from home for him now.
Percival smiled as he imagined leaving the court in little over twenty-four hours, having been cleared of the terrible crimes for which he'd been accused. Maybe it would even open the door for him to return to Northumberland, should Loretta agree.
He was just about to go back to his paperwork when his phone rang. He always preferred to give out his mobile, knowing that the landline was more susceptible to nuisance calls, so knew whoever was on the other end was either a salesman or someone with valuable information. Glancing at the caller display, he ascertained it to be the latter.
"Reverend Jeffries, it's D.S. Mellor."
"Oh, thought it might be. And how are you?"

"Can't complain. I just wanted to wish you luck for your court appearance tomorrow."

"Oh, thank you very much."

"I've briefed the jury and I've been assured that there will be no problems this time. It's going to be the formality the last one should have been."

"That's reassuring to know, thank you."

"Well, I just wanted to let you know there's nothing to worry about. So get a good night's sleep and start looking forward to a new life."

"Thank you, very much."

"Bye then, must dash. Things to do and all that."

"Bye, Mellor. And thanks. For everything."

"Who was that on the phone?" Loretta asked, walking across the study to her husband's desk.

"Mellor."

"Oh, him again. I hope he's kept his word this time. I don't trust him."

"Oh, he's OK. And yes, he has."

"Do you trust him?"

"Yes. Despite what happened last time."

As instructed, Percival Jeffries did sleep well that night. He'd been getting himself more and more worked up as the hearing approached and Mellor's phone call had made the world of difference. Now, safe in the knowledge that he was not going to be convicted, he could sleep easy and, to use Mellor's words, look forward to a whole new life where he wasn't the subject of suspicion each time a child came near him.

The first thing Jeffries noticed was that it was an entirely different jury.

The same evidence as before was read out, but the prosecuting solicitor didn't quite carry the same conviction. The boy had refused to attend, having made the point that once was traumatic enough for anyone. Therefore, when it came to his own solicitor's turn to cross-examine, and Jeffries himself was called to the stand, there were no hissed accusations or muttered insults from the public gallery. His lawyer went through his list of questions, and when the prosecutor stood up, Jeffries looked at him, trying desperately to conceal the smug grin which he felt must be present on his face.

Jeffries just went through what he had said many times before, that he had taken a shine to the boy and they'd got on well, but there was never any kind of sexual contact. Much to Jeffries' surprise, the prosecutor just smiled, said thank you and returned to his seat, without asking a single question.

When the hearing was over, court was adjourned while the jury considered their verdict. This time there were no concerned or anxious looks. He just sat with Loretta in the waiting room, sipping tea and discussing their plans for dinner. Ten minutes later they were called back in, and the Jeffries resumed their place on the bench behind their solicitor.

Back in the car, Jeffries couldn't help grinning as he absorbed the fact that he had cleared his name. In the end, there just wasn't enough evidence to convict him. In this respect, justice had been done. Now he'd served his penance and God had repaid him. They both felt more certain than ever that God wanted that Thomas woman to go to prison, so they made a joint decision to offer the police any further help they needed.

CHAPTER THIRTY

Crowe opened out his copy of The Burton Mail atop his desk and read the article about the Jeffries carefully. On the face of it, they seemed like good people, and part of him felt pleased that Jeffries had been relieved of his burden. This despite the shame he felt for being involved.

The protestors may have temporarily faded from public view, but as Sexton kept on reminding him, should they fail with their task, someone would have to suffer the consequences. Crowe knew Sexton to be a laid back, amiable man, but he also had an iron streak. If anyone was going to suffer, it wasn't going to be him.

By all accounts the companies involved were no longer pressurising the government to end the protests, having renegotiated their backhander. Now the pressure was coming from the public who were demanding answers, and from within The Force itself.

He still hadn't acted on Sexton's advice to have Thomas arrested for conspiracy to blackmail. Things had moved on between them and he'd forgiven her for humiliating him with the compensation money. In the end, he'd probably succumb to the pressure and have her arrested, although, it felt like he was being forced to apply for a job that he had no chance of—.

The phone. Crowe glanced up at the clock before reaching across his desk. It was approaching eleven, meaning it was unlikely to be Sexton. He let it ring eight times while he considered who it might be, before picking up, only just beating the answer phone to it. "Inspector Crowe speaking."

All he could hear were slow, evil sounding breaths.

"Hello, Inspector Crowe speaking."

"I heard you the first time."

"Who is this?"

"You owe me money, Crowe."

Crowe would recognise this slow, slithering voice anywhere. "Symons."

"Got it in one."

"I don't owe you a thing."

"Let me remind you. A while back, you asked me to do a job for you. You asked me to rough up that officer of yours, a calling card from the protestors."

"What? That's ridiculous? The protestors hounded her." Crowe was ashamed of the way he'd convinced himself this was true.

"You owe me two hundred pounds, Crowe. You'd better pay up or—I could make things very difficult for you."

"Are you trying to blackmail a Police Inspector, Symons?" He was already starting to think that two hundred pounds was a small price to pay to keep him off the scene.

Symons laughed a low, rustling laugh. "I know."

Crowe laughed. "What, do you know?"

"A few months ago, you were leaving your cards syndicate when—."

"Cards syndicate? Now I know you're off your rocker."

Symons' patience snapped. "Don't play games with me, Crowe! I saw you, with my own eyes. You were leaving the club in your car."

"You were intoxicated, no doubt."

"No, I wasn't. Unlike you."

Crowe felt a bolt of fear rip right through him. "Okay. You can have your two hundred pounds. But I want your assurances that I'll never hear from you again."

"Absolutely, Crowe. Give me the money today, and you'll never hear from me again."

"And you won't tell anyone about this—intoxicated hallucination?"

Symons laughed. "Very good, Crowe. I can see why you've done so well in the police force. I give you my word."

"OK. Here's where I want you to meet me at—twelve o'clock sharp . . ."

As soon as the minute hand struck ten to twelve, Crowe got to his feet, marched through the building without saying a word to anyone and, after glancing round to make sure no-one was looking, crossed the road, taking approximately twenty steps left to the cash machine. With the wad of fresh notes tucked firmly away in his wallet, Crowe turned round and went back the way he'd come, turning right instead of re-entering the police station.

After a few yards, Crowe turned down a side street, where he walked along the litter strewn dirt path, past the back entrances of the shops, until he came to an alleyway. There, leaning against the wall, looking just as despicable as ever, was Symons.

Symons immediately turned to face Crowe and smiled. Waiting until he could see the whites of Crowes eyes, he said quietly, "Punctuality. After the ability to make up the most outrageous of lies at will, just about the most important trait of a police officer, I'd say. You're destined for great things, Crowe, you really are."

Crowe shrugged. "I've got your money."

"Are they genuine notes?" Symons said with a grin.

Taking his wallet from his trouser pocket, Crowe resisted the temptation to tell him not to push his luck and, without saying a word, extracted the notes from the back of his wallet. While slipping his wallet back into his trouser pocket with his right hand, he handed Symons the cash with his left.

With the notes firmly in Symon's grasp, Crowe drooped his head and turned to be on his way.

"Wait a minute. I don't trust you. I'd better count it before you go." Crowe stopped in his tracks and turned around. "What? You gave me your word. There's two hundred pounds there, I withdrew it from my bank account just a few minutes ago."

"Won't take a minute."

Crowe stood rooted to the spot, while Symons counted the money aloud. Once he'd counted the final note and confirmed he was in possession of the agreed amount, Crowe, assuming the upper hand, demanded Symons' assurance that this would be the end of the matter.

Symons shook his head. "Just wait a minute."

"What? You have your money, now—."

"Three hundred?"

"We agreed two."

"Call it interest, for messing me around. I'm a busy man, you know."

"Now look Symons, don't push it. You'd get five years for blackmailing a police officer."

"You'd get at least ten. They'd throw the bloody book at you."

Crowe paused to think about this. It didn't take him long to realise that Symons was right. "OK. Same time, same place tomorrow and I'll give you another hundred. But that's your lot."

"Deal." Symons offered Crowe his hand.

Crowe shook his head, slapped Symons' hand aside and turned to leave.

"Same time tomorrow, Crowe," Symons called out, to Crowe's back.

Feeling completely numb, Crowe trudged back to the police station, calling at the sandwich shop on the way. Back in the solitude of his office, he locked the door, sat down at his desk and dropped his face into his hands while he went over the exchange. Even if Symons did testify against him, it might not spell curtains. It would be just his word against Symons' and the judge was far more likely to believe an upstanding member of the community than a low life, who probably had a record as long as your arm. He knew how things worked. Providing no one else testified against him, he'd be OK.

Taking his sandwiches from their triangular box, he suddenly lost his appetite. Having compromised all his principles, allowed himself to be blackmailed, bought off a potential witness to add to the way he'd treated Thomas, he could no longer look at himself in the same way. If he didn't need the money so much, he might ring Sexton and give him his resignation.

He spent a good ten minutes sat, chin in hands, contemplating, staring at the sandwiches before eventually lifting them to his lips.

Five minutes later and he was staring at the crumbs in the box, resisting the urge to light a cigarette, when there was a knock on his door. He never did get to smoke that cigarette, because from that moment on he was rushed off his feet for the remainder of the afternoon.

By the time six o'clock came around, he'd forgotten all about Symons and went home with his dignity restored, feeling more confident than ever in his ability as a police officer. It wasn't until he found Susan holding Johnny's hand that his spirits once again took a dive. He'd woken up feeling sick, giving Susan no choice but to keep him off school. Crowe felt aggrieved that she hadn't thought to call and tell him, but decided to keep it to himself.

This was a deep concern for both Crowe and his wife. Since that first day, their son had been found short of breath many times and had been sent home from school on a regular basis. Despite this, the doctor couldn't find anything wrong with him and seemed happy to go on offering the quick fix. Neither of them liked pumping him full of painkillers on a daily basis, but they trusted their doctor and hoped that eventually they'd give a diagnosis and the painkillers would stop.

Crowe arrived at his desk the following morning having forgotten to call at the cash machine. Lighting up his customary morning cigarette, he gave the matter some thought. He felt like a different person to the imposter that had sat at his desk the day before and wholeheartedly regretted his attempt to pay Symons off. Recognising he could be a danger if not handled correctly, Crowe decided to phone Symons to straighten the matter out once and for all.

"Hello?" Symons grunted in Crowe's ear.

"It's Crowe."

"Oh. Hello, Inspector Crowe. What can I do for you? Got a job for me?"

"Not exactly."

"You want to give me an extra hundred to make it a nice even number?" Symons laughed a slithery, croaky laugh.

"Not exactly. I want to keep it at a nice even number. Two hundred, the amount we agreed. And not a penny more."

"You what? You can't do this, Crowe. We had a deal."

"I can and I am doing this. I'll pay you two hundred and you can count yourself lucky to have got that much."

"So you're not bothered about going to prison. And that son of yours—what's he called? Johnny? You won't see him again until he's all grown up."

"It's your word against mine, Symons. I know who the judge is more likely to believe. You leave my family out of this."

Symons laughed. "OK, you're the boss. Whatever you say."

"What? So you're going to take your payment and leave it at that?"

"We'll see. Maybe you need a shot across your bows. Just to let you know I'm not playing games."

"What you talking about?"

"You'll see. Have a good day, Crowe."

Crowe hung up, placed the phone back in its cradle and sat back. He felt relieved more than anything that he'd stood up to Symons, but feared, deep down, that there'd be repercussions. However, it was true that no judge would believe Symons in court. He only wished that this thought had surfaced before he'd paid Symons the money. Turning to his right, he noticed the mountain of paperwork and so at last found time to make a start.

Two hours later and he was making good progress, with the done and to do piles on an even keel. That's when there was a knock.

"Come in," Crowe said, annoyed at the disturbance.

"Sir, I thought you'd want to see this." A constable entered, carrying a document. As soon Crowe could read the title, he stifled a groan. He knew exactly what it was, the only question being who it was from.

"Thank you," Crowe said, taking the document from the constable. Waiting for the door to close and the footsteps to recede, Crowe held up the complaint to eye level and began reading line by line, resisting the temptation to turn the page to see who it was from.

It soon became apparent that this complaint was from Mrs Brady. She was unhappy with the treatment she'd received and the outcome of the police's internal enquiry. She felt she'd been subjected to a cover up and was filing the complaint again. She most strongly objected to the way Inspector Crowe had dealt with her case, saying she'd been made to feel like her daughter didn't really matter.

This, in itself, wasn't a problem. He could easily get on the phone to the complaints commission, offer to make a small donation to the charity of their choice, and the matter would be forgotten about. No, the problem would arise if this was leaked to the press.

Getting to his feet, Crowe marched through the station, peeking round doors, seeking out the constable that had brought him the complaint document. When he found him, he was stood at reception, taking the specifics of a burglary. "Constable, could I have a quiet word, please?" Crowe called across reception.

The constable apologised to the person he was dealing with and joined Crowe in the solitude of the corridor.

"Constable, that complaint form. Where did you get it?"

"From Mrs Brady herself, Sir."

"She brought it in?"

"Yes, Sir."

"Was there a tanned looking man with her, possibly mid-twenties?"

"No, Sir. She was on her own."

"You sure he wasn't waiting outside in a car?"

"Yes, Sir. She drove herself here."

"You sure? Think, damn it. This is important."

"Yes, Sir. I'm absolutely sure."

"And who else saw the form? Anyone?"

"No, Sir. I brought it straight to you."

"OK. Thank you, constable. You did the right thing."

No sooner had the constable apologised for the interruption, then a car pulled up outside. Crowe stood watching from the safety of the corridor, and when D.C. Oplitova emerged, a knowing grin appeared on his face.

"Alena," he said, nodding and smiling as they passed. Observing her walk straight into the kitchen, he followed her along the corridor, hoping he'd get chance to talk to her on her own.

With the roar of the kettle filling the room, Crowe stepped into the kitchen, glanced round to confirm they were alone and stood beside her at the sink. "Alena," he said, ensuring he could be heard clearly over the kettle.

Oplitova let out a short scream and jumped round. "Inspector Crowe. You frightened me."

"Sit down." He pointed to the square table that occupied the centre of the room. "Let me make the tea."

"Oh, err, thank you. Sir."

Placing a white mug with pink spots in front of Oplitova, he took the seat opposite, drinking from a pale blue mug that looked like it had been around for ever.

"What have you been up to this morning?" Crowe said, trying to sound casual.

"I've been out, investigating a domestic disturbance, Sir."

"And that took all morning, did it?"

"Pretty much, Sir, yes. There was a lot of sorting out to do. You see, the woman's son—."

"Oh, spare me the details."

"Sorry, Sir."

"So how are you feeling, these days?"

"Oh, very good, Sir."

"I heard you had some visitors while you were off. From the protestors."

Oplitova looked confused, perhaps wondering how he had come to know about it. "Oh, yes, Sir, but—."

"They deserve to be behind bars, the lot of them."

They continued to drink in silence, Oplitova being the first to rap down her mug and stand to leave.

"So what are your plans for this afternoon?"

"What? Well, I have—."

"How about doing some work with me?"

Oplitova grinned. "Yes, I'd love that, Sir. Thank you very much, Sir."

"I have a stack of paper work to get through. You don't mind lending a hand, do you?"

"Oh, no, Sir."

"Well, come on then. Let's make a start."

Once in his office, Crowe offered her a seat and gave her some instructions. "You do this pile here and I'll do these," he said with a smile.

Oplitova gradually became less talkative as the afternoon wore on, looking at him with suspicion each time he attempted to make small talk. Roughly two hours later, she got to her feet and said she was just going back to the kitchen for a glass of water.

"Come on, Alena," Crowe replied, "there isn't much to do now. I have another job for you once this has been done."

"But I won't be—."

"No, I'm going to have to put my foot down. Get this finished, then you can drink."

"Oh, OK then."

With the mountain of paperwork finally finished, Crowe glanced up at the clock and noticed there was still ten minutes to go before The Burton Mail's four o'clock deadline.

"Well, done, Alena. You deserve a cup of tea, come on, let me make you another."

"No, no, I have—. "

Crowe waved a hand. "I insist, Alena, come on."

This time the kitchen was full of people, all of whom looked at Crowe suspiciously as he made his entrance. There was a queue for the kettle, so by the time it got round to Crowe's turn, it was past four o'clock and he lost all interest.

"Oplitova, go on, back to work. There's too much wasting time drinking tea in this place."

An hour or so later, Crowe was sat at his desk, contemplating leaving work early for the day, feeling satisfied that he'd stopped the mole from leaking the story. A knock. "Come in," Crowe called out.

It was the same constable that had brought him the complaint document earlier. This time he was holding the late edition of The Burton Mail.

"Thought you'd want to see this, Sir." The look on the constable's face told Crowe he should be worried, but that didn't prevent the headline from eating his words.

The constable had only just left the room when the phone rang. "Inspector Crowe."

"Inspector Crowe. Guess who?"

The croaky voice was a dead giveaway. "Symons. What can I do for you?"

"Just wondered if you've had chance to see this afternoon's edition of The Burton Mail yet?"

"Y—yes. I have a copy right in front of me."

"Does it make pleasant reading for you?"

"What? Symons!"

Symons roared with laughter. "Yes, it was me. Doesn't look good, does it? I expect you'll have the Chief Constable on your back in the morning, demanding answers."

Without uttering another word, Crowe hung up and left for home. He had a sick son to worry about.

CHAPTER THIRTY-ONE

Fortunately, Sexton had stopped calling first thing on a morning. This gave Crowe a few hours to consider his options. They'd had a friendly relationship until now, but Crowe knew that didn't mean a thing. He'd made it pretty clear often enough that somewhere along the line someone was going to have to be accountable for the fiasco, and Crowe knew it would be him in the firing line.

In the end, it wasn't a difficult decision to make. Smiling to himself, Crowe sat back in his leather chair, extended his legs and lit a cigarette. There was about an hour until people started to arrive, giving him time to think things through properly and act on the document that had appeared on his in tray as if by magic.

As soon as he heard things getting busy in reception, Crowe got to his feet and left the confines of his office. He was feeling in high spirits despite everything and so knocked gently on each door he passed, looked in, and told the occupant good morning. Oplitova was in the room right at the end of the corridor.

"Oh, good morning, Sir," Oplitova, who was sat at a desk with her back to the door, looked over her shoulder and smiled politely.

"Can I have a quick word?"

"What? Oh, yes, Sir, of course." Oplitova put down her pen and stood up.

"Oh, no, stay where you are. This shouldn't take long." Ensuring the door was closed securely, Crowe took two steps forward and sat at the desk beside Oplitova.

"I want to have another stab at booking Thomas."

Oplitova fought in vain to stifle her sigh. "Oh, Sir, do you think that's wise? I mean, there's absolutely nothing on her. We've pretty much exhausted all the possible avenues."

"Not all the avenues. We haven't arrested her for conspiracy to blackmail—yet."

"And you want me to do the honours?"

"Well, you were the officer assigned to the case. Unless, of course, you don't think you're up to it."

"Of course I'm up to it. I just—don't agree with it."

Crowe was about to suggest taking her off the case when a thought struck him. She was right, there was little chance of Thomas being charged, it was just another token gesture to make it look like they were doing something. Someone, though, was going to have to take the blame for another failure and if he took her off the case, fingers would be pointed at him.

"Well, we all have to do things we don't agree with, occasionally. Tell you what, I'll get Mellor to go with you. You don't have to do the questioning if you don't want."

Crowe checked his watch. "With any luck, she'll still be in bed and she won't be thinking straight. She'll be wondering what the hell is going on. Hopefully, that dog of hers won't bite you." He laughed.

Closing the door behind him, Crowe continued to walk along the corridor, knocking on each door he passed, then looking in, until he found Melllor.

The second Crowe was back in his office and sat down at his desk, he reached across and picked up his phone. At last, he'd cottoned on to the fact that he had to beat Sexton at his own game if he was going to survive the axe when it inevitably fell.

"Chief Constable, it's Inspector Crowe."

"Oh, I was just about to ring you, Bobby."

Crowe laughed, pretentiously. "I just wanted to give you my news, Sir."

"Your news? Yes, I—."

"It's about Thomas. Mellor's gone to bring her in for questioning."

"Oh. What made you change your mind?"

"Well, I'd been thinking about what you said, Sir and thought it was about time I acted on your advice."

"Do you think you can make it stick this time?"

"Absolutely certain, Sir." As soon as he said this, Crowe realised for the first time just what it would mean if they were able to arrest Thomas. For a start, the headlines would be deflected from him and any pending further inquiry would be delayed, perhaps indefinitely. And if he could take the glory, then it would surely influence the outcome of the inquiry if, and when, it eventually came.

"Glad to hear it. Now, about the other matter. What I was going to call you about."

"Other matter? What other matter?"

"Well, not to put too fine a point on it, Brady."

"Oh, that."

"Yes, that."

"Well, what about it, Sir?"

"I don't know how it got leaked out, but I suggest you find out pretty damn quick. To save your own neck as much as anything."

"Oh, absolutely, Sir."

"There's going to have to be another inquiry, you understand that don't you?"

"Yes, Sir. It's the only way forward as far as I can see."

"Good, because it's your neck on the block again. However, in light of your news, I think it might be wise to delay this until after Christmas at the very earliest."

"Yes, good idea, Sir."

"Well, we want to be grabbing the headlines in a positive light. If we launch another inquiry now and go public, it's likely to overshadow what you're doing. And we don't want or need that, do we?"

"No, Sir, we most certainly do not."

"Good. Glad we're singing off the same hymn sheet about this. Good luck with the arrest, Bobby and I look forward to hearing about it on the six o'clock news. There could still be a promotion in this for you, if you play your cards right."

"The best Christmas present ever, Sir. Chief Inspector Crowe. Has a certain ring to it, don't you think?"

"It certainly does. Well, cheerio then, Bobby."

"Cheerio, Sir."

CHAPTER THIRTY-TWO

Jane was in the kitchen doing the dishes. She'd had some friends over the previous night and had awoken to find a stack of washing up by the sink, plus the odd cup and plate scattered around the living room. It was a kind of tradition that they went through every Christmas. So much had happened over the previous twelve months, much of it positive, that for many of the protestors, it felt like a celebration. Jane, however, couldn't help but think about the innocent party. For them, nothing much had changed. She'd tried to make the point several times to her friends the previous night, but as the wine began to take effect, her protests were dismissed and eventually she allowed herself the luxury of forgetting about her troubles and joining in with the fun. It had done her good to make merry, there was no doubt about it. It was just that now, in the cold light of day, she just wished she'd made them tidy up after themselves.

As the final glass entered the hot, soapy water, she started to think about her plans for the day. It was only ten days to Christmas and she always enjoyed looking round the shops when they were decorated, despite being acutely aware that it was all designed to make people part with money they didn't really have.

The doorbell. Bemused, she walked across to the window and, on seeing the police car, felt her heart sink.

"Hello," Jane said with a polite smile, feeling slightly out of breath from her dash down the stairs. Recognising D.S. Mellor, her false smile quickly went the same way as the high spirits she had woken up with.

"Jane Thomas, I'm arresting you for conspiracy to blackmail—."

"What?"

"You have the right to remain silent . . ."

Mentally reciting her rights before Mellor reeled them off, Jane stood there patiently and waited for him to get on with it.

"I have a warrant here to search the premises." He handed Jane a blue piece of paper with black hand-written notes.

"You'd better come on in then," Jane said, once satisfied that everything was legit. The journey up stairs was decidedly more challenging than the descent and she struggled to keep up with the barrage of questions. Once back in her flat, she needed to take a moment to get her breath back before she could continue.

Mellor noticed she was struggling, but decided to ignore it. He proceeded to examine every nook and cranny of Jane's flat, going through her cupboards and private things like they were little more than rubbish at a tip.

Once satisfied that she was not harbouring whatever evidence it was he was searching for, he walked over to her computer and declared he was confiscating it. "I'll be needing your phone as well," he said, once Jane had finished disconnecting her computer and got up off her hands and knees. Without comment, Jane grasped her mobile phone and planted it firmly into Mellor's waiting hand.

With the computer under his right arm and the phone in his left hand, Mellor made Jane go in front. After Jane had locked the door and tested it to ensure it was secure, Mellor nudged her in the back and she descended the stairs. Once her computer and phone were in the boot of his car, he turned to her, grinned and said he needed to see inside her garage.

He treated the garage with no more care and respect than he did her flat. Jane looked on while he emptied the contents of cupboards and shelves onto the floor, kicked over old cans of paint and laughed when he came across anything remotely personal. It made her wonder if he really had to make that much mess and what kind of a man would enjoy doing this as much as he clearly was. She rarely ventured inside her garage as she kept her car in the car-park, but as she had no idea what he was looking for, couldn't say for certain that he wouldn't find anything incriminating.

When he emerged shaking his head, Jane momentarily felt relief, before the full extent of the mess he'd just made came into view, and all she could feel was indignation.

With the garage secure, Jane, who knew the drill only too well, got in the back seat and prepared herself for another gruelling day of going over and over the same old stuff.

Once at the police station, Jane was shoved into a hot, stuffy waiting room with hard seats and bare walls and made to wait for her solicitor to arrive. She was due to take her medication at quarter to nine, and, to begin with, still harboured hopes of being able to do so. However, as the minutes became hours, the consequences of missing encroached her thoughts. It had passed eleven by the time her solicitor, John Sinclair, arrived.

Sinclair spent a few minutes trying to reassure his client and giving her what he deemed to be the most appropriate advice, before disappearing into the video suite to examine the evidence. It soon became apparent that this would be a lengthy process, so Jane once again slumped down and did her best to pass the time without going insane. It came as a relief as much as anything, when, at one pm, Sinclair re-emerged and took her into the interview room next-door but one.

There were two of them. D.C. Lane, whom she was not familiar with and D.C. Clarke, who had interviewed her previously.

After starting the recording, and everyone had introduced themselves, Clarke turned to Jane and asked her to give her full name and date of birth. Feeling almost robotic-like, Jane did as he asked.

Clarke then went through the formalities, informing her of her right to legal advice and to take a break if she needed it. Finally, he reminded her that she didn't have to say anything, but, if she didn't, it may harm her defence and asked her if she understood why she was being cautioned.

"Yeah," Jane replied.

"Do you understand the meaning of it?"

"Yes."

"Do you just want to tell me what that is, in your own words?"

"Well, you know, if I don't tell you and it goes against me in court."

"Right, do you want me to tell you, how I see it?"

"No, I know what it means."

"Okay."

"I don't know if I can express it to you what it means, but yes, I know what it means."

"OK. As long as you're quite happy with that. I know that there are some medical concerns in respect of yourself, is that correct?"

"Yeah."

"While you're at the police station there's some medical concerns?"

"Yeah."

"And what's your position with medication at the moment?"

"Well, I should have taken a tablet with my breakfast about quarter to nine."

"Right."

"I have to have this to keep the cancer away and I have to have them every day."

"Right."

"Whether this will put me out of, I don't know the effects after, because I never take it after quarter to nine."

"No, when you take it at quarter to nine, how does it affect you then?"

"Well, you just have the ordinary side effect."

"Which are?"

"Ooh, hot flushes, plenty of things."

"No, I just want to know, what if you're taking your tablet later on today and you're in the middle of the interview and you start saying this is wrong, that's wrong. I want to know what to be looking for and what to be—."

"Oh no. It won't affect me like that."

"You know?"

"Doesn't affect the mind or anything."

"I don't want to be sat in an interview room with you and you're obviously in some form of discomfort or—. "

At long last, Lane decided to speak up. "You start feeling sick or—."

Clarke continued. "Pain or whatever."

Jane eyed up the desk in front of her and thought about hitting her head against it. "No, it doesn't affect you like that."

"You know, that's what I want to be wary of."

Time for Sinclair to shine. "If you do, we shall tell you."

"Okay Mr Sinclair, that's great. Do you fully understand the reasons for your arrest, Jane?"

"Not really, no."

And so it continued. Jane said she understood she had been arrested for conspiracy, but, when questioned, said she hadn't a clue what that meant.

They then went through first Jane's and then Clarke's definition of blackmail, Sinclair making the occasion supportive interjection on Jane's behalf.

Eventually, Clarke described what he termed the strict definition. "And it is a view to gain for yourself or another, or with intent to cause loss to another you make unwarranted demands."

Jane, who was slowly losing all will to live, replied, "Yeah."

"Yeah, now what we're saying is actions by yourself and others which is the conspiracy side. Yourself and other people have caused financial loss."

"Yeah."

"Well, that's the meaning, that's the purpose of the arrest. As long as you're aware of exactly what that is, because it goes a lot further than your definition."

Eventually, Sinclair decided to do something about the repetition, saying to Jane, "I think my advice at this time is just tell the officers what you intend to say and leave it at that. Not a lot to say."

"Well, I've been involved with this campaign from day one. I've gone up there when permitted, I've acted within the law and I've done whatever the police have instructed me. I've done what you're allowed to do by law. If the police have told me I've acted inappropriately, I've stopped doing whatever and that's it, that's my involvement. That's all it is."

Clarke needed more answers. "Right and you say your involvement is from day one. When was day one?"

"September '99"

"Right and what happened in September '99 that brought all this to a head?"

Jane continued to answer the questions as best she could.

"So, you've started going up. Who was involved originally? Who were you first meeting up with there?"

"I'm not prepared to say."

"From the first. Your first visits up there?"

"I know there was a chap called Mellor that was an infiltrator."

"An infiltrator was he?"

"Mmm. But we spotted him quite quickly."

"Be Careful, Jane," said Sinclair. "My advice to you is be a bit careful."

Ignoring the interruption, Clarke resumed. "I was going to say, how did you know he was an infiltrator?"

"You don't have to answer," said Sinclair, before Jane could open her mouth.

"No comment."

Clarke changed tack. "At the time when you started going up there, was the protest known under its current name or was that something that came afterwards?"

"I can't recall, to be honest."

"Right and you're not prepared to tell me how you found out about it. Oh, you're saying it came from the papers, yeah? You found out."

"Well, the media, yeah."

"You found out from the media coverage right. Not amongst members."

"Mmm."

"And you accept that there's been various publications on the Internet etc., in connection with that now."

"Yeah."

Forty-five minutes had passed by the time Clarke stopped the recording, got to his feet and said they'd resume later. It had been a gruelling session, testing everyone's powers of endurance and it was obvious that none of them could quite believe it hadn't even lasted a full hour.

Jane was taken back to the room she'd been in earlier. Sinclair sat with her at first, giving advice as he saw fit and explaining what he thought was likely to happen next. He'd just finished briefing her when Clarke reappeared, informing her that they were taking a break for something to eat.

By the time Sinclair had been through the CCTV evidence and they were ready to resume the interviewing, it was approaching a quarter to four.

Clarke pressed the record button, read out her rights and asked if she was feeling OK.

He started by asking about Jane's phone. If she had a mobile, if she knew the number and whom she conversed with. Jane sighed as the pointless questions came thick and fast. How many numbers she had saved on her phone and whether it was just her mobile or her home number too.

Clarke then read out a number and asked if Jane recognised it, to which she replied that she did not.

"Right, what other numbers have you got in your phone memory then? How many are we talking about, roughly?"

"Oh, ten, fifteen, twenty."

"And who might they be?"

"Anybody."

Clarke reeled off the names of some known protestors.

He then wanted to know the specifics of her mobile phone. What brand it was, her network provider, whether she used the messaging system and if it was contract or pay as you go. He even asked her how many calls she'd made and received in total, acting surprised when she didn't know the answer.

"What I don't want you to do is suddenly say at a later date, you've added these names, you've taken these names off, because you've got this conspiracy theory and I wouldn't want you to—."

"What do you keep looking at my solicitor for, quizzically, when you say things like that?"

"I'm waiting for him."

Sinclair spoke up. "He's waiting for me to explode and tell him for God's sake get on with this."

However, Clarke continued with his line of questioning for some minutes, before switching to Jane's car. When, finally, he got round to the campaign, Jane and Sinclair were as relieved as each other.

The second interview of the day lasted for a further forty-five minutes. At its conclusion, with the police making little, if any, progress, Jane was informed she could have another break before someone would come and fetch her for a third time. At this point, she still hadn't seen the fresh evidence that was the reason for her being there.

There were another four interviews, each lasting approximately forty-five minutes. It wasn't until the final interview, which started at twenty-five past seven, that Jane finally got to see the incriminating video evidence.

The video was of a young-looking woman who skipped across the screen, bent down, stood back up and skipped out of sight. There was then five minutes' footage in which Jane recognised herself, a small, plump, sixty plus female. No one in their right mind would think that the two shots were of the same person, but a walking expert had pointed out some similarities. Furthermore, the young woman on the first clip was allegedly planting a bomb outside a house. They were claiming this young woman was Jane. If it hadn't been such a stressful day in which her patience had been stretched to the very limit, she might well have laughed at how preposterous this sounded.

No one was surprised when, at ten past eight, Jane was released on bail. The bail date was set for 30th January, giving her the Christmas holidays to come to terms with being labelled a blackmailer. The Burton Mail did not hesitate to further degrade her reputation.

Christmas came and went with minimal fuss for Jane. She enjoyed the festive period as much as anyone, but without any children to dote on, it was largely spent chatting with friends and watching the usual drivel on TV.

Like anyone else, by the time New Year had faded into the dim and distant past, her thoughts had turned to the year ahead. Uppermost on her agenda was the fate of the innocents, the reason why they'd all been spending their Sunday afternoons protesting for the past six years. Her upcoming bail appointment at 10 am on 30th January didn't rear its ugly head until the middle of the month. Once it did, however, Jane could think of little else. Not that she was worried that she might be convicted or even face a court appearance. She was far too experienced a hand to concern herself with that possibility. If they'd found anything incriminating, they would surely have charged her before Christmas. No, what she was dreading and what was becoming particularly galling was the way they assumed she had nothing better to do all day than sit around waiting and answering the same old questions over and over again.

She reported in at Burton Police Station reception at ten am on 30th January, as instructed and was promptly subjected to almost an exact replica of 15th December when she'd been arrested for conspiracy to blackmail. Late that afternoon, she was released on bail until 27th February.

However, on the afternoon of the 24th February, Jane's solicitor phoned to say that her bail had been cancelled and there was no need to report into the police station on the 27th. Her solicitor did warn her though, that the investigation had not been brought to an end and they were waiting to hear about a number of enquiries that might result in her being seized for questioning again.

After hanging up, Jane smiled to herself as she considered how little had changed from one year to the next.

CHAPTER THIRTY-THREE

27TH FEBRUARY 2006

For what was probably the first time in his career, Crowe left home already late for the Monday morning team meeting that he had called the second he heard about Thomas' latest release without charge.

Make no mistake about it though, Crowe's tardiness was not his fault and he felt sure every member of his team would understand if he felt inclined to offer an excuse, which, in all likelihood, he would not. Johnny had been sent home sick from school the previous Friday and had spent all weekend in bed. Both Crowe and Susan were starting to face up to the fact that he was undoubtedly a sick boy and craved a diagnosis more than anything.

Yesterday afternoon he'd been really sick, making his pillow squelch as his stomach pains led to tears of agony. Fortunately, Johnny was not having trouble sleeping, so Crowe could not use that as an excuse for his red-ringed eyes or for the way he went back to sleep after knocking off the alarm. No, his wife had been so distressed about it that they'd laid awake holding each other and talking intermittently as Crowe did his best to reassure her that it was probably something and nothing and that by the time his next birthday came around, he'd be outside playing with his friends like any normal seven-year-old.

While he felt confident he could ignore the inquisitive looks he was bound to receive (only Sexton would dare question him and he wasn't going to be present.) Crowe was worried that his mind felt clouded over. He wished he'd had the foresight to plan the meeting for a little later, say eleven o'clock, which would have given him time to re-familiarise himself with the intricacies of the case. With the details absent from his better judgement, he would hardly be in a position to uncover what went wrong, which would be the platform with which to devise an alternative strategy.

Although he had no intention of saying it, secretly, Crowe was determined cut Thomas some slack, and he was willing to fight his corner when inevitably, Sexton called to find out what the hell went wrong. Maybe it was time to admit defeat and put that little stunt down to a gross misjudgement. If they were to run the operation again, he'd ensure there was a credible suspect first and not rely on the creative questioning of his staff, however skilled they might be.

He was determined that they were going to move on, put the affair behind them and do their best to help it fade away from public view. What they needed instead was to make a statement. A few marquee arrests with serious convictions that would reassure the public that everything was in order.

Sexton, when he came calling, would let him off the hook if he could come up with a credible plan of action, he felt sure of it. The problem was convincing the troops on the ground that they were doing an excellent job, maintaining morale without disclosing to them the truth. Parking his car neatly in between a green BMW and a red Fiat, Crowe turned off the engine and looked over his shoulder at the entrance to the police station. As far as he could recall, it was the first time he had sat there in his space, observing people coming and going. It was also the first time he'd had to squeeze out of his car on a morning. It felt like he was stepping into an alien world.

"Good morning," he said to the duty sergeant, who was busy searching for something on the shelf below the desk.

"Oh, good morning, Sir," the sergeant replied, waiting for Crowe to turn into the corridor before glancing at his watch.

Approaching his office, Crowe heard chatter, with the odd burst of laughter thrown in for good measure. By the time he had his hand on the handle, he knew everyone was in his office waiting for him to arrive. With a mischievous grin, he held his breath and turned his ear to the door. Just as he'd thought, he was the butt of everyone's jokes. Feeling more determined than ever to make this morning tardiness a one off, he silently opened the door before bursting in and making a grand entrance. This time it was he that was laughing as everyone suddenly fell silent and sat upright like they'd been waiting for him patiently in exam conditions.

"Good morning, everyone," Crowe said, marching towards his desk and acknowledging the mumbled greetings one by one. He did notice when one of his officers whispered something in the ear of the officer sat next to him, causing him to burst out laughing, but on this occasion, chose not to draw attention to it by making him explain the joke to everyone as his old headmaster might have done.

Being the senior officer present, Crowe exercised his right to keep everyone waiting. Grasping the top few documents from his in tray, he pretended to be reading them while he attempted to tune up his mind ready for the day ahead. It wasn't long before it all came flooding back, just a couple of minutes, so eventually, after clearing his throat as a ploy to gain everyone's attention, he opened the staff meeting.

"OK everyone, sorry for keeping you all waiting. As I'm sure you're all aware, we've failed miserably in our attempts to arrest Jane Thomas." He glanced round at everyone, holding his gaze slightly longer on the officers that conducted her most recent questioning.

"The goal posts have shifted slightly and we're no longer under so much pressure to bring these—thugs to justice, but last year we created a situation for which people are still waiting for a resolution."

A round of nodding and grunted agreements ensued before Crowe continued, unchallenged. He couldn't help letting his internal smile flicker across his face as he observed the way in which they were all pretending to know what he was talking about in order to save face. He loved this feeling of power. For the first time in months he was reminded of just why he'd joined the force to begin with and all the self-doubts that had been manifesting evaporated, temporarily at least.

"So, I have decided to forget about Thomas for now and focus our attention on those that have some kind of back story." Crowe was surprised at how this appeared to lift everyone and, as if by magic, they suddenly became more engaged.

"Do you have anyone in mind, Sir?"

Crowe nodded and listed four of the most notorious protestors.

"Oh, good idea, Sir."

"I'm hoping that this shift of emphasis will help to ensure that our shortcomings—go unnoticed. If we can get these hefty jail sentences, people might just assume their involvement in the incident we err—created and it will be left as another unsolved crime, leaving us free to finally put this to bed."

Crowe got to his feet and, grinning from ear to ear, took a pantomime style bow as everyone cheered.

Waiting until he once again had everyone's attention, he added, "And, make no mistake about it, anyone directly involved in bringing the famous four to justice will have my personal recommendation for honours."

This got everyone even more excited. Feeling pretty proud with himself at the way he had not only overcome difficult circumstances, but also given his troops a much-needed morale boost, Crowe brought the meeting to an end. Watching them stand up and bid him good morning one by one, Crowe half expected to hear a chorus of For He's A Jolly Good Fellow.

Once he was firmly sealed in his office and the footsteps and chatter had receded along the corridor, Crowe walked across to the window and let in the spring like atmosphere of the day outside, before returning to his desk, whistling a few bars of For He's A Jolly Good Fellow, and lighting a cigarette. The long, slow drag seemed to hit the spot with pinpoint accuracy on such a fine late winter / early spring morning.

True, he had a long day ahead. The paper work on his in tray wasn't going to sort itself out and Sexton was bound to call later. But the thought of what could be a difficult conversation only served to fuel his sense of self-satisfaction, after the way he'd acted to save his own skin. Now, when Sexton served up another reminder that the pressure was mounting, he had a potent return.

It was mid-afternoon when Sexton called. Crowe took great delight in once again changing the focus of the conversation onto what they were planning next rather than their latest abject failure to deliver the killer punch.

Sexton did succeed in bringing Crowe crashing back down to earth, although, ironically, it had nothing to do with Thomas.

"How's your son these days, Bobby?" Sexton asked, demonstrating his knack of sounding genuinely concerned while making it pretty clear that this was a leading question.

Feeling himself plummet down a dark and bottomless pit, Crowe was momentarily lost for words.

"Bobby, is everything, OK?"

"Oh, yes, Sir. Everything's fine. Johnny, my son is—fine too, Sir. Thanks for asking. And err, how's your son?"

"Oh, he's won an award . . . "

CHAPTER THIRTY-FOUR

MAY 2006

Crowe took a swipe at the alarm clock that was blasting out his moment of reckoning, informing him that it was time to pay for the previous night's misdemeanours. After sending it tumbling to the floor, and turning on the radio in the process, Crowe turned over, smiling like a sadistic rat-catcher that had just found four huge, elusive animals in his carefully laid trap.
"You'll be late," Susan said quietly, conscious of the fact that Johnny was laid fast asleep in the next room.
"I—I'm not going in to work today. I have a wee headache."
Susan smiled. In all the time she'd known him, he'd never been hung-over before. "Well, I'm glad you enjoyed yourself, but—."
"Shhh!!!!!" Crowe thrust his arm across his wife's chest as the radio presenter announced it was time for the six o'clock news. Beaming, he leaned out of bed and cranked the volume up. Susan immediately protested that Johnny was asleep, but Crowe wasn't listening. At that moment, not even an earthquake or an onrushing mega-tsunami

would have grasped his attention. Seeing her protests were in vain, Susan put her hands over her ears and turned to face the window.

"Four protestors were jailed for a total of forty years at Nottingham Crown Court yesterday . . ."

Still smiling, Crowe sat up. He'd been listening to this radio station pretty much all his adult life and he could remember when this particular news reader was a junior presenter. Never before, though had he felt such an adoration for her silky, almost erotic voice. Glancing at his wife, he wondered if or when she was going to say something to send him into such a spin.

Stretching a leg across the warm void that his wife had just left in his bed, Crowe came to terms with the fact that he had to get up. He couldn't go taking time off whenever he felt like it. And anyway, once at the station, he'd be surrounded by people that understood how he was feeling. Sitting up straight, he was about to clamber out of bed when a bolt of pain struck his temple. For the first time that morning, he realised that he might have to take the day off, so once again slid under the covers.

Some time had passed before he next opened his eyes. The light coming in through the gap in the curtains was that bit stronger, his headache felt a little less dagger-like and in his mouth, the saliva had turned extra thick. He was starting to wonder if he'd dreamt up the whole thing when the door opened and Susan burst in. She was carrying a glass of water and a foil strip of tablets.

"Come on, take these. I'm not having you moping round the house all day. Believe me, you'll thank me for it later."

Crowe glanced at the alarm clock, which had been picked up and placed on top of the drawers by his side of the bed. "But, I'm already late."

"Nonsense. Take these and get off to work."

Five minutes later, when the water had settled in his stomach, Crowe decided he'd had enough of lying in bed and forced himself to get up. The second he stood up straight, he knew he'd made the right decision and started whistling 'Zippedy doo-dah' while getting dressed.

Finding himself stuck in traffic, Crowe leant forward and beat the steering wheel in frustration. He glanced across at a woman in the car next to him. She had a car full of screaming kids and was trying to keep them entertained by singing a song. Racking his brains to find a song with a suitable melody, for some reason, Crowe stumbled across the image of Buster Bloodvessel doing the can-can. That's when it all came flooding back. Resting his forehead against the steering wheel, he cringed as he came to terms with the fact that he just might have made a bit of a fool of himself the previous night. Even worse, he seemed to recall ordering everyone to attend a team meeting in his office. They were all going to be sat round his desk waiting for him. On the positive side though, he wouldn't have to explain to anyone why he was late.

After breezing through reception and taking a few steps along the corridor to his office, Crowe heard voices emanating from behind his door. As he got closer, he could clearly tell that they were laughing, talking about the previous night as much as the convictions. Crowe would later go on to remark that he didn't know why he did what he did; it just felt like the right thing to do at that moment.

Crowe flung open the doors and, seeing that all eyes were on him, immediately started singing the Can-Can, "da, da, da . . . " Then, pinching the material at the top of his trousers, just above the pocket on his hip, he pulled his hem upwards, revealing about four inches of bare, hairy leg above his black ankle socks. The others looked on agog as he proceeded to dance the can-can all the way from the door to his desk. By the time he sat down, he was red as a beetroot and struggling to get his breath back.

"Good morning, everyone," Crowe said, once he'd fully recovered.

"Good morning, Sir." Everyone replied, trying to ignore the awkward atmosphere.

"So. We had some good news yesterday. Would anyone care to remind me what it was?"

Everyone laughed.

"Anyone?"

Eventually, a young sergeant, who had not witnessed Crowe's drunken antics the night before, got to his feet and read out the four convictions.

"Mark Holgate twelve years."

Everyone cheered. "Hooray!"

"Linda Finch twelve years."

"Hooray!"

"Phillip Bleasdale twelve years."

"Hooray!"

"Jessica Bolton four years."

"Booooo."

Deciding it was time to reassert his authority, Crowe gestured for everyone to be quiet. When he had their undivided attention, he said, "OK, well done everyone. I'm going to see to it that everyone involved in these arrests gets some recognition. I think you can all give yourselves a big slap on the back."

Everyone nodded and smiled before recommencing with the chatter. "Ok, so go on, get back to your work. Trust me, you will all be rewarded for this."

As soon as the door closed and he was alone, Crowe lit a cigarette, pushed his chair right back and took a long, slow drag, this time with his boots up on the desk. He'd waited a long time for this moment and it felt even better than he'd imagined, even though Thomas had got off Scott free. Reflecting on the way he'd felt earlier, he was glad he'd motivated himself to go to work; it had been well worth the effort. Susan had been right. Maybe on the way home, he'd call in at the florists and buy her something to say thank you.

This celebratory atmosphere continued for the rest of the day. In all the time Crowe had been with The Force, he'd never known a day like it. The nearest thing would be the Friday before the Christmas holidays when everyone, even the criminals, were in high spirits and feeling unusually generous to all they came across. To Crowe, this was a vindication and meant that he could stop worrying about losing his job and falling behind on his loan repayments.

It was approaching three when the phone call came, by which time Crowe had stopped worrying about Sexton as a threat, and had convinced himself that he could still be in line for promotion.

"Bobby!"

"Oh, Chief Constable. Nice to hear from you, Sir."

"Well I heard about the convictions and was just calling to congratulate you. I always had faith in you. I knew you'd get there in the end."

"Really? I was starting to worry— ."

"Never going to happen, believe me."

"Oh, thank you, Sir. That comes as a great relief."

"So what's the plan of action?"

"Plan of action? Afraid I'm not quite with you, Sir"

"Well, there's still a few odds and ends that need tidying up. There's the small matter of the—."

"Of Course." Crowe felt himself blush. "I'd completely forgotten."

"Perfectly understandable. That's why The Force needs someone to remain aloof and focus on the bigger picture."

"And you do a splendid job at that, Sir. The Force is truly blessed."

"Take my advice. Get it sorted, pronto. Blame it on the protestors and it will look like an admission of guilt—and defeat. Just say that one of the convicts came clean in an interview and get your man to break the news to the Jeffries."

"Oh, good idea, Sir."

"Oh, and just one more thing."

"What's that, Sir?"

"I've been under increasing pressure to reopen the enquiry into the Brady affair. I managed to delay it until after the court case, but I'm afraid I can't put it off any longer."

"Oh." Crowe felt himself plummet from the clouds and hurtle towards a particularly busy stretch of motorway.

"Bobby? You OK?"

"Yes, Sir. Why wouldn't I be?"

"You went quiet. And your voice has gone decidedly flat."

"Can't imagine why. I hadn't realised, Sir."

CHAPTER THIRTY-FIVE

Making yet another of his mid-morning starts, Crowe breezed into work, said hello to the sergeant behind the reception desk and made his way along the corridor to his office. He'd only taken a couple of steps, when the roar of a boiling kettle began to fill the air and he noticed the kitchen door was wide open. There were no voices though, meaning that whoever was there was on his or her own.

Feeling unusually nosey, as he passed the kitchen, Crowe couldn't resist looking in. "Oh. Alena. How are you?"

D.C. Oplitova was sat at the table reading the newspaper as she waited for the kettle to boil. Startled by the interruption, she looked over her shoulder and smiled at her superior officer. "Good morning, Sir. I'm very well, thank you."

Crowe noticed that she didn't return the compliment, perhaps suggesting that she didn't really feel like talking, but decided to approach her anyway. Standing behind her, he read the newspaper headlines which were all about the Jeffries. "She's home now, I see," Crowe said sympathetically.

Oplitova shrugged. "It should never have happened in the first place." She turned to look him in the eye and for the first time, Crowe noticed she'd been crying.

Placing a hand on her shoulder, he said, "I know. But they're in prison now, where they belong. I—I can't believe anyone would stoop so low. Those, they're not people, they're—. "

Oplitova got to her feet, sending his hand hurtling towards his hip as she stood. "This has nothing to do with the protestors. You ruined the lives of so many people, for what? For your own gain. Inspector Crowe, I'm not sure I want to—."

Crowe sighed. He really liked Oplitova. She was a good, honest police officer, a bit too honest for her own good. Unfortunately, she had to be stopped before she became a problem. "Alena, you're upset. You don't know what you're saying."

Ten minutes later, he was smoking his morning cigarette when he noticed his answer machine was flashing. For some reason, he felt a chill. When people leave messages it's rarely good news. It could be Susan about Johnny or—. It was Sexton. He was starting the inquest and he was coming down later to discuss it. This wasn't the start to the day he'd been hoping for.

Things hadn't got any better by the time Sexton arrived in the afternoon. He'd had constant disturbances and, following some arrests for domestic violence, there'd been lots of shouting and screaming.

"Oh, good afternoon, Sir," Crowe said as Sexton made his entrance. Crowe could tell straight away that he was in no mood for jokes or making small talk. The steely determination in his eyes said he was determined to get to the bottom of this once and for all and that Crowe could be in for a rough ride.

"Good afternoon, Crowe," Sexton said, making himself comfortable in the chair at the opposite end of Crowe's desk.

Sexton spent a good half hour going through the formalities, asking over and over if Crowe understood what the allegations were and why he was being investigated. Crowe noticed the subtle change in phrasing. Last time Sexton had hinted that it was the whole station that was under investigation and that the outcome was a foregone conclusion. This time, however, his tone was entirely different. Indeed, at times, it even felt like they were in an interview, with Crowe being the suspected criminal party.

Sexton concluded by saying that just as before it would take roughly a month to complete and he should not be around during the process. This time, however, there was no offer to pay for a holiday in the South of France. Sexton just looked at him grimly and said, "I'm suspending you with full pay until the inquest is complete. Do you have any questions?"

"No, Sir."

Without warning, Sexton's demeanour change. "Bobby, we've known each other a long time. I don't want to do this, nor do I want to find you guilty of any wrong doing. I fully expect you to emerge from this completely unscathed. Go home, put your feet up and unless you know something I don't, relax."

This did nothing to reassure Crowe, who was beginning to suspect that he was in deep water. Once he arrived home, however, Susan gave him all the reassurances he needed. She was overjoyed to hear he was taking some more annual leave and immediately started making plans for decorating the living room. Crowe smiled and wished he'd given more thought to the possibility of going on holiday. Sexton might have stumped up again if he'd at least tried.

CHAPTER THIRTY-SIX

Crowe had a whale of a time while he was suspended. Susan, overjoyed and constantly swooning after being informed that he was taking time off to spend with her, was treating him like a god. At first, it seemed that Johnny too, after seeing how happy they were, had shaken off whatever it was that was troubling him, but he soon started feeling sick again when Susan tried him without the painkillers.

It only took them two days to decorate the living room, which took them up to the weekend when Susan's parents came round to make a fuss of Johnny on his birthday. When they heard about Crowe's thoughtfulness, they were hugely impressed and suggested Crowe and Susan make use of the time by decorating the kitchen too. So, the following Monday, they went straight to the D.I.Y. store and picked up some paint, kitchen tiles and new taps for the sink.

By lunch time Thursday, they were applying the finishing touches to the kitchen. It was a fine day, so Crowe went to the nearby shop, returning with a bottle of chilled wine for them to enjoy in the garden when Johnny was in bed. Susan, who was applying a second coat of emulsion to the walls thanked him, and, laughing uncontrollably, painted a stripe all the way from his fringe to his chin. She was still doubled over with laughter when the knock came. When they both turned to head for the door, Susan pointed at the paint stripe on his face and told him to stay put.

Crowe sat down at the kitchen table, and, thinking about how much fun they'd had over the past week, started laughing to himself. An old man, walking his dog, caught his eye through the window. He was looking quizzically at a police car parked outside Crowe's house. Feeling a sudden chill, Crowe held his breath to try and eavesdrop on what was being said at the door. When he heard Susan say, "Wait a minute, I'll just go and get him," his worst fears had been confirmed. He waited for what seemed like hours, but was no more than ten seconds, for his wife to appear at the door. All the joviality of a few minutes earlier had vanished, in its place an expression that was a hideous mix of shock and fear. "It's for you," she murmured, looking him right in the eye. "I'll err, just go and look on Johnny."

Crowe was astonished to see D.S. Mellor and Sergeant Clarke stood at the door. "Hello, boys," Crowe said with a nervous grin. "W—what brings you here? What can I do for you?"

Mellor took the initiative. "Robert Crowe, I am arresting you on suspicion of failing to report an accident in which you were involved. You do not have to—."

"Yeah, yeah. I know what I don't have to do."

Mellor continued. "Say anything, but anything you do say . . . "

When Mellor had finished reading him his rights, Crowe just stood there in stunned silence, while Clarke shifted from foot to foot nervously, perhaps wondering if he was going to have to use force.

"Oh, I get it. This is a joke, right? Oh, come on, lads, very funny. Now go on, 'oppit the pair of you."

Once again, it was Mellor that spoke. "If you'd just like to come with us to the station."

"What? Oh, come on. You can't be serious."

Clarke finally spoke up. Pulling a pair of handcuffs from his pocket, he said, "You're not going to make me put these on you are you, Sir?"

"What? This—this isn't a joke, is it? You're genuinely arresting me." The pair silently nodded.

"Well, in that case, come on. Let's get this sorted." He glanced over his shoulder. "Let me just go and tell the missus what's going on, OK?"

"OK. You've got two minutes, Crowe."

Swallowing his fury at Mellor's disrespect, Crowe marched up the stairs, turned left and continued into Johnny's room. Susan was stood in silent contemplation at the window. "I err, just have to go to the station, Love. There's just something that needs sorting out."

"They've arrested you, haven't they?"

"What—n—."

"Haven't they?"

Crowe nodded. "Yes. But—."

"I don't want to know. It's from when we were separated, I know it is. I always wondered how you managed to get back on your feet so suddenly and now—."

"It's nothing to do with that. But you're right, it's a misunderstanding about something that happened when we were living apart. It won't take long."

Susan shrugged at precisely the same moment that Mellor yelled up the stairs that his time was up.

"I've got to go, Love. Like I said, it shouldn't take long." With that, he turned around and stepped down the stairs, making a point of not moving too quickly.

"Come on, Crowe. We haven't got all day. Some of us have got homes to go home to tonight." Mellor said, with a grin.

Crowe walked in front of Mellor and behind Clarke along the driveway, getting into the back seat of the car, beside Clarke. It was just a ten-minute journey to the station, during which Crowe imagined every pair of eyes he saw was looking straight through the window at him.

Once at the station, Crowe walked between them as he had before, this time keeping his eyes affixed to the floor in front of him, desperately trying to avoid making eye contact with everyone that he came across. He was bundled into Interview Room Four, a room that he'd always hated and, after informing them of his intention to represent himself, was told to wait.

Without a watch, phone, his wallet or shoe laces, Crowe sat there staring at the plain walls, thinking about the cigarettes in his drawer just along the corridor. Would they let him smoke in prison if the worse came to the worse? Crowe felt sure they would.

From the light coming in from between the slats of the vertical blinds, Crowe guessed it to be around six pm by the time the doors burst open. Mellor and Clarke entered, the latter carrying with him a tape recorder which he placed on the table in front of him before sitting down.

"Can you start by stating your full name, please?"

"Inspector—Robert—Crowe."

"Robert Crowe, you have been arrested under suspicion of failing to report an accident in which you were involved, which could have prevented the death of Lisa Brady. Do you understand what this means?"
"Yes."
"What, in your own words, does this mean?"
Crowe repeated back to him the official definition of the offence.
"What were you doing on the night of 3rd December 2004?"
"I was playing cards."
"After that?"
"I went straight home."
"Did anyone see you?"
"No. It was about three o'clock. The roads were deserted."
"Would you be surprised if I told you we have a witness that claims he watched you get into your car and then knock over the victim?"
Crowe smiled. "No. You've been talking to Symons. He has it in for me."
"The witness has a grudge against you?"
"Yes. He err, claims I owe him money."
"And do you?"
"Most certainly not. He is trying to get me back for refusing to give in to his attempted blackmail."
"He claims you gave him money to try and buy him off."
Crowe laughed. "Oh, that's ridiculous."
"Inspector Crowe, using money to attempt to pervert the course of justice is no laughing matter. It is something to be taken very seriously, and as well you know it."

"Look, Sonny. I have worked at this station for nigh on thirty years with a hitherto unblemished record. Are you seriously telling me you're going to take the word of a lowlife piece of scum like Symons over mine? Do you think any judge in the land will buy this?"

Mellor thought about this for a second and, appearing to see Crowe's logic, said, "We have to follow every line of enquiry. You know how it is."

"Do you have any more evidence? Anything that might prove that I was buying him off rather than being blackmailed? Or any further evidence that I was involved in the hit and run?"

Mellor glanced down at the desk in front of him. "No, Sir."

"Then can I please go home and attend to my sick child?"

Mellor got to his feet. "Just one minute, Sir."

They left him alone in the hot, stuffy room to consider the ramifications. A judge would not take Symons' word over his. So, as long as they didn't find any other evidence, he had nothing to worry about. Crowe started to think about what he was going to say to Susan when he arrived home shortly, having done what he said he was going to do.

However, Crowe soon realised that when Mellor had said a few minutes, he meant forty or fifty. When, eventually, he returned, he was carrying a document, which Crowe knew to be his release papers.

"Sorry for the delay—Inspector. I err, had a brief chat with Chief Constable Sexton. The upshot is that we're releasing you on bail until one month today. Should any further—. "

"Yeah, yeah. I know the score. What did Sexton have to say?"

"He said, that he saw no reason to prolong your suspension and you should resume your duties as soon as the inquiry is over. Which, we expect to be sooner than anticipated."

"Ah. Splendid."

"So. You're free to go. See you back at work, Monday morning."

"Splendid, Mellor. Good man."

He'd never felt more pleased to see Susan. She was cooking dinner, with the table laid in the garden. Crowe was pleased that she'd taken him at his word that he wouldn't be too long, but he'd been a bit lucky on the face of it. He could have been at the station all night, and then her efforts would have gone to waste.

"I made this to say thank you for finding time to spend with me," Susan said after the meal, sipping a glass of the white wine Crowe had bought earlier.

"Don't mention it. I've enjoyed it."

"Yes. We've had a good time, haven't we?" She took a deep breath and glanced up at the twilight sky. "Shame it's coming to an end."

Crowe smiled, pleased that he at least didn't have to come up with an excuse to explain his early return to work.

"When are you going back?"

"Monday."

"Oh, at least we've got tomorrow then. And the weekend." She laughed. "You'd better get that paint off your face before then."

Crowe's hand shot up to his nose. "It's still there?"

Susan nodded. "Of course it is."

"Great. That's just great."

"Oh. Can't believe I nearly forgot to tell you."

"What? Tell me what?"

"The doctor's surgery phoned. They want to do a blood test on Monday."

"Oh. That's good news, isn't it?"

"Yes. It's just that I was hoping you'd be with me. Never mind."

"No. I want to be there. I can get time off."

"No, you can't. You have things to take care of at work."

CHAPTER THIRTY-SEVEN

Back at work, Crowe soon got back into the swing of things. The first day felt a little awkward. He still couldn't look at anyone that had witnessed his arrest, but as time passed, he soon came to realise that people saw it as just another arrest. As if nothing could surprise them about the world.

Someone had been going through his stuff, that much was obvious. Indeed, that was probably how they'd ended up with Symons' number. They'd been going through his contacts one by one, asking if anyone knew anything. And Symons, still feeling he had a grudge to bear, had said yes.

Sexton phoned to give him an update pretty much straight away. He'd said they hadn't found a thing other than what Symons had to say, but they had left some feelers out for more information. His tone was as reassuring as ever, and Crowe didn't suspect a thing, not even when, at ten thirty on Monday morning, he gave Crowe notice that he'd be down Wednesday afternoon to chair a staff meeting. It was evident that things had to change if they were ever going to restore what people perceived as being a tarnished reputation. Sexton assured him that there was nothing to worry about, but Crowe felt uneasy nonetheless. It wasn't the first time that Sexton had decided to make an appearance in a blaze of glory, but he'd never before given Crowe two days' notice. Something wasn't quite right.

Come Wednesday afternoon, and Crowe was in a panic. A bad feeling hung in the air, as if the entire building was waiting for him to get his comeuppance. Crowe couldn't quite put his finger on why he was so worried. Symons could be routinely discredited in court. The cards were stacked so high in his favour that it wasn't really worth pursuing.

When Crowe arrived back in his office from the sandwich shop, he found a few people already there, waiting for the meeting to proceed. Technically, people were not allowed to eat food at their desk, that was why there was a kitchen, although everyone did it. This made Crowe feel a little awkward as he crushed up alongside them and removed the cellophane wrapping from his roast beef sandwiches.

Crowe had never felt the weight of three people's presence more as he ate his lunch in silence, doing his best not to drop any crumbs. Five minutes later, Crowe screwed up the box into a tight ball and dropped it in the bin. Only then did he feel the need to break the ice, but he was saved from the trouble by a new arrival.

The downside to having the biggest office was that it was frequently used for meetings. Crowe wasn't always keen on having to relinquish some of his privacy, but it was a worthwhile price to pay. Quite typically, Sexton swanned in half an hour late, and Crowe had to bite his tongue as he took his place at the head of the table, demoting Crowe to the role of minute taker.

Crowe sat there in glum silence while Sexton went over the findings of the inquiry. When he got to Crowe's arrest, Crowe just grinned awkwardly at everyone in turn as he wished the ground would open up and swallow him.

In Crowe's opinion, Sexton was not great at chairing meetings. Not as good as he should be, anyway. He just went through the agenda as Crowe would have done himself. It took him an hour to reach Any Other Business, at which point everyone shook their head and started thinking about packing their notes away.

Sensing proceedings were drawing to a close, Sexton stood up and gestured for everyone to remain seated for a second longer. He then concluded the meeting by saying. "I'm going to be outside in my car for the next thirty minutes or so. If anyone has anything they want to add to the inquiry in confidence, now would be the time to do so." A brief round of chatter followed as people considered if they had anything to say. Crowe felt relieved when everyone shook their heads and said there was nothing. Crowe's gaze was then drawn to the window as, for the first time that day, his thoughts turned to Johnny. When he looked again at the table, there was an empty chair where Oplitova had been sat.

CHAPTER THIRTY-EIGHT

Making the short journey home from work that Friday night, Crowe found himself stuck in traffic. It had been a difficult week all in all, and he just got the feeling that the Brady inquiry could yet come back to bite him. Leaning forward, he beat the steering wheel in frustration at the traffic. There'd been some kind of accident, that much was obvious.

Despite the fact that he'd had to skip lunch and so his stomach was rumbling even more than usual at this time, Crowe was happy to have the thinking time his current predicament presented to him. It wasn't often he got the chance to think since he'd started arriving into work late every day.

There were two things foremost on his mind that needed urgent attention. The first was Johnny. He felt bad about having had to miss the doctor's appointment. They were now waiting for a follow-up consultation at the hospital. His wandering mind led him to think about what the consultant might tell them. Worst and best case scenario. He'd hate himself if it was bad news and for some reason, he couldn't be there to support his wife. No, he had to make that his top priority. Sexton would understand in any case.

A familiar car appeared in his wing mirror, stationary, four or five cars back along the road. After racking his brains, trying to work out where he'd seen the car before, he peered long and hard into his mirror to try and get a decent look at the driver. An evil grin surfaced as he recognised the driver as D.C. Oplitova. If only he could get a closer look at the registration, it might come in handy.

The traffic obviously wasn't going to move anytime soon. Crowe turned off the engine, opened his door and stepped out onto the road. The second his car door let out a resounding thud, the traffic in front started moving, prompting all those behind to sound their frustration at the hold-up. Chin up high, he walked briskly along the road until he came to D.C. Oplitova, who was leaning forward, attending to her radio.

"Oplitova," he said, rapping on the window.

"Inspector, Crowe," she called out, startled.

Crowe motioned for her to wind down the window as the car behind emitted a long, sharp and aggressive blast of its horn.

"You too," Crowe said, looking over his shoulder. "Oplitova. I'm glad I caught you. I had word from Sexton today. He's asked me to do an audit of all the cars. He wants to know who drives what, how many hours per day, average petrol consumption, that type of thing."

"Really? That's strange."

"All down to cost cutting, no doubt. Do you have your ID papers?"

"Yes, wait a minute." Oplitova leant forward and, after spending a couple of minutes rummaging around in the glove compartment, pulled out a laminated ID card with a photo of the car next to its particulars.

"Thank you," Crowe said, taking the ID card. "I'll err, make a copy Monday morning and get it back to you. Sexton will be pleased that

I've managed to catch you tonight. He's a bit of a workaholic you know."

"I can imagine, Sir. Thank you."

"Thank you, Oplitova," he said, turning to face his car further along the road. The drivers he passed were even more aggressive on the return journey, a couple of them winding down their windows just to hurl abuse at him. Crowe smiled as he wondered how they would react if he suddenly produced his badge. As it was Friday though, and he was now more hungry than ever, he decided not to. He made a mental note of the registration numbers though, just in case he should come across them again.

When, eventually, his car started to move, Crowe wondered how best to utilise this new found knowledge. It wasn't until he passed a car lot, the one owned by a member of the card syndicate, that the thought occurred to him. Whatever Oplitova had told Sexton, it could send him to prison. By hook or by crook, he had to find a way of silencing her.

By the time he arrived home, Crowe was famished. He was delighted to find a smile and his food on the table waiting for him. It made everything worthwhile.

"I have a date from the hospital," Susan said, sitting beside him at dining the table.

"When is it?"

"Thursday afternoon."

"Great. I'll let Sexton know."

"I'd appreciate that, really I would."

As Susan was clearing away the plates, she stepped from the dining room into the hallway, reached to the small table her mother had bought them for an anniversary one year and dropped a letter in front of him. "This came for you today," she said with a smile.

Eyeing up the thick brown envelope and ascertaining it to be from the CPS, Crowe felt his spirits sink, he felt short of breath and palpitations pounded his ribcage.

"What is it?" Susan asked, noticing his sudden change in expression. Crowe ripped open the envelope and pulled out a letter. It was a summons to attend court the following Thursday afternoon.

"Ohhh!" Susan buried her face in his arm as she expressed her frustration at the clash of dates.

Crowe smiled awkwardly. "I err, have to go out tonight."

"What? Where?"

"There's just something I have to do. Please don't ask questions."

"Oh, well OK. What time?"

"About ten."

"Will you be long?"

"Shouldn't be more than an hour."

***

Stepping inside the club he'd last visited over a year before, it all came flooding back. The dim lights, the thick cloud of tobacco, the barmaid's perfume and the sound of raised voices in a function room along the corridor.

"Inspector Crowe! Haven't seen you in a while. A whiskey is it?" The barmaid asked him with a smile.

"Oh, no—not for me, thanks. I'm err, not planning on staying long."

The barmaid gave a knowing smile, stopping short of muttering, That's what they all say.

"Is err, Pedro in tonight?"

"Pedro? Yes, he arrived about half an hour ago. You're in luck; he doesn't come every week anymore."

She started laughing. "Or maybe you're out of luck!"

"No, no. I'm lucky."

"Oh well, it was good to see you. Maybe I'll err—catch you later."

With the barmaid's scent following him, Crowe left the bar and walked along the long and winding corridor, thinking about all that had changed since he was last down this way. He didn't owe a thing to anyone for a start. At least no-one apart from the bank. Recalling how Pedro had once made him do favours, he paused, hand on the door handle, listening to the conversation on the other side of the door. At that point, he felt relieved that he hadn't brought his wallet. He stood, ear to the door, eavesdropping for a good thirty minutes until they started bickering and Crowe determined that they were between hands. "Surprise," he said, bursting in.

"Crowe," each one of them muttered without batting an eyelid.

"Pedro, my old friend. Could I have a word please?"

The car dealer got to his feet and glanced at everyone awkwardly. "I err, think I'll sit this next hand out, folks. I'll be back in a minute."

Crowe led him further along the corridor until he came to the emergency exit. He lowered the bar, pushed the door open and stepped outside. Pedro followed. Once he'd looked round to confirm they were alone and there were no eavesdroppers, Crowe said, "Pedro. I err, see you've been having a spot of bother with some of my colleagues."

"Yeah. They seem intent on punishing me for selling-on stolen cars. Wish all policemen could be more like you."

"I bet you could do without the law breathing down your neck in your line of business."

Pedro grinned. "What do you have in mind?"

"Tell me, do you know anything about cars?"

"Do you mean can I repair them? Sure? I started out as a mechanic."

"So you would know how to say, cut a brake wire. And make it look like an accident?"

Pedro's jaw dropped. "I—I know how to, but—."

"I could have all charges against you dropped and make damned sure the boys in blue don't come sniffing round again."

"Well, OK, but if I get caught—."

"You won't. I'll make sure of it."

Leaning in until his mouth almost skimmed Pedro's ear, Crowe gave him his instructions.

"And if I do this, you'll have all charges against me dropped?"

"I give you my word."

"How will I know which car it is?"

Crowe delved into his inside pocket and pulled out the laminated ID card that he'd got earlier from Oplitova.

Pedro scanned the ID card and grinned. "OK, you got yourself a deal. Pleasure doing business with you," he said, offering Crowe his hand.

"Likewise."

Crowe felt immersed by a massive wave of satisfaction as he stepped into his car. Last time he'd been sat in this car park, he was living by himself in a studio flat, with no family to call his own. Now he had a beautiful wife, a son and a house in an exclusive part of town. On top of that, he'd just taken measures to ensure he'd never lose them again. Feeling that somehow he'd learnt a valuable lesson, Crowe reversed out of the car park and turned on to the road. Straight away, two teenagers appeared from nowhere, causing Crowe's heart to miss a beat. When he calmly applied the breaks, stopping in good distance from the girls, he felt another demon exorcised.

Happy that he'd kept his word, Susan was overjoyed to see him. She flung her arms around him, kissed him passionately and told him over and over how much she'd missed him. Crowe smiled and said he'd missed her too. It just felt natural, then, for them both to climb the stairs and have a look in at Johnny who was sleeping soundly in his bed.

"Robbie, I know I don't tell you this that often, but you are a great husband and father. I know you have things to do, things that I don't really want to know about, but you always make time for us."

Crowe was about to reply when Johnny stirred. "Hello, Soldier," Crowe said scooping him up in his arms. "Daddy's fixed it so you're gonna have the best possible start in life."

Suddenly overcome with emotion, Susan extended her arms to take Johnny, whose head had dropped across his shoulder as his eyes closed.

Clasping Johnny's head in her bosom, Susan wiped her eyes and said softly, "Robbie. On Thursday. What are we going to do—if it's bad news?"

CHAPTER THIRTY-NINE

For the first time in weeks, Crowe arrived into work early the following Monday morning. He'd done a lot of thinking over the weekend, and he'd realised that he was starting to let himself slip again. He'd struggled to resist the temptation of the card game and had come to see that as a wakeup call. If he'd taken money with him, he might well have joined in. In Crowe's world, the margins were that fine.

Yet again, he hadn't slept well. Ever since he'd been arrested, he'd been having vivid dreams. Now and then, he'd been waking up, drenched with sweat and had to push the duvet right down until he dried. Secretly, he was beginning to suspect that something was wrong, but didn't want to burden his wife with any more bad news. She was struggling to cope with everything as it was.

That wasn't the only reason he found himself alone in the station at six thirty am. No, he wanted to find out more about the investigation into Pedro's car lot. He'd been lucky that for once there were no overnight detainees, meaning the station had been completely unmanned when he entered the building. As there was always someone lurking somewhere, this was an opportunity not to be missed.

As an inspector, people were duty bound to keep him abreast of what was going on. His signature was often required too, which was the reason for the vast pile of papers in his in tray. He knew that somewhere in there, was a document about the car lot—that's how he'd come to find out about it in the first place.

Once he found it, he could then trace the details using the crime reference number. The trouble was, the pile was so vast that it might take him all day to find it again. Glancing at the clock, which had already moved on more than he'd imagined, he sighed. If he was to make the most of this opportunity, he would need some luck.

His luck was in. Pedro's case was the fifth document he came to. Reading the case notes silently, Crowe tutted and shook his head. Pedro, it seemed, was a very naughty boy. The police officer part of him jumped to the fore, and he got the sudden urge to see him locked away for years. Then he remembered the deal he'd made and the reason he'd made it. He had to go through with it for Johnny's sake. Making a mental note of the crime reference number, he filed the document away at the bottom of the pile and left the confines of his office. The eerie silence produced an exaggerated echo as he made his way to the back office where all the original forms were kept.

Finding the filing cabinets locked, he went into the side room and fetched a huge bunch of keys. One by one, he tried them in the filing cabinet lock, with the clock seemingly on fast forward, until, eventually it turned.

It didn't take him long to find the original notes. He pulled out a pile of them, enough, it seemed, to fill about half a telephone book. He'd read roughly half before noticing that his heart was pounding extra hard. Furthermore, he couldn't work out why. Should someone come in and catch him, he was doing nothing more than reading up on a case. There's nothing wrong with that. Indeed, he might even argue that he was just being professional.

When he'd finally reached and read the final sheet, Crowe smiled, put them back in the cabinet, locked up and headed back to his office, feeling mightily relieved. Now, when he brought up the subject at the team meeting, he could justify the case for dropping the investigation. Should he fail in his quest, then the deal he'd made with Pedro would be void. Everything depended on Pedro receiving notification that the case against him had been dropped by nightfall. And there would be no second chances.

Back in his office, he sat sweating profusely under the open window for a couple of minutes before lighting up and digesting the new information.

At ten thirty on the dot, Crowe stepped into his office—he'd found arriving last gave him a grand entrance— and took his place at the head of the table. It felt strange to be chairing a meeting without anything concerning the protestors on the agenda. It felt even more unusual to be in a meeting where he didn't feel under much pressure. The first few items on the agenda were just the usual formalities. Health and Safety, legislative updates, that kind of thing. Then he arrived at items five and six, which he considered more interesting. After explaining to everyone that Sexton was conducting an audit of the cars and wanted everyone to leave them in the car park overnight (and successfully quelling the outrage), he progressed to item six, which was long running cases.

"It seems to me, everyone, that we have too many cases that we just don't have enough evidence to pursue. Following the business with the protestors and the successful conviction of those that we knew we could get from the start, I think we should make it our new policy not to waste time on cases we can't close. Does everyone agree?" Everyone nodded, smiled and said it sounded like a great idea.

Crowe continued. "Earlier this morning I took it upon myself to find some cases that are, to put it bluntly, a waste of police time. And I came across one—Pedro's Autos—that has been running for almost two years. From what I can see, there just isn't enough evidence to form a case."

The officer responsible spoke up. "But, Sir. Pedro is a known crook. Everyone knows that. It's just, I can't seem to—."

"Exactly. That's why you should be concentrating on cases you can close."

The officer nodded. "Well, I suppose."

"So, this morning, you can go round and tell him we're dropping the case."

"You'll need to sign a form for that, Sir."

"No problem." Crowe reached under his desk, produced a form, scribbled in some details, signed it and handed it across for the officer to complete. "And, sergeant, will you do me a favour?"

"Yes, Sir?"

"When you get back from Pedro's come and tell me what he said."

"Will do, Sir."

Observing everyone's faces as they filed out of his office, Crowe got the feeling, once again, that his new policy was going to be popular.

CHAPTER FORTY

Crowe soon started to form the impression that none of the others knew about his upcoming court appearance and he had Sexton to thank for that. He should really take it more seriously than he was. On the face of it, he could be about to go to prison for a very long time. If he didn't know better, he should be running round, frantically trying to arrange representation. That's when the thought occurred to him; he'd place far too much trust in Pedro. Trust which, so far, he'd done little to earn. As the girl had later died in hospital, if found guilty, the charge could well be escalated to manslaughter.

Somewhere between one and two pm, the sergeant Crowe had been talking to earlier came to report back that he had given Pedro the all clear.

"That's great news," Crowe said with a smile, "now you can get on with solving solvable crimes. What did he say?"

"He didn't say much, really. Just said to thank you and went back to his client. It was almost as if he was expecting it, Sir."

"Nah. Why would he be expecting it? Typical Mediterranean type, if you ask me."

"Yes, that's probably it, Sir. Not much sun or sea in this neck of the woods."

Feeling distracted, Crowe was grateful for the slow afternoon. Approaching six o'clock, he told himself that he would stop thinking about the prospect of going to prison once he arrived home and saw Johnny, that he'd be able to allocate its proper place in his priorities. But by the time he arrived home, he was more distracted than ever. Too distracted, even, to eat the meal which Susan had prepared for him in between looking after Johnny, who'd had another bad day.

She'd had his teacher round during the afternoon, and consequently, was now worrying about the amount of school time he was missing. Susan was obviously distraught, he could tell from her tone of voice and he last thing she needed was a husband with a sack of problems. At one point, Crowe thought about taking a trip to see Pedro, but decided it would be far too risky. If someone saw them together or any evidence that they knew each other was found, his cover would be blown and he wouldn't see Johnny again for a long time.

Surprisingly, he did manage to get some sleep that night, but not until Susan had been sleeping for hours. He just lay there awake, listening to the rain pattering against the window as he kept going over and over the various permutations of what he'd asked Pedro to do. Maybe with the weather being the way it was and with him being the Mediterranean type, he might decide it was too much of a bother and leave him entirely in the lurch. He should have planned for this. He should have had a solicitor waiting in the wings should plan A fail. On reflection, that was his problem. He had no plan B. It wasn't long after coming to this conclusion that his eye lids grew heavy and he started to doze off.

It was light when he awoke, drenched in sweat once again. Susan was still asleep, the birds were singing outside and his alarm clock told him he didn't have long. He gently reached across, knocked off the impending alarm and stepped out of bed.

Of all days, he'd wanted to ensure he wasn't late today and he recalled worrying about missing his alarm the night before as he lay awake, mulling things over.

It was roughly eleven when he heard female voices in the corridor outside his office. Leaving his desk, he went to investigate, finding Oplitova stood chatting about a case to another female officer. She was saying that she was going out to take the details of a reported burglary. And, as the crime was some distance away, she might be gone for a while. Crowe slipped back into his office, hoping he hadn't been noticed.

The rumble of Oplitova's car had only just faded away into the distant traffic when there was a knock on the door, and a young PC entered, wanting help with a case. Crowe was only too happy to help, as it was just about the only means of taking his mind of what was surely about to happen. He'd had no word from Pedro that the job had been complete, but he just got the feeling that the job had been done.

The young PC was with Crowe for just over an hour, at which point Crowe suggested he go for some lunch. No sooner had he left then the phone rang. Crowe swooped across his desk and grabbed the handset. "Inspector Crowe," he said down the crackly line and held his breath while palpitations pounded his ribcage. Much to his annoyance, it was a recruitment agency, ringing to see if he needed any help finding the right people. Crowe told them no, in no uncertain terms, and slammed the phone down.

Later on in the afternoon, Crowe had his head buried in some paperwork when once again he heard female voices in the corridor. He dashed across his office and opened the door to get a look. This time Oplitova and friend noticed him.

"Hello, Alena, how are things?" Crowe said, feeling a tad embarrassed.

Oplitova coughed, said she was OK and broke eye contact, looking down at the floor in front of her.

Crowe's initial reaction was relief, but once seated behind his desk, he thought about what her presence meant. It meant that either Pedro hadn't cut the brakes or that she'd been lucky. Up until that moment, Crowe hadn't considered that even with faulty brakes, Oplitova might still be able to testify.

The following day—the day before he was due in court—was virtually a carbon copy. After another difficult night, Crowe arrived early, kept an ear towards the door and sat chain smoking while Oplitova was out on a call. And, just like the previous day, the call from the hospital never came. She breezed in, mid-afternoon, totally oblivious to what was going on. Crowe was even starting to think that maybe she was in cahoots with Pedro.

Time was running out. He had to risk a conversation with Pedro before it was too late. "Sergeant, I'm just paying a visit to our friend Pedro, make sure he's behaving himself," Crowe said to the duty sergeant on his way out. He didn't often get to leave the station during the day, especially since the protests had fallen off the agenda. The sun was out and the birds were singing. It felt just like he was going for a mid-afternoon jaunt in the countryside, until he turned off the main road and into Pedro's car lot. Pedro, who was outside, showing a motor to a customer, grimaced.

Crowe parked his car and sat waiting patiently for Pedro to finish with his customers before making a move. When finally, he saw them pull out of the yard in a car which he recognised from the files as being stolen, Crowe stepped from his own car and closed the door as quietly as possible before venturing across the yard to the office, where Pedro was sat with his back to the door, filling in some forms.

"A-hem."

Pedro put down his pen and turned round, startled. "Crowe?" he whispered, "what are you doing here?"

"We had a deal, Pedro. My officer came round on Monday to explain we're dropping all charges. You were supposed to do something in return."

Pedro got to his feet and approached Crowe, who was stood in the doorway. Once he was close enough for Crowe to see his gold fillings, he whispered, "Yes, and I did."

It was Crowe's turn to whisper. "No, you didn't."

"I did."

"Then why is she still walking round?"

"Because your instructions were—you told me to make it look like an accident."

"What's that supposed to mean?"

"It means that the wire is frayed, not cut. It will snap eventually, you've just got to give it time."

"I don't have time, damn it. I'm appearing in court tomorrow. She could send me down for a very long time."

"You never said. Maybe it would have been better if I'd severed the wire completely."

"Well, you never said it might not have any effect on the car. Wait a minute—how do I know you're telling me the truth? I can easily have the case against you reopened. And don't tell me you're not selling stolen cars, because I recognise that car that your customers drove off in from the database we keep."

"I thought you might need some proof, so I took these." Pedro showed him some pictures of the frayed wire he'd taken with his phone.

"Give me that." Taking the phone from Pedro, he looked at each of the pictures closely before pressing the trash can icon.

"Ok, I believe you, Pedro. I'd best be making tracks."

"You've just got to be patient. With luck, it will snap in time but if not, well, you'll just have to try and get a retrial won't you?"

At last Crowe had a plan B. Feeling as much relieved as anything, Crowe left the car lot and headed back to the station.

Once back at his desk, Crowe realised that he had no choice but to leave early. Hopefully, Susan would still be at her mother's with Johnny, giving Crowe time to try and find some legal representation. Just as he'd hoped, the house was deserted. With the phone book on the couch beside him, he began calling each solicitor one by one. Eventually, at almost six o'clock, when he'd given up hope of even finding anyone still open, a man called Jacobs said he was available to represent him in court the following day. He advised Crowe to visit his office for a briefing as there were documents to sign which couldn't be done over the phone.

Jacobs had thick black hair, wore spectacles and spoke with a vague hint of a Geordie accent. It was evident from all the pictures on the walls that he'd been around the block a few times, knew what he was doing. Fortunately, he was the kind of man that didn't mind working long into the night if it improved his chances of winning a case.

By the time Crowe stepped outside, it was completely dark. Feeling somewhat reassured, he drove home, looking forward to seeing his wife and hopefully his son too, if he wasn't already asleep. That's when he remembered. His son had a big day tomorrow too. He wished that he could do something to give him the kind of reassurances he'd had from Jacobs.

Johnny was in bed, but Susan was sat up in the living room, waiting for Crowe to return. Crowe could tell straight away from the look on her face that she was worried about the trip to the hospital. He took her hand and told her it would be OK. It was all the reassurance he could give her, but it seemed to do the trick.

Needless to say, the following morning was frantic in the Crowe household, with everyone vying for the bathroom at the same time. Crowe wanted to scream out that he was in trouble and could they please give him some space to prepare, but knew he had to keep it to himself. He didn't have to endure it for long. At nine am, Susan and Johnny departed for the hospital, leaving Crowe with a further thirty minutes to psyche himself up.

CHAPTER FORTY-ONE

Coming home after a brisk morning's walk, Jane unclipped Suzie's lead and made herself comfortable on the couch. It was such a beautiful day outside that it felt a shame to waste it indoors. There must be something she could do outside that would give her skin a bit of colour.

Descending into a dream world, looking out through the window, Jane's train of thought had just taken an unexpected turn towards the protests, when the phone rang.

"Hello?"

"Hello, Jane, it's Stephen Smith. I represented you—. "

"Oh, hello, Stephen. What can I do for you?"

"I have some news which you might find rather err, interesting . . ."

"Go on."

"I've just been informed by my colleague, Peter Jacobs that an old friend, or should I say adversary is up in court today."

Despite her intrigue, Jane was indifferent. "Do you have a name?"

"Yes. I err —. "

Jane laughed as the anticipation began to bubble over. "Come on man, spit it out."

"Robbie Crowe. Inspector Robbie Crowe."

Jane gave a short scream as the phone slipped from her hands and tumbled to the floor. She could hear Smith talking as she stooped to pick it up. "Sorry about that," she said, embarrassed.

"I told you you'd find it interesting."

"Mr Smith, I can assure you that that is the most interesting thing I've heard this year. May I ask what the charges are?"

"I'm afraid I'm not at liberty to say, but you are of course perfectly entitled to follow proceedings from the public gallery. The hearing is due to start at eleven am. I know it's short notice but—. "

"Not at all. Mr Smith, thank you very much for informing me, but I have to go now to start getting ready."

"Of course."

Twenty minutes later, Jane was sat in the driver's seat of her blue Nissan Micra. She should really phone the others to let them know, but there hadn't been chance. Maybe if there was a hold up she'd take the opportunity to call round.

Jane couldn't understand why she was so happy, practically floating on air. Maybe it was because there was a keen sense that everything was about to unravel. Then a thought struck her. Usually, when a police officer is up in court, the media are swarming all over. For some reason, they'd managed to hush this up. This was fortunate for her, because if the whole world and his wife knew about it, she'd never get into the public gallery. But then, if she'd known beforehand, she'd have spent the night camping on the street to ensure she got the best view.

She arrived at Birmingham Magistrates Court in what seemed like no time at all. All the roads had been clear affording her the easiest of journeys. This did mean, though, that she hadn't had chance to phone any of the others, so she'd have to do the honours later.

On leaving her car, she walked to the front of the building, saw the queue and felt her heart sink. After glancing round, trying to think on her feet, she decided to join the back of the queue, because, however unlikely, that way there was more chance of getting in than if she turned around and headed straight back home.

She waited outside in the sunshine that was starting to become slightly too strong for her, until someone at the front heard a call and everyone began to move. Five minutes later, she was inside the building and five minutes after that, she could see the packed benches of the public gallery. When the final bench, the one right at the back, began to fill, Jane looked at the number of people in front and, noticing that there was an especially slender woman, thought she might just make it.

The clerk was looking increasingly worried that she was going to have to turn people away as she beckoned the waiting public forward, one by one. When Jane was front of the queue, in all honesty there didn't look to be enough room for anyone else. To her credit, the clerk spoke to a woman who had placed her bag beside her and space for one extra person was created. Walking into the court room, Jane was overcome by a strange sense of déjà vu. However, being in court without anything at stake personally felt strange.

The woman beside her looked decidedly well to do. She wore a dark summer dress and had long grey hair, tied in a plait. On her lap was a leather hand bag that looked as if it had cost more than Jane's entire outfit. "Busy, isn't it?" Jane said to the woman, eager to break the ice.

"Yes. It'll be because of the news. That's why I came, was it you?"

"What? Oh, no, my err- solicitor phoned."

"Oh!" The woman sounded most put out by this revelation. "Then haven't you heard?"

"I haven't heard any news today. What's happened?"

"Apparently there's been a car accident. One of the witnesses' brake wire snapped. A police woman by all accounts." The woman lowered her voice. "Very convenient, wouldn't you say?"

"What about the police woman? Is she OK?"

"Well, she's not in any imminent danger, but they do say she's lost some memory."

A sudden thought occurred to Jane. "Did they say her name?"

"Yes. Oppertov or Olitob or something else Slavic. Something starting with Op."

"It was definitely a woman?"

"Yes."

"Was it, Oplitova?"

"Could have been."

The man behind Jane tapped her on the shoulder and confirmed her fears.

The magistrates made their entrance, prompting all chatter to stop. At the front, Jane could see Crowe sat beside a stout, almost Dickensian looking man with thick black hair, whom she assumed to be Jacobs. When the chief magistrate stood up to read out the charges, it occurred to Jane that she still had no idea what they were. Failing to stop and report a traffic accident—hit and run. She never would have guessed that in a thousand years.

After pleading not guilty, Crowe was then asked by the prosecution to give his account of what happened on the night of 3rd December 2004. "As I've previously stated, I went to a card game, then went straight home."

"Your one bedroomed studio flat that you'd been renting because you'd lost your house in a game of cards?"

Crowe's forehead glistened with perspiration. "Err, yes. That is correct."

Once he had finished his cross-examination, the prosecutor, Hobbs, called his first and only witness. A dark skinned, well-set man with bulging muscles. Taking his place in the witness box, Symons struck Jane as being a truly nasty piece of work. Realising what this meant for the chances of prosecution, Jane stifled her sigh.

"Mr Symons. Could you tell me what you were doing on the night in question?"

"Yeah. I was err, out, on a stag with an old friend of mine. We went on to a club, so we finished later than planned. Then, on my way home, I noticed a young girl that I'd seen dancing in the club, staggering across the road. Then a car appeared from nowhere and err—slammed right into her."

"And what happened then?"

"I was waiting for the driver to get out of the car and call for an ambulance, but he didn't. He took a good long look through the windscreen and then err – drove off."

"Did you get a look at the driver?"

"Well, it was dark, so it's hard to say. But I recognised the car."
"Who did the car belong to? Can you point him out?"
"Yes. It belonged to—Inspector Crowe." Symons pointed at Crowe.
"No further questions." Hobbs returned to his seat and Jacobs took to the floor.
"Mr Symons, you said you'd been out 'on a stag' could you elaborate on that please?"
"Yeah. My friend was getting married the next week, so we'd been out celebrating his last night of freedom."
"So, you'd been drinking?"
"Well, I err, don't often drink, but on this occasion, just one or two. I know what I saw, though."
"Mr Symons, would you mind telling the court what you do for a living."
"Yes, I work in a dry cleaners. Simon's. My old man owns it."
"Is that your only line of work?"
"Well, I do the odd bit of—private investigating too."
"And what does that involve?"
"Well, people have problems and they pay me to err, sort them out."
"And does this ever involve violence of any kind?"
"Not violence, no."
"But you do use intimidation tactics?"
"Whatever the case calls for."
Excited whispers swept around the room as a rather smug looking Jacobs returned to his seat. From the public gallery, Jane observed him smile and exchange words with Crowe who was looking a lot happier than he had when he left the stand.

Just as the chief magistrate was about to call for order, Hobbs got to his feet and said he had further questions. The magistrate granted him permission to continue and a hush descended.

"Mr Symons, would you mind telling the court how you came to know the car belongs to Inspector Crowe."

"We've err, done business together."

"Done business? You mean he frequents your dry cleaners'?"

"Err, no. Occasionally, when he wants to get people to do or say something, he calls me to err—put pressure on them."

"No further questions."

Once again, the fat magistrate in the middle was about to adjourn when Hobbs stopped him in the act. From the public gallery, Jane watched him approach the bench and participate in a heated conversation with all three magistrates. This time it lasted around five minutes. When Hobbs left the vicinity of the bench, the Chief Magistrate called for Crowe to return to the witness stand.

"Inspector Crowe, " said Hobbs, "have you heard about the unfortunate road accident that happened earlier today?"

"Err, yes." Crowe glanced at the floor.

"And what do you make of it as the superior officer of the officer involved?"

"Well, it's a tragedy. I do hope she's OK."

"You wouldn't know anything about it then?"

"If you're asking me, do I think it was a stitch up, then the answer's no. But, she was receiving a lot of unwanted attention from the protestors that we'd been dealing with. So maybe they had something to do with it."

It was clear to everyone that Hobbs had Crowe on the run. Jane couldn't help but smile at his desperate tone of voice.

"Inspector Crowe, would you mind telling the court why you'd ordered D.C. Oplitova to leave her car in police grounds under the order of Chief Constable Sexton, when Sexton categorically denies giving the order?"

"I err—no comment."

"No further questions."

Crowe walked back to his seat, looking like a man that had the weight of the world on his shoulders. Hobbs, by contrast, strode across the court to approach the bench. After another heated discussion, the Chief Magistrate, rather reluctantly recalled Symons to the stand.

Hobbs once again took to the floor. "Mr Symons, have you ever done any work for Inspector Crowe that has involved D.C. Oplitova?"

Symons looked across the room at Crowe and grinned. "Yes. He asked me to rough her up and make it look like it was the work of someone else. Some protestors or something."

Jane could hardly contain her elation that the truth had finally come out and acquired some strange looks when she silently clenched her fist and gave a mini air-punch.

"And did you carry out this work?"

"Yes."

"How much were you paid?"

"Two hundred pounds."

"Thank you. No more questions."

As Symons left the stand, Hobbs again approached the bench. This time the conversation went on for a good ten minutes with all three of the magistrates making excited contributions. People around Jane in the public gallery started whispered discussions with the odd burst of laughter thrown in for good measure. Finally, the chief magistrate stood up and waved a hand. The court fell silent. He announced a thirty-minute recess while they consider the verdict and the new information that had been brought to their attention. Jane, however, like most people around her, didn't move a muscle.

Feeling like the only person in the public gallery that was directly involved in the case, Jane sat in silence as the gossip buzzed around her. The bench was hard, there were no cushions and she'd been toiling to make herself comfortable for the past thirty minutes. Just as it was becoming unbearable, the magistrates and solicitors reappeared and a hush descended.

"Robert Crowe, we find the evidence brought against you insufficient to charge you with failing to report a road accident, so we find you not guilty."

An excited chatter spread like wildfire around the court room. After roughly one minute, the chief magistrate held aloft his hand and the room fell silent again. "However, we do find there to be sufficient evidence to warrant a further trial, for the crime of conspiracy to pervert the course of justice. I therefore order the defendant to be tried for the aforementioned crime, seven days from today."

CHAPTER FORTY-TWO

To Crowe, it seemed like the whole world's media was waiting for him as he fought his way to his car, through the flashing cameras, while ignoring the multitude of microphones that were thrust in his face by reporters with just about every foreign accent under the sun.

It was a far cry from just a few hours earlier, when he had entered without a reporter in sight. When he finally made it round the back of the court building to his car, he sat for a minute in silent contemplation. He wasn't sure whether to celebrate or not. He'd got off Scott free for the crime he was being charged for, but the hearing had opened a whole new can of worms.

Once he had made his way on to the main road, he soon realised, however, that everything could be fixed with one phone call to Sexton who would surely stand up in court and back him.

By the time he pulled up on his driveway, he'd convinced himself that he was in the clear. Nonetheless, it had been a close shave and he needed some support from his wife more than ever.

The second he opened the door and took an expectant sniff, it became apparent that if it was support he was after, he was going to be left wanting. He trudged up the stairs, wondering where Susan was and wishing that on tonight of all nights she had been thoughtful enough to make him something special to eat. He found her, not in Johnny's room, but in their bedroom. She was sat on the bed, chin in hands, elbows on knees, staring at the floor. As he got closer, he saw that she was crying.

"What is it?" he said, sitting down beside her and placing an arm around her shoulder.

Susan buried her face in her hands and collapsed into his chest. "I've been waiting for you to come home all afternoon," she said, in between sobs.

"Why? What is it?"

Pulling away, she removed her hands and glared at him. "You've forgotten, haven't you?"

"Forgotten? Oh—Johnny. You went to the hospital this morning and . . . " His own ball of sobs ate his words. "That's it, isn't it? It's bad news."

Susan nodded. "Leukaemia. Our son has cancer of the blood."

"Oh, dear God, no."

CHAPTER FORTY-THREE

This time, everyone knew. There was no need for her solicitor to call, although he did the day before. By that time, though, Jane, along with several other protestors, were on their way to Birmingham Crown Court. They'd each brought with them a sleeping bag, having decided against the idea of forking out for a hotel. The last thing they wanted was to leave without seeing for themselves the action unfold.

Fortunately, it was a dry summer's night. Sat on the pavement outside the court, Jane talked about old times with the others. The common consensus was that everything had been leading up to this moment and that Hobbs, the solicitor working for the prosecution, deserved a medal for reinstating their faith in British justice.

Feeling very sore, Jane got to her feet at seven am on the day of the trial and, knowing she was among friends that would save her place, went for a walk around the block, returning laden with provisions.

An hour later and the media began to arrive. Many interested parties were there, most of them disappointed to see the queue of people that had been ready and waiting all night. The case was due to start at ten, so there was another hearing first thing, which, fortunately, proved to be a straight forward affair.

As the church clock in the distance chimed, people started to grumble, wondering what the delay was. That's when a woman appeared and gestured for them to follow her into the court room. This time, Jane was the first person to be seated, so she found herself on the front row with the best view in the house.

Once the legal teams and chief witnesses had taken their places in the front benches, it wasn't long before the judge and jury arrived.

Crowe was first to be called to the witness stand, who once again pleaded not guilty. Jacobs began the cross-examination, drawing attention to his unblemished record in the police force and the good work he had done in sending four protestors to prison. He used the kind of language that Jane had been hearing ever since she started protesting. Hate campaign, terrorists, criminals, and just like the others, he got away with it unchallenged. Then, he sat down and Hobbs took the floor.

"Inspector Crowe. One week ago, the court heard that you employed the services of a—hitman— to rough up one of your colleagues in order to further tarnish the reputation of the Save the Newchurch Guinea Pigs Campaign. Would you like to give me your reasons for doing that?"

Looking down from the public gallery, Jane saw before her a broken man. She'd read about his son in the newspaper and felt a strange affinity with him. Like they'd been through so much together and now everything was caving in on him. She wanted justice, but not for his son to get leukaemia. Some might say that this was God's punishment for the things he'd said about her in the newspaper, but not her. She'd never taken the idea of God very seriously, so why should she use it to justify what she deemed to be a twisted viewpoint?

"Inspector Crowe?" Hobbs was getting impatient.

"I err, was acting on orders from above."

"Orders from whom?"

"The Chief Constable, but—."

"Chief Constable Sexton, you mean?"

"Yes, but he was acting on orders too, right from the top."

"By right from the top, do you mean the Prime Minister?"

"Yes. He claimed he'd had instructions directly from the PM to put a stop to the SNGP."

"Put a stop to it? You mean sabotage the protest."

"Yes. Invent crimes, twist public opinion, that kind of thing."

"Inspector Crowe, let me get this right. You are claiming to be part of a conspiracy theory against the SNGP, originating from the Prime Minister?" Sniggering, Hobbs looked away, without making much of an effort to hide his incredulity.

At the back of the room, Jane noticed a man, perhaps a reporter, talking to someone on the phone, giving them live updates on the proceedings. When Hobbs ended his line of questioning, he marched along the centre aisle to Chief Constable Sexton, where he stooped to whisper something in his ear.

Hobbs appeared to wait for the man to resume his place at the back of the room before calling Sexton to the stand.

"Chief Constable Sexton, you have heard the allegations made against you by Robert Crowe that you were involved in a conspiracy to tarnish the reputation of the SNGP. Are these allegations true?"

Sexton shook his head. "Not at all. The man's an incompetent, clearly in need of a break from his duties."

"Why would he make such an outlandish allegation?"

"To save his own skin. He has some twisted views about animals and will stop at nothing to prolong their suffering. I think he gets some kind of kick out of it."

"In your opinion, is Crowe capable of paying a thug to terrorise a fellow police officer in order to increase the chances of further arrests and keep innocent people in prison?"

"Absolutely he is. And as for these conspiracy theories then—he's clearly living in cloud cuckoo land, Sir."

"Thank you, Mr Sexton. No more questions."

"Please, if I may, your honour, I wish to say something." Sexton called out to the judge.

"Very well, I'll allow it."

"On the night of 5th October 2004, the body of Gladys Hammond was taken from her grave. This was all Crowe's doing. He wanted to get back at a pensioner that had successfully filed a compensation claim against him and to tarnish the name of the SNGP once and for all. So, he ordered two of his officers to dig the body up and take it to Cannock Chase. He then claimed that a pensioner dug it up alone and dragged the body up four flights of stairs without leaving any evidence. And he didn't stop there. He went to the national newspapers and had the audacity to call her a hypocrite for choosing to have cancer treatment that was tested on animals. God knows what kind of sick thrill he got from this, your honour. If you need any further example of how far Crowe is willing to sink to fuel his —perversions—then this is it."

Jacobs immediately recalled Crowe to the witness stand.

"Inspector Crowe, can you clarify your involvement in the Gladys Hammond affair?"

"Certainly. In October 2004, I was contacted by Chief Constable Sexton, who told me he'd had orders from above to put a stop to the Save the Newchurch Guinea Pig Campaign, outside Darley Oaks."

"Darley Oaks being the farm in Yoxall, Staffordshire, where guinea pigs were bred for medical research?"

"That is correct."

"Inspector Crowe, I know this story was subjected to extensive coverage in the media, but for the purposes of clarification, could you just remind everyone present who Gladys Hammond was?"

"She was the mother in law of the Hall family, the family that owned the farm."

"And did Chief Constable Sexton instruct you to dig up the body of Gladys Hammond?"

"No. That—was my idea. I had to come up with something. I was told I could do anything bar having them bumped off." Crowe went bright red and became suddenly short of breath.

Jacobs looked concerned. "Inspector Crowe, is everything OK?"

"Yes. I err—." He mopped his brow with the back of his hand.

"Inspector Crowe, would you say the pressure put on you to put a stop to the SNGP was unreasonable?"

Crowe blinked, swallowed hard, took a deep, deep breath and said, "Yes. I'd say so. Yes it was." He lunged forward, resting his head on his folded arms atop the stand.

"Inspector Crowe, are you sure you're OK to continue?"

With a renewed sense of purpose, Crowe raised his head and stood up straight. "Yes, I'm OK. I don't need a break, no."

"Very well. Would you say you were encouraged to lie to secure a conviction?"

"Oh, all the time."

"Any examples come to mind?"

"Yes. On Sunday 31st October 2004, I approached Jane Thomas and asked her about the incident. She said to me in a jokey kind of way, 'you took her up, you find her.' I want to make it clear now that I misreported this. I said that she said 'Go dig up some graves'. I also doctored the date to make it read like she said it the day after the body was found."

"And you made this false representation of the facts under pressure from Sexton?"

"Yes, I would say so."

"How was this pressure applied?"

"Well he'd phone me and say that unless we secured a conviction, someone would have to carry the can. And unless I could find someone to blame it would be me."

"So let's get this right. In order to save your own skin, he encouraged you to blame someone lower down the ranks?"

"Yes. This—." Crowe took another deep breath and ran the back of his hand across his glistening face. "This is standard practice. If something goes wrong, blame a lower ranking officer."

Jacobs turned to face the judge. "No further questions, Your Honour."

In reply, Hobbs did his best to discredit Crowe, once again bringing to attention his attitude towards animals.

"Inspector Crowe, would you call yourself a supporter of vivisection?" Jane fought of the urge to cough as everyone waited for his reply in silence.. "Yes. I agree with experimenting on animals to further our understanding of medical knowledge."

"In your view, is it acceptable to sacrifice the lives of animals in such a way?"

Again he paused. "Well, I used to think—."

Hobbs repeated the question, more firmly this time.

"Well, I was brought up to believe that man was created to rule over animals, but—."

"So you disagree with groups such as Animal Rights, despite the fact that so many people, including myself, love animals and secretly support their principles? Instead choosing to brand them as terrorists in order to promote your own twisted agenda against them?"

"Well, I wouldn't say . . . " Crowe, clearly unwell, once again mopped his brow before spending what seemed like an age letting out deep breath after deep breath.

"Inspector Crowe—."

"No comment." Jane read his lips but heard no sound.

"Thank you, no further questions."

The judge then announced a recess while the jury considered their verdict.

Little under an hour later, Jane sat and watched in disbelief as Crowe was sentenced to five years in prison. At first, she felt surprised at how eager the judge had been to believe the evidence against Crowe, but then it dawned on her that someone had to take the blame to stop the truth from being heard—or believed. Feeling slightly aggrieved, she left the building wondering what she could do to help Crowe.

Once outside, though, her spirits lifted. As far back as the eye could see were protestors, chanting and holding placards, demanding the government act to stop the testing of drugs on animals. News had spread fast and now the media were using Animal Rights to protect the establishment. Picking up a newspaper from a seller on the street corner, she was surprised at how many famous figures had crawled out of the woodwork in support of Animal Rights and were clamouring for justice for animals.

When she arrived home, the first thing she did was check her phone. There were at least twenty messages from her friends and fellow protestors. It quickly became apparent that the court case had shifted the tide of public opinion and there could, consequently, be some momentum behind a fresh campaign to have testing drugs on animals outlawed. They decided to plan another march through the town centre to test out this theory.

Much to Jane's surprise, the authorities agreed straight away, so the following Saturday lunch time, two hundred of the hardcore turned up, but with the additional support picked up on the day, their number multiplied three-fold.

Following the extensive and for once positive coverage this received, there were similar campaigns right the way across the country and an online petition was started. When the number of signatures topped two million, it was debated in the house of commons. With a majority of over a hundred the bill was passed and it was written into that year's Queen's Speech that animals would no longer be used for testing or trialling drugs. What didn't make the headlines were the possible alternatives under consideration.

CHAPTER FORTY-FOUR

JANUARY 2007

"Are you absolutely sure you want to go through with this, Jane? You don't have to, you can cancel or just not turn up."

Holding her phone to her ear, Jane cast her eyes down at the document on her lap. It had taken three months to process, and in that time things had moved on. Now she had to see him, to give him the news and let him know that he had an ally.

Helen, one of her closest friends from the Animal Rights lot, was struggling to see her logic. She, along with the rest of them, still saw Crowe as the enemy. She thought he was getting everything he deserved and after all, what he was experiencing was nothing compared to the suffering the animals had had to endure. She just couldn't work out why Jane was being so generous to him.

For her part, Jane couldn't get the image of the forlorn and broken man being taken away for doing as he'd been told. He'd had the courage to stand up and tell the truth, and for that, they'd thrown the book at him. Jane couldn't understand how anyone could believe Sexton and not Crowe, but there were millions that did. Especially after the article in the Sunday Times. This included some of her oldest friends.

"No. I'm going. And there's nothing you or anyone else can do to dissuade me. He might not even know, about—. "

"Probably not. Are they allowed newspapers in prison?"

"I don't know. Probably not, but I've saved him a copy, just in case."

"Oh well, if there's nothing I can say to make you change your mind—."

"There isn't."

"Good luck."

"Thank you, Helen. That means a lot, really it does."

As it turned out, she almost forgot to take the newspaper with her the following morning. The engine of her blue Nissan Micra had just struck up a stationary roar, when she realised, and promptly dashed back up the stairs to her flat, noting, not for the first time, how hard it would have been for a sixty-two year old woman to drag a body up there alone without leaving any kind of evidence.

That was in the past now, but not forgotten. Today was part of the healing process. Her name had been dragged through the mud, simply because she was an inconvenience to someone. That woman that had spat in her tea, the man in the mall that had told her to fuck off, part of her wanted to find them and extract an apology, but she knew that would be sinking down to the level of those deemed to be of more importance than her. Crowe for instance. He'd let the fact that she got one over on him drive him to distraction, and now he was paying the price.

There was some justification in trying to seek compensation from the police, though. That's why she'd filed another complaint. There was a letter on her writing desk, informing her that her claim had been rejected and her arrests had been wholly justified. In other words, the old boy's network, of which Sexton was evidently a member, had stuck together once again, just as they did in court when it was Crowe that paid the price.

With the newspaper on the back seat, Jane started the car and turned on to the road. It wasn't a particularly long drive, no more than forty minutes with a clear run. Owing to the time of her appointment though, nine am, she would inevitably find herself stuck in traffic at some stage of the journey. The delay came sooner than she was expecting, pretty much as soon as she'd turned onto the main road that led into town.

Sat behind a blue car that was blurring out rap music, Jane's thoughts turned to Alena Oplitova. That poor woman that had become so disillusioned with the police. That was one thing she couldn't forgive Crowe for. In a culture of blame shifting, it was evident that he'd done his best to lay a trap for her, should the net fall in. she couldn't come to terms with how one human being could frame another just to save his own skin, but then, she wasn't a police officer or a politician so she wouldn't understand. The lights changed and finally, the car in front started moving.

Stafford prison was an intimidating red brick building with huge iron gates. After showing her identification to a man in a white booth, she was allowed in. On leaving the confines of her car, a sudden chill hit her. This prison was old school.

After much pleading, she was allowed to take the newspaper with her into the visiting area. This was a room about the size of a school hall, full of tables at which were sat some of the meanest looking men—and women—Jane had ever set eyes on. She was taken to a table slap bang in the middle and told to wait. Roughly five minutes later, Crowe emerged through the heavy doors and immediately started scanning the room to see someone he might know. Jane waved to catch his attention and he made his way across to join her.

To begin with, a wall of ice stood between them. "You're looking well." Jane hated lying to anyone about anything. But despite everything she had planned to say, once he was there in front of her, she felt strangely lost for words. His finger nails were yellow, he stank to high heaven of cigarettes, and his voice had a smoker's rustle. Furthermore, he had a cough that surfaced after every sentence he spoke.

"Am I? So are you."

"How are they treating you?"

His eyes appeared to glaze over. "Jane, I'm sorry."

"What for?"

"For the grave robbing thing, for all those times I detained you without any evidence, for dragging your name through the mud." He hung his head. "For saying the things I did to the newspapers." He let out an almighty, deep, rumbling cough. Then he doubled over, hand on chest.

"Are you OK?" Jane asked, concerned

"Oh, yes, just a bad chest that's all. Most likely a result of the inferior living conditions."

"It's OK—about the grave robbing thing. That's not why I applied for a visiting order."

"I—just assumed that you'd come for an apology. God knows you're entitled to one. So, what was it then?"

"I wanted to see if there's anything I can do to help at first—."

"You want to help me? After everything I've done? Why?"

"Because I owe you. You stood up in court and told the truth. That took courage, and for that you were sent to prison."

Crowe shook his head. "No, you don't owe me anything, but thanks. It kind of feels like all my friends have deserted me right now. I need all the help I can get." He broke into a grin. "You should put in a claim for the way you've been treated."

"Well, I've just had a claim for compensation turned down as it happens. I intend to take it further though. How's your son fairing?"

"Oh, that made the papers, did it?"

Jane nodded.

"Not so good. He . . ."

Jane reached across the table and grabbed his hand, attracting the attention of a police officer, who started watching them like a hawk. "He's started treatment. You know, the chemo." He broke down. "Jane, I'm so sorry."

"It's OK—Robbie. It's all in the past now. Your son will get better soon. I did."

Crowe smiled and looked up. "Yeah. Thanks, Jane."

"There was something else that I have to tell you." Given his state of mind, Jane felt reluctant to tell him about Alena and had visiting orders been a bit easier to come by, she might well have left it for another time.

"What?"

"D.C. Oplitova. She err—." Jane folded the newspaper to enable easy reading of the article. "Here," she said, passing it across. "Read this." After five minutes' silent reading, Crowe looked up, lost for words. Jane thought the poor man might be about to crumble. He opened his mouth and half whispered, "Why?"

Jane shrugged. "They say she wasn't herself after the car crash."

Crowe swallowed hard before replying. "But that doesn't explain—."

"Who knows what's going on in someone else's head. I always got the impression that she was a good police officer that cared. Maybe this was the problem. Maybe when the truth came out, she couldn't bear to know that her whole world had been a lie."

"Well, she did have this idyllic impression of the police. Everyone else seemed to know. She objected to the Gladys Hammond thing."

"Did she?"

"Yeah. She never quite got it that policing is about protecting the establishment."

"What a shame."

"It says here that she was found dead at home on 6th December and that the subsequent inquiry concluded she'd hung herself."

Jane nodded.

"And that there'd been a police inquiry that she was waiting to hear about."

"Mmmm."

"What was the inquiry about? That's what I want to know."

"I don't know. It doesn't say, does it?"

Crowe shook his head, and for a moment, Jane thought he was going to break down in tears. "Poor Alena. She had nothing to do with it. I—Jane, just go."

"What, why?"

"I don't want or need your help. Just go, please."

"What did you mean, she had nothing to do with it?"

"Nothing. Poor Alena, poor Gladys. Poor—you. Jane thank you for coming, but I don't want your help. Please don't apply for another visiting order. If you do, I'll say I don't want to see you."

"OK, if that's what you want. But I don't understand why."

Crowe got to his feet, once again drawing the attention of the guards. "Please Jane, just go. I need to be by myself."

CHAPTER FORTY-FIVE

JULY 2008

Jane was still smarting at the way she'd been treated. Several months previously, she'd lodged an appeal against the rejection of her compensation claim. The trouble was, this involved going to court and legal expenses that she couldn't pay. Living in a democratic state, the government had thought of this scenario and allocated public funds to those that can't afford to pay legal costs themselves. Jane was, however, turned down for legal aid and now, three months after appealing the decision, she was holding in front of her a letter informing her of the outcome of her latest appeal.

Before tearing open the envelope, she'd felt a wave of optimism, telling herself that eventually she'd come across someone sympathetic to her situation and, by the law of averages, this must happen soon. However, on extracting the letter from the envelope and holding it to eye level, this optimism had evaporated inside two seconds, to be replaced by embarrassment. She felt embarrassed for having hope. Hope that she'd receive the same entitlement as any other citizen, despite the many vested interests that would have objected.

She'd had her appeal turned down once again, because the likely benefits of the case, the restoration of her good name, did not justify public funding.

With the letter folded along the original creases and back inside the envelope, Jane's thoughts, for some reason, turned to Crowe. The last time she'd seen him, he'd apologised. As it had become increasingly apparent to her that she was never going get anything from a system that only looked after those with power, Crowe's apology had escalated in importance. Maybe some time soon she'd put in another application for a visiting order. Now that they were on the same side, it would be good to see how he was doing.

So she got straight on the phone and asked Stafford prison for an application form, which she completed as soon as it arrived roughly one month later. Once again, the reply didn't deliver the news she'd been hoping for.

CHAPTER FORTY-SIX

2009

"Crowe, the governor wants to see you," the prison officer said, unlocking the door to his cell, which Crowe shared with one other man, and stepping inside. Crowe climbed down from the top bunk. This was the most action he'd seen in weeks.

He didn't often get to leave his cell, so any trip, however short, was much appreciated. All the cells in the prison were identically unadorned. Just a bed, two bunks if it was a double cell, a writing table and a toilet. He could understand how men had gone mad just lying there with nothing to do but count the bricks or catch the cockroaches as they scurried across the bare, concrete floor.

He must have sent many a man, some good and some bad, to this prison in his time as a police inspector, but as luck would have it, he had yet to come across any, despite being three years into his five-year sentence.

The picture Johnny sent a year or so back caught his eye on his way out, prompting the guard to lose patience and say, "Come on Crowe, get a move on. I haven't got all day." Johnny was alive and kicking, but he wasn't getting any better. He'd turned into one of those kids that practically live inside hospitals and are forever having sharp things stuck in them. Poor little mite. He was a very sick boy and, despite having his own tutor who attended every day, missed being at school with his friends. Judging from the look on Susan's face last time he'd seen her, about six months previously, the prospect of him returning to school was a very long way off.

With the clang of his cell door still resonating along the corridor, the guard took Crowe up the stairs to the governor's office. Once inside, the guard left them and told the governor he'd be waiting outside should he need anything.

Crowe knew this was code for I'm here to give him a kicking if he steps out of line, but didn't let it worry him. He just stood there to attention, hands crossed behind his back, waiting to be addressed. The governor delighted in keeping him waiting as long as possible, just to let Crowe know who was boss.

"Good afternoon, err—Crowe," the governor said, finally putting down his pen.

"Good afternoon, Sir."

"Now, the reason for bringing you here is that I have a proposition for you. I understand that while you've been here your conduct has been nothing short of exemplary, so when this came up, given your circumstances, I thought of you." He handed Crowe a flyer about the government's new initiative on cancer research.

Crowe read it with interest. Once he'd reached the bottom line, his enthusiasm had taken residence on his face.

"Thought you might like it," the governor said.

"I do, Sir."

"And would you, like to volunteer?"

"Yes, Sir. But not because I want to get out early, Sir."

"I understand Crowe, but you wouldn't say no to that added benefit would you, Crowe?"

"No, Sir."

"Good. Go back to your cell and I'll make the arrangements then."

"Oh, thank you, Sir."

A week later, Crowe was sat on the top bunk, smoking and coughing his guts up, when the lock rattled. He looked up to see three men in white coats enter. One of them was carrying a needle. "Crowe?" The needle man said, approaching the bed.

"Yes?" Crowe swung round.

"Oh, no, don't get up. I believe you've agreed to participate in some tests—for cancer research?"

"Oh, yes. Whatever I can do."

"Well, I just need a quick blood sample before we start. If you wouldn't mind rolling up your sleeve. Lie down if you prefer, it really makes no difference."

Crowe did as the man asked. Lying down on his bunk bed, Crowe gritted his teeth, well aware that having a blood test is one of those things that people profess doesn't hurt when they get older, but in actual fact hurts just as much as it did as a child.

Thirty seconds later, the man withdrew and wiped the needle before sealing the sample and putting it in the pocket of his white doctor's

jacket. "Thanks for this. I'll err, be back in touch. It usually takes a couple of days for the tests to be completed, unless anything arises."
"Oh, thank you."
The man handed Crowe a plaster to put over the leaking vein on his arm before he left. Laid on his bed, sleeves rolled down over the plaster, Crowe wondered what he meant by 'if anything arises'. Surely if he had any kind of chronic condition, he'd know about it or at least be aware of the symptoms. This thought kept him occupied for several hours until his cell mate returned with tales of what had been happening in the kitchen.

***

Three days later—Crowe had long since stopped using day names, as in prison every day was the same—, needle man returned. This time his demeanour was noticeably more downcast, and he appeared to be showing Crowe more respect than he'd become accustomed to. Furthermore, he closed the cell door behind him, creating the illusion that they had some privacy.

"Crowe—Robbie isn't it?—I'm Dr Marsden. I don't believe I introduced myself before. Mind if I err, sit down?"

Crowe nodded.

Dr Marsden made himself comfortable at the writing desk and nudged out the other chair with his toe. "Please, take a seat."

Without uttering a word, Crowe did as he was instructed.

"I'm not a prison employee. Let me make that clear," the doctor said. "I'm employed by Cancer Research and I'm also a specialist in Oncology. Do you know what that is?"

"Yes. My son—. "

"Of course you do, please forgive me."

Crowe shrugged and began to wish that he'd get on with it, and say whatever it was that he had to say.

"You remember on Tuesday morning, I came in and took a sample of blood from you?"

Crowe nodded, resisting the temptation to throw in some sarcastic comment about him being too busy to remember insignificant events like that.

"Well, I have the results. And I'm afraid it's not good news."

Crowe woke from his slumber. "What? What have you found?"

"Robbie, brace yourself."

Crowe felt every muscle in his body tense. "OK."

"You have lung cancer. Do you smoke?"

Crowe nodded.

"Well, there's your answer."

Crowe found it ironic that right at that very moment all he wanted to do was smoke his way through an entire pack.

"So, will it go—if I give up?"

"Well it would help, but—I was hoping you wouldn't. Stop smoking I mean."

"So you can see if the treatment works?"

"Exactly. And if we find a treatment for your cancer then, there's no reason why it couldn't work for—cancer of the blood, too. Do you see what I'm saying, Robbie?"

Crowe smiled. "Yes, Dr Marsden. I'd be helping find a cure for my son."

"Indeed. So, in many ways, your cancer could be seen as a blessing in disguise."

Crowe nodded, not knowing whether to feel elation or not. Being happy to hear you have a chronic disease didn't feel right.

"So, tomorrow I'll be back and this time you'll have to come with me to the research ward of the prison hospital, where you'll be spending the next week."

When he was once again alone in his cell and the echo of Dr Marsden's footsteps had ceased to consume the entire corridor, Crowe laid on his bed and gave some thought to the bigger picture. With everything he'd been through, he knew that if these trials proved successful, someone in higher places would have a lot to say on the subject.

If they found a cure for cancer, that meant they could tell people to smoke all they wanted, meaning more tax revenue, meaning they could tell the pharmaceutical companies to stick their money where the sun don't shine. He knew in reality the government was far too greedy to do that, but it was an interesting thought. One that Jane would be interested to hear. He made the decision there and then that if, and when, she applied for another visitor's order, he'd agree to see her. He hadn't had any visitors at all since he'd decided to stop seeing Susan.

The following afternoon, Crowe found himself lying in a hospital bed being poked and prodded in every department as he waited for the man with the evil grin to arrive with the big needle. He was beginning to discover for himself just how Johnny must be feeling.

As soon as Johnny entered his head, everything felt OK again. He didn't mind the indignity of it all because he'd been offered the chance to actually do something for real. Most parents of sick children would kill to be in his position.

However, when the man with the needle came, he did have an evil grin and from where Crowe was lying, the needle looked a bit oversized. He could feel it ripping into his vain already.

"Won't feel a thing, he said as he slid the needle into Crowe's arm."

Crowe gritted his teeth and screwed his eyes as the alien object entered him, recalling how the doctor had told exactly the same lie when he'd had his T.B. jab as a thirteen-year-old.

When the doctor removed the needle, Crowe's hand shot towards his arm. The doctor flashed another evil grin and wiped the blood away with a damp swab.

"We'll have to repeat the process again tomorrow. Hope it didn't cause too much discomfort. Oh and, you might feel one or two side effects. Just let a nurse know if you do, OK?"

Crowe wanted to ask him about the side effects, but already felt light headed, as if on a roundabout that would detach itself at any moment and fly off down a long black hole.

"Crowe? Did you understand what I just said?"

"Yes."

"What? Did I just say?"

"Side effects. Tell nurse."

The doctor glanced over his shoulder at the nurse and they both started laughing. "Oh, that'll do," the doctor said and turned to leave the ward.

Feeling his temperature sore, Crowe informed the nurse that he wasn't feeling well. She went away and promptly returned with a case full of medicines, which she administered one by one until Crowe felt like he would start to rattle.

After shoving a thermometer under his tongue and loitering by his bed for a couple of minutes, she removed the thermometer, made a note of his temperature, closed the curtains around his bed and left Crowe to sleep off what he hoped were the temporary side effects of his injection.

***

So for the next six months, Crowe spent one week a month in the research wing of the prison hospital. At first, it felt like a thankless chore, which left him without the use of his arm for the following week as well as his cough, which, if anything appeared to be getting worse.

Then, one day about four months into the treatment, Marsden emerged into the ward grinning from ear to ear. He told everyone, about twenty men in all, including two others that had cancer to start off with, that they'd done some experimenting in the lab and they were confident they'd reduced the side effects. He also hoped that this time they might see some positive results.

The guinea pigs laughed aloud, many of them saying they hoped the side effects wouldn't be as bad. Truth be told, everyone had started to notice a hint of despair in Marsden's eyes as he and the nurse administered the injections. His demeanour had rubbed off onto everyone else, and as a result, people had started to question why they'd agreed to be treated like human guinea pigs. Lending yourself to a worthwhile cause was one thing, but feeling you were being used to satisfy someone's curiosity or worse still, their ego, without any real hope of scientific progress, was another thing altogether.

On noticing the smaller needle, though, the size most doctors used, people's attitudes changed. This time there were no side effects, meaning Crowe and the rest of them had little to do all day but lie in bed, bored out of their minds. They were even relieved when Marsden returned and said they could return to their cells early. A further day had passed before Crowe's cell mate commented that it was good to finally get some sleep. When Crowe asked him what he meant, he replied, "Because you're not coughing anymore." Crowe just laughed this off, but when he thought about it, he realised his cellmate was right.

When the time came for the next round of experiments, Marsden reported that everyone had shown at least some signs of improvement, so this time they took a sample of blood from everyone and sent them back to their cells. Of course, many of them were somewhat disgruntled that they'd lost out on the chance of a soft bed and some female company for a few days, but Crowe was almost as happy as Marsden.

The following day, when he came to visit Crowe in his cell, Marsden could hardly contain himself. Indeed, he looked to be quivering with excitement as he spoke. "Robbie, I have some great news, Pal. Your cancer has gone," he blurted out from the doorway of Crowe's cell.

"What? Completely?" In all honesty, Crowe was expecting Marsden to realise that he'd just got a bit over excited and make his follow up statement somewhat more conservative in an attempt to save face.

"Completely. Not a trace. How's the cough?"

Crowe felt a grin stretch from ear to ear. "Gone."

Marsden sat down at the writing desk and said to Crowe calmly, "OK, everyone else has shown the same results, so we need to do another test, just to make sure. The last thing we want to do is announce we've cured cancer and then end up with egg on our faces."

Crowe nodded in agreement.

"So, what I'd like to do, if you're willing and I have to stress that you don't have to do this if you don't want, is, inject some more cancerous cells into you and then repeat the dose in two weeks' time. Are you willing to go through with this?"

"Yes. Count me in."

"Oh, I knew you'd say that. You stay there and I'll be back in a jiffy." Marsden disappeared, leaving Crowe to sit and wonder if he'd just helped to find a cure for his son. Five minutes later, Marsden returned, carrying a black bag. He told Crowe to sit on the bed, delved into his bag and extracted the evil looking needle.

Of all the injection's he'd endured, this was by far the worse. He felt like he was being invaded, from the moment the needle pierced his vain and the evil substance made its way into his bloodstream.

It seemed to take Marsden an eternity to slowly push the syringe until all fluid was drained from the barrel. By the time Marsden had his finger on Crowe's arm to stop the bleeding, Crowe felt like his arm was about to burst. He examined it carefully, surprised it wasn't swollen in the least.

"OK, thanks for agreeing to this, old chap. In a day or so, you might notice your cough returning. Sorry about that."

"Small price to pay."

"Exactly. Well. I'll err, see you in seven days."

For the next week, Crowe had little else to do, but lie on his bed and wait for the cancer cells to spread. Six days later, he was coughing his guts up—quite literally. It even reached the stage where the cough stopped him from putting a cigarette in his mouth, much to the annoyance of his cellmate. On one occasion, Crowe's cellmate got up in the middle of the night, slumped down at the writing desk in the dark, before turning to Crowe and hissing, "if the injection doesn't cure you and the cancer doesn't kill you, I'll kill you myself."

"Sorry." Crowe just about managed. "They're coming for me tomorrow—. "

"Halleluiah."

"Hopefully the injection should make me stop."

"And if it doesn't?"

"Well, then by all accounts I'm a gonner."

His cellmate tittered. "Sounds good to me."

After a night in which neither of them slept at all, the lights went on and they got out of bed. Crowe hoped for everyone's sake that the injection would work and that it would have an effect by the time his cellmate returned from the kitchen later that afternoon.

Quite typically, it was approaching lunch time by the time Marsden showed up. He took one look at Crowe, who was sat coughing his guts up on the top bunk and said, "oh dear. I didn't think it would make you this bad. I'm so sorry."

Crowe explained that neither he nor his cellmate had had any sleep for the past few nights before following Marsden to the prison hospital.

There was a smaller group this time, perhaps because not so many had agreed to have the cancer put back into their bloodstream. Crowe did notice that among the ten to twelve men present, there was included the two other genuine cancer sufferers. Perhaps they felt that bit more strongly than the others.

Crowe laid atop the covers as instructed and waited for Marsden and the nurse to do the rounds. Hopefully, there would be no need to keep them in the hospital overnight, Marsden explained, as the injection shouldn't have any side effects. This was greeted with cheers by some and grumbling by others.

Just like before, the injection was completed with minimal fuss. After all the tusk-like needles he'd had stuck in him, this regular needle was a cinch.

Just as before, there were no side effects, but worryingly, the cough persisted through the night. Just when Crowe and his cellmate felt they could take no more, Crowe fell silent for five minutes. Both of them commented and laughed when he coughed again, but from that moment on the coughs became increasingly sparse until, two days later, they stopped altogether.

When Marsden confirmed that once again all traces of cancer had gone, the prison sent out a press release stating that they had found a cure for cancer.

***

Despite only having a matter of months left to serve, Crowe decided that he was once more open to seeing visitors. Susan was the first to arrive. To his dismay, she had heard about the prison's discovery and was sceptical. He had been hoping to give her his own enthusiastic account of the story and see her face light up.

She had no idea that he'd been involved though and this information appeared to make all the difference. She left looking positively radiant, and Crowe got the feeling that he'd just made her day.

CHAPTER FORTY-SEVEN

Clutching her visiting order, Jane stepped down the stairs and entered the car park, where her car was waiting patiently for her next journey. Truth be told, she'd all but given up on Crowe and had completed the visiting order more in hope than expectation. Now that the day had finally arrived, she found that she didn't really have much to say to him. Of course, she'd heard about the cancer cure, but was as sceptical as the next person. No-one in their right mind was going to risk making themselves look foolish by falling for this publicity stunt. She was hoping Crowe might know something about it, but wasn't really confident that he would.

It was exactly the same process as before. She was taken into a huge hall that reminded her of her school days in the dim and distant past. Then she was led to a table and told to wait for Crowe. When he showed up, the first thing she noticed was how well he looked.

"You're looking well," she said, with a grin, this time telling the truth.

"Oh, thanks. I feel it. It's all down to this new cancer treatment."

"What? You were involved?"

"Yes. Oh, you don't know, do you? I was diagnosed with lung cancer myself. And it cured it."

For the first time, Jane thought the new treatment just might be the real deal. "How's err, your little boy?"

Crowe's face lit up. "Cured."

"Oh, Inspector Crowe. That's wonderful. I err, don't really know what else to say."

"Well, you could have said I told you so."

"Come again?"

"Well, correct me if I'm wrong, but this is the first time research for cancer, or any chronic condition, has been carried out on humans — not animals—and, it's been effective. Straight away."

"Well, when you put it that way—."

"Jane, I'm so sorry for everything I did."

"Oh, don't mention it. You're forgiven."

"And thank you."

Jane smiled.

"Thank you for being so understanding, for forgiving me and for helping to find a cure for my son. Without your campaign, it would never have happened."

"Don't mention it."

"I'd err, like us to be friends, when I get out."

"Sure."

"They cut a year off my sentence you know. I get out next month." He started laughing. "Changed your mind now, have you?"

"No, I err—Inspector Crowe, that's great news. It's the second best news I've had today."

CHAPTER FORTY-EIGHT

About a month later, Jane was sat reading a book in her flat when there was a knock. She'd been trying to finish the book for weeks and felt frustrated at there being yet another interruption. However, once she walked to the window and saw Inspector Crowe's car parked outside, she smiled and walked down the stairs to greet him.

He soon persuaded her to get in his car and he promptly whisked her home to meet up with Susan and Johnny. Once there, they all sat in the garden, glass of wine in hand, while they went over the events of the past few years. Right back at the start, when they let out all the guinea pigs and Jane first joined the protests, no one could have envisaged how it would turn out in the end.

Then Crowe laughed to himself and said while he was in prison he'd had a thought that he wanted to share with her.

"What was that?"

"Well, I figured that now they've found a cure for cancer, they'll no longer put the health warnings on cigarette packets so that they can get extra money on them from all the tax."

"Makes sense."

"So they could use that money in place of the bung they get from the pharmaceutical companies . . ."

Jane started laughing. "I see where you're coming from."

Crowe leaned back in his chair and roared with laughter. "Figure that one out."

EPILOGUE

Without the intimidation, unlawful policing and blatant lies of the following, this book would not have been possible:

The Hall family
The Chief Constable of Staffordshire
Detective Chief Inspector Nick Baker
Chief Inspector Brett Oakes
Chief Inspector O'Leary
Inspector Jolley
Inspector Hallam
Inspector Bird
DS John Bloor
Sergeant Farrington
Sergeant Malone
Sergeant Moore
Sergeant Midwinter
WPC Stanslake
WPC Lynne
PC Taylor
PC McCann
PC Atkins
PC Mather
PC Cairns

PC Rushton
PC Wilson
Judge Pert
CPS Chief Prosecutor Harry Ireland
CPS solicitor Richard Johnson
Police solicitor / barrister Michael Griffiths
Vicars Jenny & Peter Lister
Halls' solicitor Timothy Lawson-Cruttendon
Villager Peter Clamp
Ex PM Blair

The vicars supposedly retired due to the strains of the protest. In fact, they were once again 'moved on' by the church, to a place where Peter helped the children of prisoners.

On 7th October 2004, Gladys Hammond was stolen, 17 March 2005 the injunction failed, January 2006 Darley Oaks farm closed, 4th May 2006 Gladys was found. It should be noted that Staffordshire Police wasted 2.3m pounds of tax payer's money on the campaign.

Finally, I would like to give a mention to DC 532 Heather Williamson, who was an honest police officer and for a short time became my close friend and confidant.

Janet Tomlinson

The foregoing symbolises only a fraction of the abuse of power to which all animals are subjected, including mankind.

This case highlights the extent to which those in authority will go, in order to achieve the power they crave i.e. political control and influence. Had it not been for a few "just" and compassionate people, the injustices in this campaign would never have been exposed. This particular episode of horrific cruelty and abuse was relentlessly challenged and finally came to an end, but sadly the deplorable and horrendous cruelty and abuse to animals continues.

The Bristol School of Veterinary Sciences in 2011 surveyed for the first time the number of cats and dogs in UK rescue organisations. They found that there were 131,070 cats and 129,743 dogs in these rescue centres. This does not include the feral cats and stray dogs that are running wild, un-spayed, un-neutered and starving. Why are these animals allowed to be sold to anyone who will impulsively decide to have one because they look "cute" when they are young, and subsequently "disposed of", when they tire of them or they become "inconvenient."

The study highlighted the need for further investment in neutering and spaying as well as education in responsible ownership. The care of these abandoned animals is left solely in the hands of charities which receive no government funding, despite the latter being solely responsible for the problem. Politicians boast that "we have the best welfare standards in the world "– this is a figment of their imagination!!! Pets are sold in pet shops as if they are toys and frequently bought by people who buy them for young children. These defenceless animals are also readily available to buy online, but despite ongoing requests by various organisations to ban this irresponsible trade in animals, the Government will do nothing!

Likewise, the Government refuse to ban wild animals in circuses, despite graphic footage of the cruelty involved. Even though in 2011 64% of MPs voted for a ban on wild animals in circuses, it has never become law and circuses continue to treat the animals with contemptuous disregard of their needs. Tigers, lions and other animals therefore continue to live a life of emptiness and cruelty even though 92% of the public are in agreement with the ban.

Another area of needless cruelty supported by the Government is fox hunting. Even though it was banned in England in 2005 the law has continued to be flouted by the hunters, and at the recent election it was yet again proposed by the Government to have the ban repealed by means of a free vote.

Then there is the Live Exports issue, a most barbaric trade which is archaic and belongs to primitive times. Farm animals are transported from all over the country to ports like Dover and then transported by sea to various countries where their destiny is unknown. Again, the Government refuses to end this cruel trade despite public opinion.

I could continue in this vein - the Government has the power to improve the plight of animals, especially when they have the support of the MPs. However, they continue to remain indifferent and inactive. The charities that pick up the pieces receive no funding from the Government and subsequently rely on the public. Laws are passed such as licensing puppy farms, but these are never followed up and the footage of the conditions of many of these farms is horrific. "Puppy farming" has now spread to urban areas as it can be a highly profitable venture. Councils tend to turn the other cheek, as they do with pet shops when informed of the poor conditions in which the animals are kept, frequently out of sight of the public. One pet shop, of which the council was informed, sold cats and kittens and always told the purchaser not to have the cat spayed. Instead, they were encouraged to bring kittens back to the shop. The council in question was not interested and to this day the shop continues to operate in the same manner.

This is just a sample of the Government's negative attitude towards animals both through action and inaction. Explanations regarding the legislation for human medicines to be tested on animals may be described as incoherent and incomprehensible. When questioned as to why there are no convincing answers, they will not contemplate looking at animal replacement science. This is totally dismissed even though successes achieved have been astounding. Yet again all the scientists in human relevant medical research are funded by the public.

Printed in Great Britain
by Amazon